MAKE YOUR PEOPLE BEFORE YOU MAKE YOUR PRODUCTS

MAKE YOUR PEOPLE BEFORE YOU MAKE YOUR PRODUCTS

USING TALENT MANAGEMENT TO
ACHIEVE COMPETITIVE ADVANTAGE
IN GLOBAL ORGANIZATIONS

PAUL TURNER

and

DANNY KALMAN

WILEY

Library of Congress Cataloging-in-Publication Data
Turner, Paul, 1952 October 18-
  Make your people before you make your products : using talent management
    to achieve competitive advantage in global organizations / Paul Turner, Danny Kalman.
      pages cm
  Includes bibliographical references and index.
  ISBN 978-1-118-89958-8 (hardback)—ISBN 978-1-118-89961-8 (ebk)—
  ISBN 978-1-118-89960-1 (ebk)   1. Expertise.   2. Ability.
  3. Corporate culture.   4. Organization.
  I. Kalman, Danny, 1952-   II. Title.
  BF431.T87 2014
  658.3′14–dc23
                                                                              2014023330

A catalogue record for this book is available from the British Library.

ISBN 978-1-118-89958-8 (hbk)
ISBN 978-1-118-89961-8 (ebk) ISBN 978-1-118-89960-1 (ebk)

Cover design by Dan Jubb
Set in 10/14.5 Palatino LT Std by Aptara
Printed in Great Britain by TJ International Ltd, Padstow, Cornwall, UK

CONTENTS

About the Authors   vii

Acknowledgements   ix

Foreword   xi

Introduction   **1**

   1 The case for talent   **11**

   2 The world as an open market for talented people   **27**

   3 Defining talent   **49**

   4 Removing the 'exclusive' tag   **65**

   5 Developing a global strategy for talent   **83**

   6 The CEO as the 'owner' of the talent strategy   **105**

   7 Coordination and coherence in implementation   **123**

   8 Identifying talent   **141**

   9 Attracting talent at all levels   **161**

10 Developing the whole workforce   **185**

11 Managing talent in an age of transparency   **211**

12 Retaining talent   **227**

13 Measuring the effectiveness of talent strategy   **243**

14 Joining up the 'ownership' of talent management   **261**

Conclusion   277

References   285

Index   297

ABOUT THE AUTHORS

Paul Turner has held professorial positions at universities in Birmingham, Cambridge and Nottingham. His previous roles were President of Europe, Middle East and Africa, Employee Care for the Convergys Corporation of Cincinnati, Group HR Business Director for Lloyds TSB, Vice President of the CIPD, a Director of BT, a Non-Executive Director of OPI and Blessing White and a General Manager for Plessey in both the UK and Asia Pacific.

Paul was Chair of European Human Asset and Talent for Tomorrow Conferences from 2009 to 2012. He was a judge on the Middle East HR Excellence (2013), European HR Excellence (2011) and the CIPD People Management Awards (2009). He has spoken at business conferences around the world and is the author or co-author of *Meaning at Work: Employee Engagement in Europe* (2012), *Talent Management in Europe* (2012), *Workforce Planning* (2010), *The Admirable Company* (2008), *Talent* (2007), *Organisational Communication* (2003) and *HR Forecasting and Planning* (2002). Paul has written articles for business journals and the international press.

Danny Kalman is a Talent Management (TM) professional with extensive experience in the field. He was TM Director at Panasonic Corporation until 2013 and during his 20 years with Panasonic he had both European and global practical experiences in developing their talents at all levels of the company. Danny both chairs and speaks at conferences on leadership and talent management around the world. He is an accredited business coach and runs bespoke leadership and talent management programmes globally.

ACKNOWLEDGEMENTS

We would like to thank the many people who helped us in the preparation of this book:

From Wiley, Vicky Kinsman, Jenny Ng, Tessa Allen, Tim Bettsworth, and Emma Henshall.

From the CIPD, Margaret Marriott, Stephen Pobjoy, Claire McCartney, and Sinead Burke.

Research and helping to put together the manuscript, Jane Marie Turner and April Winstock.

Case study authors Sue Kamal, Adam J. Turner, Angela Williams, Wojciech Zytkowiak, Stephen Frost, Patty Grant and Richard Mills, Preston C. Bottger and Jean-Louis Barsoux, Stephen Pierce and Christine Cooke, Fiona Whitworth, Tea Colaianni and Julia Jameson.

FOREWORD

By Susannah Clements
Deputy Chief Executive, CIPD

There is an ongoing shift in the business landscape, caused by the scale and velocity of change in the global economy. As a result, organizations are seeking new insights about the ways they can achieve high levels of performance and growth in the face of turbulence and unpredictability.

Against this background, there is growing recognition that good people management is crucial to success. For many organizations, people are the main source of competitive advantage. For some the only source. Business leaders are striving to ensure that they deliver outstanding practices in people and organizational development by aligning their people strategies to the goals of the organization and ensuring that all employees are engaged with what they're trying to achieve. People management is a strategic as well as an operational imperative.

But this isn't straightforward because of changes in the nature of work and the dynamics of organizations. And so three priorities stand out.

The first is an understanding of the *future of work*. In essence, this means answering questions about the nature of 'work' and how it takes place. The answers will have implications for skills and job needs as well as career paths. The impact of global mobility, technological developments and new ways of working are particularly important.

The second critical factor is an understanding of the *change in work-force dynamics* caused by demographics, generational shifts, attitudes and expectations, the changing skills base and trends in learning and education. Today's workforce is both diverse and constantly changing. Insights about how these changes affect the organization's performance are critical.

The third area concerns the *culture and organization of the workplace*. This means insight into how organizations are evolving and adapting, how such evolution affects culture and engagement, and the best ways in which to organize, develop, manage, motivate and reward to ensure high levels of performance.

The achievement of success in these three areas will require insightful solutions on the part of people professionals across a broad range of subjects – from organization design and development through to employee relations and engagement. The CIPD's professional map outlines the critical skills needed in these areas, and it continues to grow and evolve to reflect these changing dynamics.

Of equal importance is the subject of talent and talent management – how to develop individuals into successful managers and leaders, and how to help those people achieve their potential.

Make Your People Before You Make Your Products deals with these areas in an innovative way by taking a whole workforce approach to talent in global organizations. Its core assumption is that talent management in the 21st century is different to talent management in the 20th century. Today, the world is an open market for talented people, which means that organizations have to work even harder to attract and retain the best at all levels.

Several important themes are covered. The first is that it will be necessary for modern organizations to take an inclusive approach to talent; losing the exclusive tag, but still maintaining excellence in areas such as high potential development and succession planning. To do so requires a broader definition within the organization and skillful management from those with talent responsibilities. The authors refer to this as an 'Inclusive/Selective' approach.

The second theme concerns the importance of coming up with innovative solutions as to how the whole workforce can be managed and developed. Creative approaches such as formal and informal combinations for talent development; adopting an openness in management through having a 'sunao' mind and ensuring that the CEO becomes the Chief Talent Officer are proposed.

But this book also deals with the fact that coherence and coordination in implementation are just as critical to success as the development of a robust talent strategy, and the third theme – implementation – focuses on how the grand designs of talent strategy can be executed effectively. Creating a powerful employer brand, employee value proposition and using these in a coherent approach to talent attraction and employee engagement are covered as part of the talent management process. And guidelines are put forward about developing measures of success.

Throughout the book, a series of case studies from global organizations give practical examples of the 'how to' of talent management in different business environments.

The book concludes that the reward of getting talent management right is the chance to create and sustain a competitive advantage that can't be copied: the competitive advantage of having a skilled, engaged and motivated workforce, which is surely a priority for all organizations.

INTRODUCTION

There isn't enough talent to satisfy demand

People management works best when the interests of the organization are coincident with the interests of individual employees. For the organization this means achieving its stakeholder objectives; for the employee this means satisfaction at work, a balanced life and visible career prospects. Investment in people at work isn't an act of faith. It is an act of business strategy. The attraction, development, management and retention of talented people are critical to the success of all organizations.

If you give your people the chance to perform at their best, if they are engaged in what you're trying to achieve and if you have a workplace in which they can develop and shine then you will have a powerful edge that no other organization can copy. Your people can be your unique source of competitive advantage.

Such a view was echoed by Konosuke Matsushita, founder of Panasonic, who believed that there was a convergence between the growth of the company and the growth of its employees. The two were interdependent. He practised this philosophy with the belief that you 'grow your people before you grow your products'. The ultimate success of the company showed that there was merit in taking this approach. But it wasn't based purely on altruism. There were real business benefits from this focus.

This is brought into sharp focus by the current worldwide shortage of talent. No one company or country has the ability to 'grow enough' (*Economist*, 2012). The imbalance between demand (increasing as the world economy recovers) and supply (remaining unpredictable because of shortages in key skills) has caused intense competition. What started as a 'war for talent' in the days of significant global economic growth (say 1996 to 2008) continues today in the post-recession environment. The language may be less bellicose, but the sentiment remains the same.

The forces at work are complex. Knowledge economies have a huge demand for creative talent, whilst in other geographies the expansion in manufacturing or services ultimately leads to a dearth of managerial, project and operational talent. Challenges caused by external labour market dynamics are exacerbated by the context within which organizations increasingly operate (i.e. a world moving in real time and in which complex networks are supplementing fixed hierarchies in organizational design).

Furthermore massive changes in the 'geography of talent' require intelligence about which skills the organization needs to fulfil its short- and long-term objectives. These include digital skills from highly-skilled technology workers; 'agile thinking', not only on the part of the organization's leadership but also through the whole workforce, to cope with rapid and sudden changes in markets; interpersonal and communication skills to facilitate cross-border relationship building and teaming; and global operating skills as organizations expand into new markets.

No old attitudes for new times

A convergence of external macro-economic factors, internal organizational dynamics and changes in attitude towards the development of the individual has created a challenging context for talent, requiring new insights from talent managers to create a winning approach.

Indeed, Klaus Schwab, founder of the World Economic Forum (WEF) and its executive chairman, has stated that in the future people will be a country's and a company's most important resource and 'investing in people is not just nice to have; it is imperative for growth, prosperity and progress'. Many have recognized this point of view. In the WEF analysis of 122 countries, Switzerland, Finland and Germany featured prominently, whilst Singapore's workforce and employment score was the second highest in the world. At a corporate level, Google, SAS, CHG Healthcare and Boston Consulting Group were amongst the 'Fortune 2013' best companies to work for; *Forbes* 'Asian Fab 50' included Tata, China Vanke and Wharf Holdings, whilst 'Great Places to Work in Europe' included Diageo, Hilti and Admiral Group. Recognition of excellence in people development spans geographies and business sectors.

People management is more complicated than rocket science.

But this is easier said than done. Managing people is more complicated than rocket science because people are more complicated than rockets. Each member of the workforce has a unique character, unique talents and unique needs. In large, global organizations, the number of combinations of personality attributes, skill levels and cultural factors will be enormous. If once we may have believed that one size *did* fit all – leading to standardized reward packages, performance management systems and group training and development programmes – it certainly doesn't now. The challenge facing all organizations is to get the most out of people as individuals as well as the departments or business units in which they work. To do so means adapting the way in which global organizations approach their people management, moving to a culture where employees are regarded as individuals within a community rather than an audience viewed from a stage. In a global context the psychological and physical logistics of such an approach are significant.

An organizational paradox

If they are engaged with what the organization is trying to achieve, employees will put their unique attributes to work with commitment, relishing the chance to be part of a success story. But they will do so in a complex global environment that is extremely competitive and fast moving and where the ground seems to shift with each passing economic cycle. They will be most committed when they can see meaning in their work, life and career – when they have some idea of what the future holds and when they can have at least an input into their own direction of travel. This represents a paradox of modern organizational life. People want more information, participation and self-management, when less organizational stability and predictability can be offered. The way that organizations shape themselves to deal with these new circumstances will be different from previous eras.

From exclusive to inclusive

In the past, one way to 'manage' such uncertainty was to have inspirational leaders who could take the organization forward to its goals regardless of what obstacles were placed in front of it. Hence, the focus was on identifying and developing those who had vision, charisma, drive and an ambition to excel. This leadership cadre would do the right things and provide the energy to carry the organization through whatever economic conditions prevailed. They would release enough information about what was going on to the support their case, preserving that which was sensitive or strategic. Few people could do all of these things. And so leaders with a proven track record in these skills were, and are, in great demand.

The urgency and necessity of getting the right people into leadership positions, combined with a perceived shortage of those who fitted the profile, led to a burgeoning of interest in talent and talent management. This mainly dealt with an *exclusive* group of people who had immediate experience to take up leadership roles or were potential successors to the board or executive team – or were high potentials identified as having the potential to move two or more steps up the organization. These were 'top talent'. The competition to attract such people was so intense during the period of economic boom (1996–2008) that it became known as the 'war for talent'. A short lull in the war during the Great Recession has now been replaced by, once again, a focus on attracting the right level of 'top talent'. It shouldn't be surprising that the dynamics of this exclusive group received the attention of corporate leaders and academics, and these have been articulated through notable books, articles and practices. A change in leadership could force the stock price, and hence shareholder value, up or down.

But increasingly, this focus on the chosen few at the top of the organization is seen as being only part of the solution. The realization that other members of the organization had talents to offer expanded the remit of talent management. Those with specialist or hard-to-find skills, those who could run projects and those who could work in multi-cultural teams were also in short supply. So, early into the war for talent there was recognition that shortages of talented people occurred throughout the organization at every level. Employee engagement of the entire workforce was seen as a necessity and began to receive as much airplay as top talent development, especially in the wake of low engagement scores in surveys worldwide (Rice, Marlow and Masarech, 2012). To make sure that as many people as possible were able to contribute to the organization's (and hence their own) success, an increasing number of people have been enveloped in the definition of talent. In more recent times this has become an *inclusive* approach (i.e. there is recognition that everyone has talent). Talent exists in more than just a few people at the top.

Today's definitions of 'talent' can be placed on a continuum between the two extremes of inclusivity and exclusivity depending on the organizational context. And in some cases the attraction, development, retention and management of talent have overlapped so much with people management in general that the two are often indistinguishable. This is both an expression of the importance of people in the organization and a source of confusion within the human resources profession. It's probably time to move on.

What does 'make your people before you make your products' mean in practice?

The debate about whether talent is an exclusive term applied to a few people or an inclusive term applied to many is one that sometimes gets in the way of delivering excellence in people management. In fact, there's an inevitability about regarding all employees as having talent quite simply because no single country produces enough to go round. Global demographic and skills changes have transcended the influence of any one company, country or region. And so organizations have to make provision for ensuring that they have a supply of suitably trained and culturally-aware managers and executives who are able to fulfil the most senior roles whilst cherishing the whole of the workforce and, through talent management, making sure they all have the chance to reach their full potential. The challenge is to do both things brilliantly.

Such a premise is the basis of this book. In order to achieve competitive advantage, all employees will need to be treated as having talent. If you don't do this, they may leave or underperform. The principle of making your people before making your products may help to build a sustainable competitive position, maximizing the skills and potential of everyone who works for the organization.

Such a principle can apply to whatever definition of talent is adopted. It matters that everyone in the organization is given the opportunity to deliver to their full potential.

To make this work means having a certain organizational ethos. Making your people before making your product means that organizations will:

- **Recognize that the world is an open market for talented people.** People are not abstract resources to be deployed around the chessboard of global competition. They are individuals, each with valuable skills and a role to play in the organization's success.
- **Create a community of talent.** Talent can no longer be regarded as an audience in receipt of a service but as more of a community that fully participates in and determines what the service actually is. Talent management is now talent management for all.
- **Include all employees in talent management.** The definition of talent embraces both inclusivity and exclusivity. Clarifying roles and integrating employees into the organization's purpose and methods are important but this also means giving oxygen to employee creativity and, where relevant, adapting the organization to new opportunities identified by employees.

- **Ensure that the CEO takes ownership of the talent strategy.** It is his or her obligation to ensure that the organization has a flow of talent at every level or network node and that every employee has the opportunity to maximize their contribution to their own and the company's success.
- **Enlighten leaders and empower managers** who not only allow the ability of talented people to rise to the surface of competitive advantage but positively encourage it. In this respect talent management is about both culture and process.
- **Give equal or greater status to global people strategy than other strategies such as product marketing or technology.** If you are going to make your people before you make your products then the focus of your company has to be as much on people as on any other traditional factors of production. People will be at the forefront of strategy and talent management will be a critical component part.
- **Integrate the 'tools' used in talent management with the tools of management.** They aren't just used when there is a high-level departure or a particularly poor set of employee attitude survey results. They are dynamic and strategic on the one hand and delivered in real time for operational excellence on the other.

For some, these criteria will mark a paradigm shift in the way in which organisations are run. Making your people before making your products will require a joined-up approach between people and business strategies.

The structure of the book

This book deals with some of the questions and issues that are facing those whose job it is to deliver an organization in which talent is harnessed and engaged at every level.

In Chapter 1 we introduce the subject of talent in global organizations, create a business case for making your people before making your products and outline some of the critical success factors in making this work.

In Chapter 2 we discuss how changes in external labour market dynamics necessitate having an outside-in perspective for modern talent management. This means that an understanding of labour markets is no longer an interesting piece of data for the talent debate but a crucial source of intelligence. In addition we talk about internal organizational dynamics and the effect these have on talent and talent management.

In Chapter 3 we look at how the subjects of talent and talent management have evolved over a period of twenty years or so and look at some of the evidence that has come to light about the perceived rights or wrongs of a particular way of defining talent and some conclusions about the position as its stands today. Our view is that there is no 'one right way' to manage talent but that the context of the organization will, to some extent, determine what can be achieved and what can't. We follow this up in Chapter 4 with a strategic overview of talent in global organizations. And in Chapter 5 we go through the key principles and actions of developing a talent strategy in an organization that has adopted the 'make your people before you make your products' philosophy.

A critical success factor for such a move is the support and active involvement of the CEO to such a move. In Chapter 6 we cover what the CEO as the 'owner' of the talent strategy means in practice together with some examples from the Most Admired Companies in the world (Brown and Turner, 2008).

Chapter 7 discusses the importance of integrating the 'tools' used in talent management with the tools of management, and in Chapters 8–12 we cover how this works in practice in the identification, attraction, development, management (using the 'sunao', or openness, approach) and the retention of talent.

In Chapter 13 we discuss the importance of those with responsibility for delivering talent management to provide insights as to what this means for their organizations. In particular we talk about moving from data through information to intelligence and then insight.

We deal with the overlaps and potential conflicts between HR and talent management in Chapter 14. The chapter outlines the roles and responsibilities of HR and talent professionals and areas in which there may be ambiguity. It then puts forward ways in which these can be resolved.

In the Conclusion we offer some insights into the findings on 'make your people before you make your products'.

We have included case studies from a range of organizations to illustrate the points being made. The case studies are exemplars of talent management from around the world.

An organization's success may depend on its ability to create the environment and opportunity whereby the initiative of talented people can be unleashed (Mackey and Sisoda, 2013), that their imagination and passion can be harnessed and that their contribution can be maximized. Making your people before making your products is a philosophy that will facilitate this success.

Chapter 1

The case for talent

Executive summary

- *People are not capital, assets or resources; they are people. People design, make and deliver; they develop intellectual property and create wealth.*
- *If you make your people before you make your products, your people will satisfy your customers, which in turn will make your company profitable. This in turn will increase the value for your shareholders and provide money to invest for growth.*
- *An engaged workforce will be active participants in achieving the organization's objectives.*
- *An organizational culture that recognizes the value of allowing talented people at all levels to flourish with abundance can be uniquely differentiating.*
- *The attraction, development and retention of the talented people in the right place, at the right time and with the right skills should be the priorities for all organizations.*
- *The choice between either inclusive or exclusive definitions of talent as extremes on a continuum looks increasingly anachronistic. Instead, organizations will try to adopt both positions simultaneously. Everyone has talent.*
- *Balancing the outcomes of the organization's global talent needs against (sometimes competing) local requirements is a challenge for most global organizations.*
- *Talent management may require a shift in the corporate mindset. People will be on a par with new product development, the creation of new distribution outlets or clever financial engineering in the list of the company's priorities.*

Treat your employees like customers

People are not capital, assets or resources; they are people. People design, make and deliver; they develop intellectual property (IP) and create wealth.

If engaged, they will be active participants in achieving the organization's objectives. That is why Facebook, with its ability to attract talent; Apple and Google, with their ability to give talented people full rein to their creativity; and more recently Yahoo, whose acquisition of Tumblr and hiring savvy developers has turned the 'former also ran into the most talked about company in Silicon Valley' (Fast Company, 2013), focus so much on their people. But it isn't just in the technology sector on the West Coast of America where talent is the competitive differentiator. The Best Practice Institute cites both the Internal Revenue Service and Avon (Goldsmith and Carter, 2010), whilst the names of Lenovo, headquartered in China; Singapore Airlines; BASF, headquartered in Germany; Tesco, of the UK; and HCL, based in India with its 'employees first' philosophy, resonate with students of talent management and its practice.

The attraction, development and retention of the right people, in the right place, at the right time and with the right skills, are priorities for all organizations. Ninety per cent of corporate leaders regard effective people development as of the highest importance and 70% spend more than

20% of their time on talent management (Scullion and Collings, 2011). 'I see my role as the chief talent officer of the company', stated the Procter & Gamble CEO, (Donlon, 2012), a viewpoint that is gaining traction.

For successful organizations, people management is a core business activity that is about delivering short-term operational needs and securing long-term prosperity. The attraction and retention of talent is an important part of this. At its best, effective talent management will lead to the creation of an environment in which potential will be fulfilled, individual contribution maximized and the workforce fully engaged with the direction and strategy of the organization. People can be the key source of competitive advantage. For many they are the only source of competitive advantage.

The classic approach to talent management

Hence, organizations will align people strategy and business strategy, and will seek to create practices designed to engage and motivate the workforce.

There are many ways to do so. But whilst there is greater choice, diversity and opportunity in the modern organization, there is also greater complexity (Sohota, 2013). So, to provide coherence, large and geographically dispersed workforces will be divided into segments or groupings with common identifiable characteristics. The workforce could be segmented by country or region, by job role (engineers, salespeople or finance professionals), job title (officers, managers or directors), organizational levels or grades based on hierarchical positions or the types of skill needed.

Each of these will provide the basis for policies within the overall people approach of the organization, which will be designed to ensure equity within groups and differentiation between them. Benchmarking is used for national or international competitiveness in such things as reward or training investment.

In turn, the workforce segments will require a supply of people who are able to fill leadership roles: executive, managerial or specialist positions. Such roles will range from chief executive to managing director, country manager, or functional directors in marketing, finance or production. This group of talented people will be selected using the two criteria of performance and potential. They are the ones covered by the classic definition of talent. They will feature in talent pools or in succession plans and will receive additional development, executive coaching or leadership programmes to ensure that they have the knowledge and skills not only for their current jobs, but also for those one or two levels above – those of strategic importance or those based on new projects.

Over the past 20 years there have been significant shortages of people within this exclusive definition of talent at various times, but particularly at the peak of the economic boom. Extremely tight labour markets meant that issues about 'top talent' were high on the corporate agenda.

Extending the reach beyond the 'C Suite'

However, the spotlight shone even brighter on talent and talent management when it became clear that talent shortages were not only at executive or managerial level but also throughout the organization. To deal with this new reality, talent managers extended their reach, bringing in new tools and techniques for a wider audience. The definition of talent initially grew to encompass those with high potential and certain specialisms within the organization, such as technology or marketing, then even further to incorporate scarce skills wherever these were to be found in the organization and at whatever level.

This extension in scope wasn't straightforward. The lack of a common definition of talent led to debates about the differences between talent management and people or HR management. There was duplication, lack of clarity and sometimes conflicts of interest between those with talent responsibilities, learning and development and HR generalists. Furthermore, each organization realized that its own perspective and definition were influenced by a multitude of factors, including history, culture, the strength of feeling about talent on the part of the CEO and the skills within the HR function to deal with the subject.

The upshot was that one talent definition did not fit all and a consistent approach to talent strategy was hard to find and even harder to achieve.

Subsequently, there have been efforts to gain consistency through benchmarking and knowledge sharing and a greater emphasis on measures of success of talent management initiatives. But this remains an ongoing process.

Whilst there may have been disagreement about how far the definition of talent should stretch, there was agreement that talented people were a scarce and valuable group that could be the difference between success and failure and therefore worthy of special attention on the part of the organization's senior executives. And so the acquisition and management of talent, however defined, has become a strategic priority.

For many, there is the belief that if you take care of the people they will take care of the future (Peters, 2013).

If you make your people before you make your products, your people will satisfy your customers, which in turn will make your company profitable, which in turn will increase the value for your shareholders and provide money to invest for growth.

Does everyone have talent?

In some organizations, an inclusive approach is taken whereby all employees are assumed to have talent. In this case, the organization will encourage employees to go beyond their normal roles or objectives and will provide the means to progress to new opportunities. But more than this, the stock talent assessment criteria of performance and potential will be supplemented by attitudinal factors. Novartis, the Swiss pharmaceutical company, for example, looks at whether an individual's key values and behaviours are aligned with those of the company (Stahl *et al.*, 2012). Talent management processes are there to facilitate the contribution and opportunity over and above what is normally expected. In such an organization the challenge is to engage the employees to apply their talents to maximum effect, to offer discretionary effort over and above that required through standard performance management measures.

A more common definition of talent is one that focuses on a limited number of 'key' people. This definition is based on exclusivity and will look to make sure that there is a pipeline to fill share price influencing positions such as the chief executive or those who are being developed to take on senior positions through succession management, or graduates and high potentials. Often fast trackers will be identified as being able to move two more levels up the organizational hierarchy. This approach is one exemplified by General Electric's 'vitality curve', which differentiates between the top 20%, the middle 70% and the bottom 10% (Stahl *et al.*, 2012).

Career Development Conversations at Jerónimo Martins

Jerónimo Martins is a Portugal-based international group operating in the Food Distribution, Food Manufacturing and Services sectors; with operations in Portugal, Poland and Colombia. The group has over 69 000 employees and annual sales of nearly €11 billion.

The Management Trainee Programme recruits high potential graduates for senior management roles through accelerated career paths. The company has developed a 12-month structured approach of which a key element is a series of development meetings to stimulate reflection on career goals and what is needed to achieve them, turning a career development process into a true dialogue.

The process starts with individual meetings that are held during the first week in the company so as to have an initial reflection on motivation and future career aspirations, followed by general business training.

As trainees get to know the various areas and functions of the business, additional conversations take place to understand career preferences and the associated motivations. Shortly before the final decision on their placement for Individual Functional Training, a further meeting is held. This is intended to discuss options, see how these fit individual preferences and explain the long-term development alternatives (career paths) that the organization believes will best leverage the trainee's potential.

(continued)

While in their functional training, the trainees' performance is evaluated with regard to future development. The trainees are asked to provide an input on their career vision, especially if it has altered.

A third meeting then takes place before the final assignment of the trainee to a function. As the trainees are in the company for about 10 months at this point, and thus have quite a good understanding of the company's structure and existing career paths, they are encouraged to speak about where they would like to be in the long term, and then reflect on what the different professional experiences (rotations) are that would prepare them for that role. The trainees are advised to be ambitious but at the same time realistic in their planning.

Even though all trainees then graduate from the programme, the meetings do not end. Each of the programme graduates attends a follow-up meeting in their second and third year in the company. During these meetings, reflection is made on the work they have been doing, focusing on how it contributes to their development and the plans that had been agreed on when they were graduating from the programme. Trainees talk about their performance, development of relevant competences and are asked to evaluate the overall experience and progress as they see it with regard to expectations that were raised in the course of the recruitment process, the programme and after it.

Career development advice is given, turning the process into an internal career counselling tool not only allowing HR to stay connected with the development of the trainees but also helping the trainees to navigate through the complexity of career development in a large organization.

Wojciech Zytkowiak, Jerónimo Martins Group, Human Resources

The top performers are candidates for programmes to prepare them for positions of greater seniority than those they occupy at the moment.

In the above examples, either dedicated talent managers take on responsibility for developing specific talent programmes or talent management activity is integrated within the people or HR organization.

Talent 4.0: The new now

The multi-generational, diverse and global nature of the modern work-force means that the choice between either inclusive or exclusive as extremes on a talent continuum looks increasingly anachronistic. Instead, organizations will try to adopt both positions simultaneously. This means having policies and practices that maximize the development of all employees whilst at the same time ensuring that there are enough people developed specifically for senior management or technical roles. Talent is becoming a non-hierarchical concept.

Whereas the preparation of succession plans might have been consid-ered as Talent 1.0, the attraction of high-flying CEOs as Talent 2.0 and the focus on graduates, high potentials and specialists as talent 3.0, the new now of maximizing the potential of a multi-generational, multi-cultural, cross-organizational, inclusive talent workforce is Talent 4.0.

Some organizations go significantly further than the standard lan-guage of employee engagement or talent management and have begun to put employees first, customers second (as exemplified by Vineet Nayar, CEO of HCL) or treat their employees with the same care and considera-tion as they would their customers. Furthermore, encouraging a culture of cooperation between talented teams, rather than competing for a few plum positions, can pay off handsomely, as shown at Microsoft where CEO Steve Ballmer made sure that 'the product groups work together instead of operating as talent-hoarding fiefdoms. As a result, Microsoft arguably now has the best product lineup in its history' (Vance, 2012). Creating an environment where people can deliver to their full potential, and making people at every level before making product, is an attractive option.

Enriching lives, rewarding achievement and delivering full potential are no longer objectives drawn out of left-field management texts but ones that are realistic and desirable. Authenticity and meaning are two of the characteristics of great organizations (Churchard, 2013). Indeed, for some, such as Volvo, 'talking about purpose, as well as performance; communi-cating a clear sense of where the organisation is heading and how it will get there' in a way that is meaningful for all are built into the people strategy (Glover, 2012). An approach to talent management that facilitates the achievement of this is increasingly recognized as a critical success factor.

Creating a context in which talent can flourish

Those organizations that are able to create a context whereby all talent can flourish will have a pool of people who can make a difference to the organization's prosperity.

Regardless of the organizational structure or the approach to strategy setting, there is a growing recognition of the fact that talent exists at all levels of the organization. Indeed, the frontline worker who is brilliant at creating solutions for customers or the back office worker who is a genius at app design, process flows or project management is regarded in today's organization as critical talent, irrespective of whether they are riding on a fast track. New companies such as those providing product to Apple and Google's apps shops rely as much on their nimble market-focused designers to produce winning products as the vision of their CEOs. Making sure that all are given the space and development to fulfil their potential is the twin talent challenge.

The onus is on the organization as a whole, and on those responsible for talent management in particular, to develop practices and a culture that maximize the contribution of all employees whilst at the same time ensuring that fulfilment of key positions is also satisfied. Organizations will acknowledge that smart talent management will create strategic value and create competitive advantage (Vaiman and Vance, 2008).

The unique challenge in global organizations

Balancing the outcomes of the organization's global talent needs against (the sometimes competing) local requirements is a challenge for most global organizations, and yet successfully doing so is one of the critical success factors that have been highlighted. Some are able to introduce global performance standards, supported by global leadership competency profiles and standardized performance appraisal tools and processes.

Others allow the decision on whether to enforce a single global standard to remain a local one, believing that the principles are more important than the processes. On the whole, a company's decision 'about how much local control to allow depends partly on the industry; for instance, consumer products need to be more attuned to the local market than pharmaceuticals or software' (Stahl *et al.*, 2012).

There is a wide range of challenges facing global organizations in their quest to attract and retain talented people. These include the well-researched areas of cultural differences and attitudinal or behavioural variations from one country to the next. A less-well-researched area is the energy needed to manage global operations given differences in time and distance. Persistence and flexibility are two characteristics of global management. Some would say core competences.

Releasing the potential of talent

The approach advocated by this book is that if you make your people before you make your products, releasing the potential of your talent as a top priority, the creativity and commitment released will generate new business opportunities that other companies may find hard to replicate, which in turn will give you a unique competitive advantage.

Achieving this desirable outcome may require a shift in corporate mind-set because people will be on a par with new product development, the creation of new distribution outlets or clever financial engineering in the list of the company's priorities. This is a different world from the one in which talent consisted of a few high potentials in talent pools to be visited at the time of the annual talent review. Now, organizations have simultaneously to implement exclusivity and inclusivity in the company's talent strategy.

Talent management goes beyond the creation of effective processes to the creation of an inclusive culture of opportunity.

If organizations can become like the talent factories epitomized by Procter & Gamble in the seminal *Harvard Business Review* article by Ready and Conger (2007), they will ensure a supply of people to fill key positions. To do so means that they will need to maintain 'a twin focus on functionality (rigorous talent processes that support strategic and cultural objectives) and vitality (management's emotional commitment, which is reflected in daily actions)'.

But it's no longer relevant for organizations to direct their talent management efforts only to the traditional 'centres of performance': senior managers and high potentials. Instead a more comprehensive and holistic view will be necessary, since recently recruited employees may be the ones who hold the key to the company's prosperity.

They may be nearer to the marketplace in which the organization is competing, have skills based on new technologies that can be developed into winning products or services or they may have a mindset of creativity and innovation. Hence, their talents are invaluable in developing and positioning a company in its market. Their knowledge and behaviours will be critical in developing the company's ethos and culture.

Talent management should embrace the potential of all employees.

A business case for talent: The organizational perspective

It is possible to justify the level of interest in talent and talent management from two perspectives.

First, there is the argument that talented people can make a difference to the organization's bottom line. This is the business case for talent. Second, there is the argument that talent management can help to maximize the contribution of talented people and ensure that they perform and develop to their full potential. This is the 'people case' for talent management.

The World Federation of People Management Associations concludes in its *Creating People Advantage* report (Boston Consulting Group, 2012) that those companies which didn't adapt to the 'new state of high volatility will be rendered obsolete by more nimble and flexible rivals'. One way to avoid this is by an effective talent strategy. There are significant business reasons for having a focus on talent.

Amongst the benefits of effective talent management are greater commitment, well-being, favourable turnover intentions and fairness (Sonnenberg, 2010). Talent has been identified as a driver of value creation, more talent and better shareholder returns. Dave Ulrich identifies four key outcomes of why talent matters (Ulrich, 2011):

- Investor confidence: total market value; better p/e than competitors.
- Community reputation: brand recognition and impact.
- Business execution: ability to implement new strategy.
- Customer commitment and share.

Amongst the objectives outlined for talent management in North American Companies (Right Management, 2012) were to ensure future leadership, plan and manage succession and to retain high-value talent. Other objectives included fostering employee engagement, developing all employees and boosting productivity. The output of these could reduce employee turnover, build the organization brand and advance diversity within the organization. Additional benefits were creativity and innovation and the ability to adapt to globalization.

In addition, a survey of talent management in European organizations (Turner, 2012) found that talent management had a variety of organizational benefits:

- Talent management programmes could enhance the organization's performance resulting in higher business performance indicators.
- An effective talent management programme could support the achievement of stretch targets by ensuring a supply of leaders through all parts of the organization.
- Giving talent the opportunity to gain insight into the company through structured development and secondment opportunities and then using this insight to build new business segments was a value-adding outcome of the investment in talent.

- The development of internationally minded leaders would support the organization's global growth.

Furthermore, the benefits of talent management in Asia were seen as integral to continued economic growth (Selvaretnam, 2013).

The business benefits of having robust talent management systems and processes are recognized worldwide. But this is only one part of the organizational case for investment in talent. The other concerns the many benefits felt by the people who work for the organization when they feel that they have the opportunity to flourish.

A 'people' case for talent: Talent management from the perspective of those defined as 'talent'

The CIPD found that 'participants on talent programmes or pools have high engagement levels and are more likely to see a future with their organization. They value personal development such as coaching and mentoring over more formal offerings and believe that the talent activities will help them to both perform better in their current roles and prepare them for potential future positions' (McCartney, 2010).

The challenge now is to extend these feelings to all employees, to create a culture of meaning and abundance throughout the whole organization (Ulrich and Ulrich, 2010). This means addressing the multiple needs of employees.

People want different things from the organizations in which they work. One study of high potentials identified interest groups (Uren, 2011) such as 'Brand Enthusiasts' who want to work in a company that has a strong reputation or brand. 'They seek opportunities to be stretched and challenged, and want the necessary support to make this happen'; 'Career Ladderists', who want promotion and are attracted to organizations with upward development and progression; and 'Connectors', for whom 'development is about having a range of opportunities and experiences, as well as having the right collaboration and support in place to make the most of them'.

One of the talent challenges will be to create the environment in which the expectations of each of these groups are understood and, if possible, met. The result will be tangible outcomes (return on investment in talent) and intangible ones (motivated and engaged employees or an increase in the value of intangible assets such as corporate reputation or IP). But this won't be enough. As Caplan (2011) points out, 'everyone is important. Make talent important for everyone'. This means focusing on the individual development of all employees.

In today's business environment talent management has gone beyond the matching of supply and demand. The traditional challenges faced by those organizations such as recruiting and retaining people in tight labour markets have in recent times been complemented by new ones brought about by globalization, demographics and attitudinal differences between generations, as well as increasing demand from within the organization to provide an economic rationale to funding talent initiatives.

The already complex field of talent management has been made more so by these developments. And so it is incumbent on the organization to have some clarity about its objectives for talent management investment, a clear strategy for delivering these and a process that is robust as a stand-alone entity but is also integrated with other organizational or people management processes.

Critical success factors for talent management

Traditional, linear approaches to talent management that have evolved over a twenty-year period have a proven track record. But there is the opportunity to add to them with new approaches that take account of external forces – globalization, demographic change and so on – and internal dynamics such as new types of organizational structure. Gap analysis and demand fulfilment through classic talent methods such as nine-box models are important but can only offer part of the solution. In addition, an organizational culture that recognizes the value of allowing talented people at all levels to flourish with abundance can be uniquely differentiating.

This has led to clarification of organizational expectations of those responsible for talent.

Combining new and more traditional talent challenges creates a revised set of critical success factors, which include:

- Using outside-in thinking to gain insights into the dynamics of labour markets and new ways of managing talent.
- Having clarity and consensus about what is meant by the term talent in the unique context of the organization.
- Prioritizing the effective alignment of talent strategy with business strategy.
- *And* the creation of new strategies based on the unique talents within the workforce.
- Ensuring that this is done in a way that leads to a return on investment in talent.
- Managing talent in a flexible or non-hierarchical workforce structure.
- Managing talent in a diverse workforce.
- Dealing successfully with generational differences and the attitudes to employment and career management.
- Reconciling organizational (cultural), management and financial (budget) tensions of delivering talent strategy.
- Integrating social media into talent management processes.

In future, sustainable talent management strategies will value 'knowledge-sharing, involvement and shared leadership, require all staff to be other-referential rather than self-referential, and value craftsmanship and experience as well as potential' (CIPD, 2011a).

Making your people before you make your products may be the key to achieving this.

But this will not take place in a vacuum. And so those responsible for talent management will also have an understanding of the context within which their organizations are operating. The demand for talent takes place in a dynamic and competitive environment.

Chapter 2

The world as an open market for talented people

Executive summary

- *There is a worldwide shortage of talent; in every geography, talent is on the move.*
- *Shortages occur at every level – executives, engineers, sales representatives, technicians, IT staff – and workers in fields such as oil and gas extraction, aerospace manufacturing and optical engineering.*
- *Demographic changes have exacerbated the problem. But for some companies and countries, the demographic edge is a genuine competitive edge.*
- *The multi-generational workforce means different expectations and outcomes for those involved in talent management.*
- *Satisfying this complex demographic picture means regarding talent as a community to be engaged rather than an audience to be addressed from a stage.*
- *This means creating meaning at work and creating 'abundant' working environments.*
- *To do so also means recognizing the different types of organizational structure that may exist. The classic hierarchy will need talent management that meets a different set of expectations than those in a networked organization.*
- *Effective talent management simultaneously requires great leadership (at all levels and not just through high potential talent programmes) and full engagement of the whole of the workforce (to ensure that all talent makes a full contribution).*

A worldwide shortage of talent

The case for making your people before making your products is accentuated by the context within which global organizations are operating. To put it simply, there is a worldwide shortage of talent. ManpowerGroup's (2013a) survey notes that 35% of 38000 employers reported that they had difficulty in filling jobs and that this could affect their business prospects.

- In Canada, the hardest jobs to fill are engineers, sales representatives, technicians and IT staff; in the UK, the number of marketing and media jobs continues to grow, while the number of available candidates is in decline; talent is increasingly dominating the CEO's agenda in India and the PwC 15th Annual Global CEO Survey 'suggests that 78% of all CEOs want change in the way they manage talent'. (PwC Saratoga, 2012).
- In the UK, over 145000 people came into the country for work purposes in 2012. China and India were the main sources of incoming talent but Australia and the US made up significant numbers also. Others in the 'top 10' included the Philippines, Japan and Russia. Nurses are recruited from Portugal, Spain, Ireland and the Philippines. There are skills shortages in railway signalling and computer gaming and in fields such as oil and gas extraction, aerospace manufacturing and optical engineering.
- In 2011, nearly 17% of the US workforce were not US citizens at birth. Where shortages are at their most acute, such as the case of highly skilled

science and engineering talent in the US, organizations have sought to off-shore some of their critical innovation work because talent can be accessed in other markets than the 'home base' (Lewin, Massini and Peeters, 2009).

- The demand for executives and managers who are able to deliver successfully in the face of intense global competition continues to outstrip supply. In China, 'people that can manage businesses, lead others, create and innovate' have critical skills that are much in demand by global multi-national corporations and indigenous companies looking to compete on the world stage. 'With the limited supply of these critical skills, firms are now competing head to head to attract and retain such talent' (Vorhauser-Smith, 2012).

In every geography, talent is on the move. Nor is it just at executive level that issues of talent supply and demand are important. In a study of the core strengths of global cities, it was noted that 'human capital gains help propel Sao Paulo, Brazil, up the rankings', because a combination of unemployment at historic lows, an increase in foreign skilled workers, an attractive housing market and excellent transport links had given the city a 'demographic edge'. Demographic change is not an abstract sociological concept, but one of significance to the achievement of competitive advantage for regions, cities and businesses (Citi, 2013).

The demographic edge is a genuine competitive edge.

An organization-wide understanding

By 2020, the world could have 40 million too few college-educated workers, and in developing economies there may be a shortfall of 45 million workers with secondary-school education and vocational training. 'In advanced economies, up to 95 million workers could lack the skills needed for employment' (Dobbs *et al.*, 2012).

It's no use having great plans for the business based on having a mix of knowledge and skills if the people with those skills aren't available, don't want to join or don't want to stay at the organization. And so the first principle of make your people before you make your products relates to an organization-wide understanding that the world is an open market for talented people. There are opportunities for most and the challenge will be to attract and retain the best. This challenge falls to everyone who works for the organization. From the CEO who will lead, create culture and guide strategy, managers who will act in a way that shows they value people and employees who will take opportunities and act as champions of the organization, to actual and potential employees as well as customers.

A feature of this is a culture in which people are not regarded as abstract resources to be deployed around the chessboard of global competition. They are individuals, each with valuable skills and a role to play in the organization's success. In global organizations this will come about by a culture of opportunity for talented people wherever in the world they work and systems that encourage the development of that talent. The position can be complex.

Talented people are in demand during times of economic growth and continue to be so even when times are slower. The former speaks for itself; the latter derives from the fact that whilst there may be more labour available on the market because of downsizing or organizational restructuring it may not have the right skills for the specific market. Or, as was prevalent during the most recent recession, those people who would have moved in fact stayed put because of uncertainty in the economic climate. Hence, the supply of talent was not sufficient to meet demand. Understanding the supply side of the talent debate is as important as highlighting demand in order to achieve equilibrium.

And more. The whole talent landscape has changed. As Andrew Benett points out in *The Talent Mandate*, there has been a shift from workers to talent which in turn means that 'success is no longer about fine-tuning production processes to churn out more products with the same number of workers; instead, it is about fine-tuning the employee base to produce knockout ideas and build a level of value that vastly exceeds what each individual costs the company in pay and benefits' (Benett, 2013).

A complex history of talent management

This is a problem with which organizations have been wrestling for some time. There is a complex recent history of talent and talent management and as a result the number of interpretations and best practices has escalated. Sometimes the advice can be contradictory. Nonetheless, there is consensus about one point: talent is scarce.

The focus on talent, as we understand it today, gained momentum during the mid-1990s when economic, social and political factors came together in an almost perfect storm to create an intensely competitive labour market, hence McKinsey's seminal *War for Talent*, with its early focus on the corner offices of corporate America, argued that at a time when the need for talent was increasing, large US companies were finding it hard to attract and retain good people; a situation that could only get worse (Michaels, Handfield-Jones and Axelrod, 2001).

In spite of a good deal of effort to resolve talent shortages, there were mixed results such that Peter Cappelli argued that 'failures in talent management are an on-going source of pain for executives in modern organizations. Over the past generation, talent management practices, especially in the United States, have by and large been dysfunctional, leading corporations to lurch from surpluses of talent to shortfalls to surpluses and back again' (Cappelli, 2008). It's fair to say that talent management continues to evolve.

Thomson Reuters: Careers without boundaries

Thomson Reuters is the leading source of intelligent information for the world's businesses and professionals. It combines industry expertise with innovative technology to deliver critical information to leading decision makers in the financial and risk, legal, tax and accounting, intellectual property and science, and media markets, powered by the world's most trusted news organization. The company has around

60 000 employees in more than 100 countries. The challenge the company faces is to ensure a supply of talented people to match the multiple demands of its global businesses.

Careers without boundaries

Thomson Reuters believes that diverse people make a difference beyond boundaries and across borders and that this is the key to its customers' success and, ultimately, the company's. It has a firm belief that careers shouldn't be confined. The breadth and global reach of its business offers virtually unlimited opportunities to shape a career path that matches the contours of an employee's talents, interests and goals. To fully leverage this, the company has adopted a philosophy of 'careers without boundaries'.

Many paths, a single commitment

In order to support this philosophy, the company aims to provide every employee with a positive working environment, continued professional development and a commitment to a work–life balance and equal opportunities. The vast network of global career opportunities, facilitated by virtual working, means that there's no single path. Employees can start in one location and decide to further their career in another (physically or virtually), or apply their expertise to a different strategic business unit from where they began.

Accelerating development

Professional development takes many forms at Thomson Reuters via a broad suite of learning and development resources and opportunities that employees can take advantage of. In addition, programmes designed to accelerate development are offered to a number of targeted talent groups. These range from programmes for emerging women leaders and leaders in Asia to the Global

(continued)

Talent Rotation Programme that aims to provide short-term rotations into and out of rapidly developing economies (RDEs), accelerating the development of the highest potential talent and allowing them to gain the global and cultural experience needed to lead in a global context.

Particularly successful has been the Generate programme, which combines a real-world business case with corporate responsibility to develop future leaders. It uses a mix of virtual collaboration and a week in an RDE focused on global awareness and innovation through the delivery of a sustainable business project for a community partner. Results have been impressive:

- Ninety-six per cent of participants agree that the programme made them more effective in working virtually and collaborating in global teams.
- Seventy-five per cent of participants received a promotion after completing the programme.
- Ninety-five per cent of participants still work at Thomson Reuters.

'A company can only grow as fast as the people within it grow. The reason I like Generate so much is that it speaks to the nature and culture of Thomson Reuters.'

– Generate participant

Sue Kamal, Global Head of HR Strategy & Change, Thomson Reuters

Companies become talent factories

There was additional urgency to address talent issues because, by the turn of the century, talent shortages went beyond the upper hierarchical levels and extended to the far reaches of many organizations. And the problem was worldwide. 'Talent and talent management thus became global phenomena and for a decade have been uppermost in the minds of both HR professionals and business managers. There was a growing consensus that organisations needed to increase their efforts in the areas of engaging, motivating and fully using the skills of their workforces.

Hence, talent shortages were perceived to be high-risk business issues. A spate of responses to the war for talent, in order to alleviate these, included Ready and Conger's exhortation for companies to become 'talent factories'. To do this required procedures in place to identify and develop next-generation leaders who are synchronized with the company's growth plans and to keep the attention of the company's leaders on talent issues (Ready and Conger, 2007).

The worldwide recession changed the talent paradigm because 'while there is a surplus of job seekers, some companies are facing shortages in critical areas where they most need to attract and keep highly skilled talent' (Erickson, Schwartz and Ensell, 2014). Just because there are high unemployment rates doesn't mean the people with the right skills are available. A talent paradox is 'raising the stakes in the competition for critical talent, with organizations trying to outbid each other for a select group of critical employees and the skills they need to succeed ... this competition is fuelling rising salaries as well as prospective employees' expectations, making it difficult to meet skill needs while keeping labour costs at desired levels' (Deloitte, 2013).

Far-reaching, strategic issues affecting talent and talent management were 'increased world-wide economic development, extensive global communication, rapid transfer of new technology, growing trade, and emigration of large numbers of people' (Tarique and Schuler, 2010) have created significant challenges in the field of international human resource management and in particular global talent management. How to address these challenges is one of the continuing foci of talent management.

One way to inform the debate is to build an understanding of the forces that are driving talent supply and demand, and from this derive insight as to how to make sure there is a balance between the two. It will not be easy to achieve such equilibrium.

Of the many forces that affect the supply of and demand for talent, three stand out. These are:

- the external forces of globalization and its effect on the movement of labour;
- demographic change and its effect on the movement of attitudes and behaviours; and
- the changing structure of organizations from hierarchies to networks.

1. Globalization, technology and the free movement of skilled people

Although the catch-all term 'globalization' is often used to describe people flows and migration of individuals between countries, there are many other reasons for such movement, ranging from the social or political – owing to war, climate change and natural disaster – to economic factors with the rapid growth of markets such as Brazil, Russia, India and China.

Talent flows and migration

In recent times the lack of equilibrium between the demand for and supply of people to deliver economic growth has also been a cause of talent migration and labour flows between countries. The fallout from this historical movement has had the most significant impact on the subject of talent. There are two-way flows as work moves towards labour on the one hand and labour moves towards work on the other.

The 'move to relocate work close to sources of plentiful and often cheaper labour' (CIPD, 2011b) has meant that organizations will have a variety of geographic centres of production or distribution. In these cases global talent management requires strategic priorities that take account of differences across national contexts for how talent should be managed in the countries where they operate. Both the importance of talent and its effective management will be critical success factors (Vaiman, Scullion and Collings, 2012). Furthermore, understanding and navigating the political, legal, social and economic climates of the geographies in which such organizations are working as well as moving into emerging markets will require an understanding of cultural differences.

The movement of labour towards work also has implications. In emerging economies talent is 'scarce, expensive, and hard to retain', whilst 'fast-moving, ambitious local companies are competing more strongly' (Dewhirst, Pettigrew and Srinivasan, 2012). This is compounded by the fact that 'Executives from developed markets, by no means eagerly seizing plum jobs abroad, appear disinclined to move' (Dewhirst, Pettigrew and Srinivasan, 2012).

- In developed economies the challenge is no easier since 'the proportion of employers reporting an increase in competition for well-qualified talent has risen threefold from 20 per cent in 2009 to 62 per cent in 2013' (CIPD/Hays, 2013) with managerial and professional vacancies being the hardest ones to fill, followed by technical specialists. Labour turnover has declined steadily since the start of the financial crisis in 2008, and 'one in six organisations reported that an absence of applicants has contributed to recruitment difficulties' (CIPD/Hays, 2013).
- From a global perspective, one of the consequences is the gap between demand and supply, which means that there is difficulty in filling key positions. The supply of leaders with a global mindset for growth who are able to demonstrate cultural sensitivity and awareness, manage diversity inclusion and respect and maximize the contribution of multicultural workplaces (CIPD, 2011b) is regarded as not being sufficient to satisfy demand.

It can be more complex even than this picture suggests. One study of creative talent postulates that there is a concentration of talent, leading to the argument that a few cities and regions 'truly matter in today's global economy' (Florida, 2005). Innovation is most concentrated in a few areas. Hence, the growth of the creative economy means that an even greater focus on attracting and retaining such talent is necessary (Florida, 2005).

Hence, globalization has had a dramatic effect on the availability of talent from the demand side as work moves towards sources of labour and labour moves towards sources of work. In addition the concentration of particular skills in a few key regions provides further complexity.

A critical starting point for those in developing people strategy in general and talent strategy in particular is a deep understanding of the dynamics of labour markets and demographic change that can inform their decision making.

Which skills are in short supply?

This point was well made when the subject of worldwide talent shortages took centre stage at the annual World Economic Forum conference in Davos, whose attendees in 2013 included the chairs of Toshiba, Coca-Cola, Embraer, UBS, Telenor and Peremba as well as Secretaries of State from Ecuador and the Philippines, the Prince of Monaco and the Secretary General of the United Nations. That such an illustrious group should have talent on their agenda shows by how much talent has become a priority among federal governments, federal agencies, nongovernmental organizations (NGOs), educational institutions and community-based organizations (CBOs) as well as corporations.

The 2011 conference highlighted a number of 'most difficult skills to recruit' including:

- combined technical and business expertise
- global experience
- ability to develop and lead others
- creativity and innovativeness
- courage to challenge
- ability to adjust to change quickly
- analytical skills
- language skills
- ability to collaborate.

An agenda item at the 2013 conference was 'how to thrive when global competitiveness is increasingly driven by talent and innovation'.

The position is that talent shortages are having a bearing on profitability and 'One in four CEOs said they were unable to pursue a market opportunity or have had to cancel or delay a strategic initiative because of talent challenges. One in three is concerned that skills shortages will impact their company's ability to innovate effectively'.

The shortage of talent is a global phenomenon. If organizations are going to deal with this effectively, they will also need a global perspective. But more than this, they will need a macro-level view of the whole economy and a micro level view of how their own region is affected.

The variability in response was particularly marked in global organizations. Although they are, on paper, well equipped to attract talented people, since they can 'tap sources of suitably qualified people around the world and attract them with stimulating jobs in different countries' there is some evidence that this is becoming more difficult with intensifying competition for talent.

2. Achieving demographic advantage

The quantitative challenge in talent management is an important consideration for organizations looking to match demand and supply to deliver their business objectives. But it will not be enough to fill key roles unless the challenges thrown up by the changing demographics of the workforce are also addressed.

Organizations need to be smart if they are to ride the demographic trends that characterize modern labour markets. This is because there are older stable populations in developed countries and younger more mobile ones in developing countries and, second, there are different approaches to work (and life) between the generations.

In the first instance there have been rapid shifts in demographic profiles in some countries as well as the incidence of declining birth rates and increasing longevity. Boston Consulting Group in conjunction with WFPMA found that populations in developed countries such as Germany, Japan and the USA will skew sharply older in the next decade, which may cause vacancies to become unfulfilled, whilst at the same time companies will lose 'valuable institutional and process knowledge'. In the meantime, rapidly developing nations are and will continue to experience skills gaps that population growth alone won't fill. This situation has created an absolute imperative of identifying, attracting and retaining talented people (Boston Consulting Group, 2012).

Talent and the multi-generational workforce

The multi-generational workforce (Buahene, 2009) means different expectations and outcomes for those involved in talent management. Four distinct demographic groups can be seen: traditionalists, whose perceived goal was to build a legacy; baby boomers, whose perceived goal was 'to put their stamp on things'; Generation X, whose perceived goal was to maintain independence; and Generation Y, whose perceived goal was to 'create life and work that has meaning'. These generational identities are translated into workplace behaviours in terms of the relationship with the organization, the relationship with authority, the relationship with colleagues, the preferred work style, the type of management style that is prevalent and the different learning styles.

Generation Y is the largest ever to enter the workforce. 'As a result of their shared social and historical experiences [they] have been claimed to be identifiably different from their generational predecessors (i.e., Generation X, Baby Boomers, and Traditionalists)' (Weyland, 2011). The result is that this demographic is 'destined to be the most high-performing generation in history. The key is to find out how to unlock their potential and develop them into the managers and leaders of the future'. This generation will want to work for organizations that are 'playing a constructive role on behalf of multiple stakeholders, not just investors and shareholders, and that can provide them with opportunities to be part of that effort' (Savitz, 2013).

The impact of this multi-generational make-up of the workforce reflects itself in the different expectations on the part of different demographic groups, as shown by Deloitte's study (Deloitte, 2010):

- Executives in Generations X and Y had job advancement as their highest expectation.
- But Generation Y had a much stronger inclination towards individual career planning. Generation X favoured leadership development programmes.
- Baby Boomers, on the other hand, had benefits (such as health and pensions) as their highest expectation.
- Employees in all three generations had promotion or job advancement high on their lists. But of the three groups, Generation Y employees (as opposed to executives) had the lowest percentage who ranked job promotion or advancement as their priority (41% as opposed to 64% of Generation X and 50% of Baby Boomers).

There are other findings about the career and development differences between the generational groupings. For example, Generation Y employees saw their career in chapters of two to three years each, expected quick reward and individual development and had low barriers to separation and high self-confidence. The traditional 'middle managers programme' may not be enough to capture the imagination of such a group.

Creating meaning at work for talented people

Creating meaning at work is an important part of the talent strategy.

The chairman of the board of directors of Alfa SAB de CV, Mexico, reinforced this point with his comments that 'our capacity to attract, retain and manage executive talent does not depend on the compensation package, but rather on our ability to create a sense of belonging to an organisation that offers a long-term relationship and a professional development opportunity, and that has a clear conception of itself, of what it wants to be, and of how to achieve it' (PwC, 2011).

In addition, Dave and Wendy Ulrich have given the examples of Old Navy and Zappos as organizations that have understood the value of creating meaning, Old Navy by weaving stories around a hypothetical 'typical customer', and Zappos by building a culture of happiness for customers around which people practice can develop (Ulrich and Ulrich, 2010).

Creating meaning at work transcends any one generational group, and developing talent strategies for the multi-generational workforce will therefore require flexibility.

Whilst bearing in mind that not everyone in a particular demographic group behaves in the same way as every other member of that group, there are some useful general characteristics and from these it is possible to reach some important conclusions for talent management:

- There is the possibility that different segments have different expectations about their work, lives and careers.
- This has implications for attraction since the employer brand will have to have different strands or emphases.
- Once attracted the retention of people will require a multiplicity of options.
- As will development: some will require individualized career planning as a priority; others will place more emphasis on flexibility.

In conclusion, massive economic change coupled with both quantitative and qualitative forces, such as attitudinal differences between generations, have created a complex labour market. These environmental forces mean that organizations have to be smart about their approach to talent. Creativity in design of talent initiatives and flexibility in how they are delivered will be critical success factors.

3. Organizational and structural influences on talent management

The third consideration arises from the significant internal challenges brought about by the inherent structure and culture of a particular organization.

The shift from hierarchies to networks implied by the forces outlined above (this assumption not only applies to dotcoms or technology start-ups but to some of the largest organizations in the world) means that traditional approaches to talent management need additional insights.

The organization's business strategy will determine organizational design; and this will in turn determine the approach to talent and talent management.

Talent management in hierarchical organizations

Classic talent management has its roots in hierarchical organizations. This still has relevance for many. Figure 2.1 represents a hierarchical organization. There is a logical, largely fixed structure overseen by a CEO,

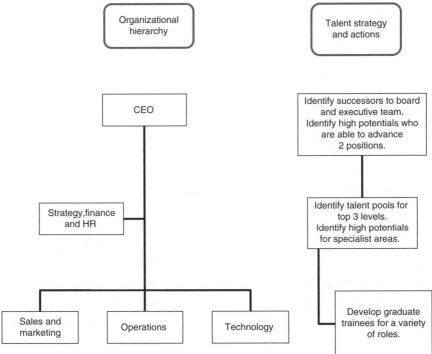

Figure 2.1: Talent management in hierarchical organizations.

managing director or president to whom functional, country-based or product group heads report. The flow of 'talent' is mostly upwards, and the management of it is planned, systematic and backed by data of progress on upward movement, the numbers who are able to do so and the resource needed to prepare them for such roles.

The characteristics of talent management in this would be:

- Identify those positions which would come under the talent remit: likely to be the CEO, the Board/Operating Committee or Group and selected senior management roles.
- Assess the suitability of candidates to fill these roles in the shorter term: the succession plan.
- Assess the suitability of candidates for the medium term: the talent pool.
- Develop programmes for each of these candidates to ensure that they have the right levels of skill today and in future (executive or management development, executive coaching).
- Assess and develop candidates for the longer term: graduate or fast track programmes.

Hierarchies lend themselves to classic talent management, focusing on a few people to satisfy executive and managerial positions.

But new organization structures require a different approach.

Talent management in networked organizations

Figure 2.2 shows a different type of organizational structure. Here, the organization may be based on networks or projects. Reporting lines are less clear, since the market may be fluid or unpredictable, demanding a rapid response, or the project terms may be changing, demanding the sourcing of new skills. The conventional definition of talent as one who can move up the hierarchy by two levels or one who is being groomed to take over a business unit or department is not sufficient to explain the dynamics of talent in this structure.

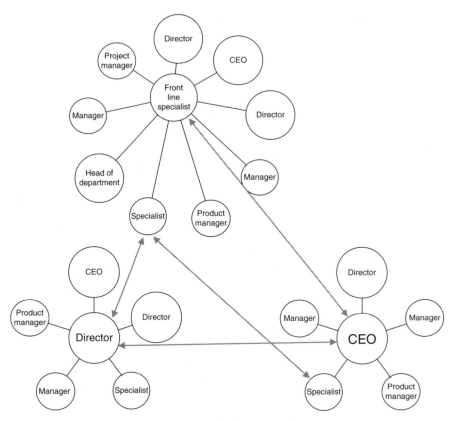

Figure 2.2: Talent management in networked organizations.

In Figure 2.2 a specialist in one part of the organization working with a specialist in another part of the organization may be critical to the successful delivery of a product, project or service. These are highly talented and skilled people. But they won't necessarily feature in a succession plan, assessment centre or talent pool. They may not be typical promotion candidates for elevation two steps up the hierarchy. They may not want to be. But one thing is certain: they have talent and the organization wants to keep them.

Developing talent to satisfy medium- or longer-term requirements is more difficult here because such requirements may change; the attraction and retention of talented people at all levels to satisfy short-term needs is a priority.

Talent management in the networked organization has the following characteristics:

- There is a need to satisfy the immediate and medium-term succession to the CEO and executive positions through succession management, recruitment and retention.
- Certain selected roles may be needed, e.g. M&A specialists in an organization growing through acquisition for which immediate and medium-term requirements will be made.
- However, in addition to these 'traditional' talent roles, there is an imperative to acquire, develop and retain specialist roles in either front of line or back office positions. In a networked organization such roles and the people who fill them will be included in the talent approach.

The arrowed lines in Figure 2.2 represent flows of knowledge to deliver business strategy. The specialist who is working to coordinate the outputs of the CEO in one part of the business and the director in another is a priority talent. Yet such a role may not be covered by traditional talent methodologies. And so a different, more inclusive perspective is needed in this type of organization.

Making your people before making your products would envisage that the specialists in networked organizations will be attracted because of inclusive talent development, retained because of the opportunities created by such an approach and will receive development that is relevant to the completion of this current role and an opportunity for further development to prepare for future roles; whatever they may be.

Both external and internal drivers of talent challenges have been identified (Tarique and Schuler, 2010). Amongst these are national culture, the prevailing economic context, politics and labour law. Internally, it's becoming necessary to recognize and clearly articulate the financial value of global talent to the organization (CIPD, 2011b). These factors set a context for talent management that simultaneously requires great leadership (at all levels and not just through high potential talent programmes) and full engagement of the whole of the workforce (to ensure that all talent makes a full contribution).

The purpose of this chapter was to put over the point that understanding labour market dynamics and organizational design are two critical success factors in the delivery of a coherent talent strategy. Insights in such areas should be as important to the organization's business strategists as knowledge about the latest technology platforms, competitor product development and positioning or alternative tax management options. It is up to those responsible for people and talent management to project this case.

It is a highly complex environment and having some clarity about what we mean by 'talent' is an essential starting point.

Chapter 3

Defining talent

Executive summary

- *The definition of talent varies from organization to organization, since history, structure and culture will have an impact. Defining what is meant by talent is an organizational imperative.*
- *For some, talent is about high performance and the potential of a selected number of people to move up the organization into senior leadership or managerial positions.*
- *For others, talent is an inclusive term which refers to all employees. For most, a successful talent strategy is concerned with both ends of the employment spectrum.*
- *The definition of talent in multi-national companies tends towards an exclusive approach which involves a focus on certain groups of 'high-performing' or 'high-potential' people, whilst for others it meant a focus on certain 'key' positions in the organization.'*
- *In the future, organizations will look to develop a talent strategy that embraces all employees but at the same time has initiatives to supply future leaders. This is a talent strategy that appears to be simultaneously inclusive and exclusive.*
- *Globally, organizations need to manage their talent supply chain with the same rigour they would with other parts of the organization, and focus on making their organizations the most attractive to the best local talent.*
- *The strategic workforce plan will inform the talent strategy.*
- *The sum total of all of the potential of individual talent in an organization will be that organization's theoretical competitive position. If these potential outputs are sufficiently different and ahead of the outputs of competitor organizations that will be the organization's competitive advantage. If these potential outputs are converted to real outputs then that will be the organizations competitive success over time.*

'Talent is a pivotal resource'. But what do we mean by 'talent'?

The above forces will affect how an organization reviews and then sets its talent strategy. And so the second principle of 'make your people before you make your products' is important such that talent can no longer be regarded as an audience in receipt of a service but as more of a community that fully participates in and determines what the service actually is. Talent management is now talent management for all.

It is understood that the performance of talented people is important for business growth since it has the potential to drive productivity. 'It can improve customer share and it can be a differentiator at a time of intense global competition' (Ulrich, 2011). Talent is a pivotal resource in delivering competitive advantage.

An individual's talent is the product of ability (competence, education, training and experience), coupled with motivation (engagement, satisfaction, challenge and wellness) and opportunity (Van Dijk, 2008).

The sum total of all of the potential of individual talent in an organization will be that organization's theoretical competitive position. If these potential outputs are sufficiently different and ahead of the outputs of competitor organizations, that will be the organization's competitive advantage. If these potential outputs are converted to real outputs then that will be the organization's competitive success over time.

To achieve this will require a range of interventions across the people management sphere: 'whereas once "talent management" was mainly concerned with recruitment, it is now a much broader "essential management practice" covering organisational capability, individual development, performance enhancement, workforce planning and succession planning' (CIPD, 2011b). Nowadays, the development of a talent strategy and 'making people your competitive advantage' are at the heart of business management (Lawler, 2008).

Defining what is meant by talent is an organizational imperative if clarity of scope and the effective allocation of resources are to be achieved. But is it possible to have a 'right' definition of talent and, if so, which one is it?

Competence, commitment and contribution

The definition of 'talent' varies from organization to organization, since history, structure and culture will have an impact. Nevertheless, it's important for an organization to spend time clarifying this point if maximum leverage is to be achieved from the best deployment of its people. A clear definition of talent will facilitate strategic focus, the optimum allocation of financial resources and the best return on people investments.

The CIPD (2014) defines talent as consisting 'of those individuals who can make a difference to organisational performance, either through their immediate contribution or in the longer term by demonstrating the highest levels of potential', and talent management is the attraction, identification, development, retention and deployment of individuals with high potential who are of particular value (Tansley *et al.*, 2007). Many organizations use these definitions of talent and talent management as the basis of their approach.

And yet, in spite of a 'decade of debate and hype' there was still a lack of clarity about the definition of talent and strategic talent management, which have been defined as 'activities and processes that involve the systematic identification of key positions which differentially contribute to the organisation's sustainable competitive advantage, the development of a talent pool of high potential and high performing incumbents to fill these roles, and the development of a differentiated human resource architecture to facilitate filling these positions with competent incumbents and to ensure their continued commitment to the organisation' (Collings and Mellahi, 2009). They also make the important point that key positions are not 'necessarily restricted to the top management team (TMT) but also include key positions at levels lower than the TMT and may vary between operating units and indeed over time' (Collings and Mellahi, 2009).

Women into senior roles at Sodexo

Sodexo is one of the largest employers in the world, with 428000 employees operating in over 80 countries. The company provides a broad range of services designed to improve the quality of life for clients and consumers, ranging from food services through to complex integrated facilities management. The strength of our brand relies on the strength and diversity of our teams.

Our talent management process helps us identify and develop talent across all levels of the organization, ensuring a solid pipeline of high-performing future leaders. A number of talent development approaches are used by Sodexo, ranging from group-based activities through to individually-tailored programmes.

In 2009, the Group CEO, Michel Landel, made a commitment that 25% of senior roles would be filled by women by 2015, and that the longer-term aim was for this to increase year on year. In addition, our ambition is to increase the number of high-potential women in senior operational roles, building a talent pipeline and bench-strength that

(continued)

will fulfil the strategy of the business globally and across all segments. This is a challenging and ambitious target.

The solution was to design and develop a bespoke programme for high-potential senior managers. This would include a broad range of formal and informal learning opportunities to allow individuals to gain the knowledge and experience needed to move into more senior operational roles. It also supported Sodexo's talent strategy, which aims to encourage the development and promotion of women into senior operational roles within the organization.

After a comprehensive assessment process, a 12-month plan was developed to provide movement between the business segments and functions within Sodexo to enable participants to stretch personal learning and experiential boundaries. Key activities included:

- executive coaching for the duration of the programme;
- planned moves across segments/functions, including participation at executive meetings;
- operational mentors for the cross-segment placements;
- participation in Business School leadership programmes;
- participation in the Challenge 24 (Collaboration Company) action learning programme;
- formal placement feedback sessions.

The initial phase of the programme has recently completed, and has shown success with movement into senior operational roles and a knock-on effect on other roles in the organization. These results demonstrate our commitment to developing and growing our own people. Feedback has been very positive. We plan to continue with this approach to build the talent pipeline further.

Angela Williams, Group HR Director Global HR Services/HR Director, UK and Ireland, Sodexo

McKinsey's perspective over time

US management consultancy McKinsey, having contributed significantly to shaping the language of talent through its 'War for Talent' research, was able to take a 10-year perspective on how talent was defined by the latter years of the last century.

Its 2008 study of talent (McKinsey and Company, 2008), presented at the CIPD's People Management Conference, outlined five possible approaches.

The first is one in which everyone who works for the organization is regarded as 'talent'. In this example, the whole of the workforce has an opportunity to develop and contribute in their own unique way. This is known as 'inclusive' talent management and may lead to engagement in the broader context of the organization. There is a downside in that such an approach is likely to be more complex in its management and implementation. The processes needed to manage a whole workforce as talent will be organization wide and there may be a cost implication.

At the other extreme, McKinsey notes that some organizations regard talent as top management, their successors and other high potentials. This tends towards the popular, traditional view of talent management. A limited talent pool and a focused talent strategy make this approach efficient and ensures that it optimizes the allocated resource. The downside is a possible feeling of exclusion of those in the workforce who aren't regarded as 'talent' in the organization's definition.

Two other McKinsey definitions reflect this exclusivity and include 'talent' to mean high potentials or specialists.

Finally, there was a definition that is related to individuals identified as high potential independent of hierarchy level.

Talent in European organizations

A European study confirmed a continuum of talent definitions. On the one hand, talent was defined as a leadership cadre, 'a future leader with deep knowledge of the industry and good interpersonal skills' and as

'Individuals who have the potential to lead in a determined timescale: 1 to 3 years'; on the other hand, the definition of talent was much broader: 'every employee has unique talents, every job requires specific talents, the key is for [the] organization to best match supply with demand, in particular for critical positions' and 'talent is anybody who has potential to succeed in our organization' (Turner, 2012). This latter perspective was also supported in a later study, which concluded that an inclusive and developmental approach, focusing on talent identification and acknowledgement, was probably the most effective.

The study concludes that 'for some, talent is about high performance and potential of a selected number of people to move up the organization into senior leadership or managerial positions. For others, talent is an inclusive term which refers to all employees. For most, a successful talent strategy is concerned with both ends of the employment spectrum' (Turner, 2012). On the one hand, the organization will need to ensure a supply of future leaders, whether this is part of a succession plan or in the development of talent pools. But on the other, and increasingly, there will be a focus on the talent of everyone who works in the organization.

The talent formula

But not all talent definitions were related to organizational structure or specific leadership roles. The interpretation of talent as a concept bound up with organizational hierarchy and job descriptions was supplemented by Dave Ulrich, in a more inclusive hypothesis. He proposed a talent formula (Figure 3.1) (Ulrich, 2011).

Figure 3.1: The talent formula.

This takes talent beyond the hierarchical and focuses it on the three important factors that ultimately determine both individual and corporate performance: competence, commitment and contribution. It is possible to assess any one individual using these three metrics, regardless of their position and status.

Global talent and talent management

As we can see from the above, there is no consistency in the way in which talent is defined at the national or regional level. And when the subjects of talent and talent management are placed in a global context the definition becomes even more open to interpretation. In fact, there is no consensus about the meaning of global talent management. Instead, it appears to depend on the context of the organization and its specific place in a global market or environment. Often this can lead to 'contradictory advice and fragmented theories' (Tarique and Schuler, 2010).

Perhaps one of the reasons for this is that 'different organisations define talent from different perspectives and by different criteria. An organisation may define talent based on the type of company, business strategy, overall competitive environment and other factors' (Zhang and Bright, 2012). As such the approach to talent is shaped by the organization's relationship with the environment or the individual context. Therefore, the definition of talent is situation specific.

And the application of talent management systems and processes is equally open to interpretation. Research in 260 multi-national enterprises (MNEs) found that 'although a significant number of MNEs have systems and mechanisms in place strategically to identify and develop their talent many more seemingly adopt an *ad hoc* or haphazard approach. For instance, less than half of all MNEs have both global succession planning and formal management development programs for their high-potentials. Consequently it seems that there is a considerable distance yet to be travelled to arrive at a universal appreciation of the need to strategically manage one's key employees' (McDonnell *et al.*, 2010). Interestingly, this study also found that 'MNEs operating in the low-tech/low-cost sectors are significantly more likely to have formal global systems to identify and develop high-potentials' (McDonnell *et al.*, 2010).

In this global context, three possible 'streams' of talent and talent management, and how they are defined and practised, were identified:

- talent management as typical human resource department practices and functions;
- talent management as HR planning;
- talent management focusing on high-performing and high-potential talent.

In spite of the variability of organizational experience a definition was put forward as 'global talent management is about systematically utilizing IHRM activities (complementary HRM policies and policies) to attract, develop, and retain individuals with high levels of human capital (e.g., competency, personality, motivation) consistent with the strategic directions of the multinational enterprise in a dynamic, highly competitive, and global environment' (Tarique and Schuler, 2010).

Hence, we have another view of talent with which to work.

To be inclusive or exclusive is a worldwide debate

The dialogue about inclusive or exclusive approaches is not confined to any one company, country or continent. In a recent study of talent management in multi-national companies the majority of those companies surveyed had an exclusive approach 'seeing TM as "integrated, selective" HRM. For some, this involved an "exclusive-people" focus on certain groups of "high-performing" or "high-potential" people, whilst for others it meant an "exclusive-position" focus on certain "key" positions in the organization'. A minority had an inclusive approach and a few emphasized 'organizationally focussed competence development', concentrating upon smooth talent flows and development, and moving towards a 'social capital' perspective which 'took cognizance of networks, contexts and relationships as well as human capital' (Iles, Chuai and Preece, 2010).

Nonetheless, 'at its heart, talent management is simply a matter of anticipating the need for human capital and then setting out a plan to meet it' (Cappelli, 2008). How to do this is the challenge facing CEOs, HR directors and those with specialist talent responsibilities. This raises the issue of which definition to choose as the 'right' one for the organization.

The definition of talent depends on the evolution of the organization in which it takes place; the unique characteristics of the competitive environment of the organization and the specific culture of that organization.

Unclear definitions: Diluted strategies?

So what can an organization do about this seemingly intractable problem? Does it matter if the definition of talent is unclear?

PwC found that many organizations were failing to understand what talent management really meant and were unclear about how to create a sustainable talent pipeline for the long term. Its conclusion was that organizations needed to manage their talent supply chain with the same thoroughness as other parts of the organization. They should make their organizations the most attractive to the best local talent.

Having clarity about what is meant by talent will inform strategy and ultimately resource allocation.

The different definitions of talent and talent management have implications for the way in which organizations go about their talent fulfilment. It's possible to conclude that:

- 'Talent' is a context-specific term. There is no one definition of talent that is relevant to all organizations. Instead, it is dependent upon the specific context of the organization. For example, a start-up technology company will define its talent as those people who can develop products and applications to take to market. As the company grows it will need more marketing and finance skills; then it will need to put in place structures and processes for dealing with its people. At each stage, there will be different talent priorities. A mature business, on the other hand, will have different talent needs, maybe focusing on the development of global markets, merger and acquisition skills or those for a management buy-out; it may require experienced project professionals who have skills in managing large public-sector contracts; or it may require people who have experience of opening service centres overseas. The definition and focus on talent in the first example will be different from that in the second.

- The definition of talent is moving from being a hierarchical concept to one that is non-hierarchical. As organizations adopt new structures and processes, the talent needs of a 'node' rather than an organizational level are different from one another. Talent pools based on the ability to move up one or two levels are being supplanted by ones where the ability is that of moving between horizontal nodes – delivering projects in different contexts – or the ability to manage cross-culturally wherever the 'talent' is in the organization.

- Globalization means that whatever approach to talent is identified (hierarchical or non-hierarchical; organizational layers or nodes) is more complex than operating talent in one country alone.

There also remains a further important question relating to how far down or across the organization talent is defined.

The different perspectives on talent across the world raises the questions of whether it is important to have a single definition of talent in the organization and, if so, why – and which one to choose? There are those who regard the subject of talent definition as something that can actually suppress talent: 'a continued obsession with identifying "the right stuff"; that magic formula that defines someone as talented, prevents organizations from asking questions which could encourage a move forward in engaging, developing and leveraging the talents of their people' (Ross, 2013).

A European study of talent concluded that 'organisations will in future look to develop a talent strategy that embraces all employees but at the same time has initiatives to supply future leaders or those in key positions' (Turner, 2012). This is a talent strategy that appears to be simultaneously inclusive and exclusive. In reality it is a balanced approach and in

Europe it is forecast that talent management will be as much concerned with employee engagement as with succession planning.

Nevertheless, different organizations will be at different stages of development and may therefore have talent priorities that necessitate deviation from this perspective.

Defining talent is like taking a snapshot of a fast-moving car

For most organizations the definition of talent will be like a snapshot of a fast-moving car. Today's priorities mean that we may have to take an exclusive focus on a few positions that have been identified as mission critical by the board: the European CEO has been headhunted; the US marketing director has resigned; we're opening a new shared service centre in Bangalore and need an experienced Head. These are short-term business priorities, and those with talent responsibilities will have to deal with them, often at the expense of other projects. In this particular set of circumstances the focal point of talent activity is the top of the organization.

But the talent snapshot may have wider organizational implications, for example employee engagement is at a high level and the challenge is to maintain this favourable position or it may be at the lowest level for five years and people don't think they have career opportunities, or labour turnover in the technology division is too high or we can't staff our sales teams to optimum levels. These are also talent issues but in what we could term an inclusive way (i.e. they relate to a wider section of the workforce than the executive cadre).

If we take these examples and place them on a global scale, we multiply the exclusivity or inclusivity challenge several-fold. The question remains as to how to deal with these talent issues when they concern those at several levels.

A solution is to regard talent management as both an exclusive and inclusive organization-wide concept, whereby executive positions and the wider workforce are given equal status in talent strategy.

Furthermore, it's important that we are able to combine a strategic perspective and helicopter above the whole organization to identify longer-term trends, but at the same time put in place micro-level talent supply processes.

Hence, global talent management is both exclusive and inclusive simultaneously. To manage such a perspective requires outstanding intelligence and insight on the part of HR and talent professionals.

How to gain a consistent understanding of talent in the organization

There is no one right way to define talent in any particular organization. Whilst there may be a commitment to the idea of making your people before making your products, the organization may have a long and established history of talent management that doesn't fit with this mantra or, indeed, any definition at all.

In order to progress to a working model of talent, therefore, those with responsibility to deliver the talent strategy will need to undertake a series of steps as follows:

- Use outside-in thinking to develop the case for talent based on intelligence and insight on external labour markets and internal organizational dynamics.
- Gain the buy-in from the CEO about the necessity of having a greater focus on talent and talent management and of having the principle of making your people before making your products.
- Secure space at board or executive committee meetings to have this discussion with a wider audience; gather views about talent and what is meant by talent in the organization.
- Gather information from the strategic workforce plan about future workforce requirements and identify any particular talent strengths or shortfall.

This is more of a data-gathering exercise than anything else and is intended to be the foundation on which a future strategy is based. This will be the point at which strategic options are developed. These options will be specific to the organization because at this stage talent defini-tion, strategy and management will be contextual. There are a range of possibilities and these will be discussed in more detail during the next chapter.

Chapter 4

Removing the 'exclusive' tag

Executive summary

- *Whereas talent was once a collection of high-potential people who could move the required number of steps up the organization and would be willing to do so, the expectations of a new generation are more complex.*
- *A new approach is 'inclusive/selective', i.e. adopting the concept of everyone having talent, as well as ensuring business continuity in selective positions.*
- *If the organization is to achieve a position whereby all employees have the opportunity to develop, it must also ensure that they believe that they have the opportunity to develop.*
- *Talent resides at all levels of the organization, and making sure that it surfaces and is converted to the creation of strong competitive positions for the organization is a critical objective.*
- *Moving from the current to the future will require insights based on labour market data and predictive analytics to show how advantage could be gained, along with a CEO who is responsive to the idea.*
- *The whole of the HR community will need to embrace and engage with the new way of thinking and ensure that there is one 'talent' voice.*
- *Developing a roadmap for crafting the transition will include presenting reliable labour market data to senior executives and initiating a dialogue with the CEO about the necessity for change.*
- *Respect for the history of the various parts of the organization and the probable different stages of their evolution will be important.*

Moving from current to future state

External forces, such as labour mobility, demographic change and the social or career expectations of people, and internal changes in the way organizations are designed, mean that the debate about talent definition can no longer be boiled down to the simple choice of: does the organization take an exclusive or inclusive approach to talent management?

Whereas talent was once a collection of high-potential people who could move the required number of steps up the organization and would be willing to do so, the expectations of a new generation are more complex. There is no longer a guarantee that once the organization has identified such people, tapped them on the shoulder and placed them into a fast track they will buy the message that is being given to them. They will want to know more, want more participation and most importantly for the setting of talent strategy will want the ability to shape their own path. And in today's labour market, what about those who are excluded from the talent selection process? Are they prepared to stay and wait for the organization's talent spotlight to shine on them? Probably not.

The CEO of US information and entertainment company AOL has stated that the right mix of talent can create corporate agility. It is the process of determining exactly what this mix is that is the objective of talent management.

Hence, talent reaches a broader group of people than before, and a group that has become less of an audience for predetermined development programmes and more of a community. And these communities are able and willing to create advantage both for themselves and for their organizations and, moreover, expect to be given the chance to do so.

However, whilst it may be understood that if the organization is going to attract and retain people who can make a difference it will have to have inclusivity in the way it goes about managing talented people at all levels, there still remains the question of the current position or short-term demand, which means that such an approach may be an ideal objective and will have to be combined with the existing process.

A cross-boundary matrix for talent

It is important that the organization deals with the issues of freeing up talent at all levels whilst maintaining a supply of people to fill executive and managerial positions. There needn't be a contradiction but to do so requires skilful management within the organization.

It's possible to synthesize the various traditional approaches about what constitutes talent into three groups. If we add the local-regional-global perspective, we can develop a working model of talent options. Figure 4.1 summarizes this.

For most organizations it will be necessary to maximize the return on investment in talent based on the current position (likely to be an exclusive approach) and attempt to move to one of greater inclusivity for future strategies.

The position of an organization as defined by its talent geography and scope will have certain characteristics:

Top managers, successors and high potentials

In this case, the talent strategy is very much focused on the supply of people to top positions such as board members and other senior executives

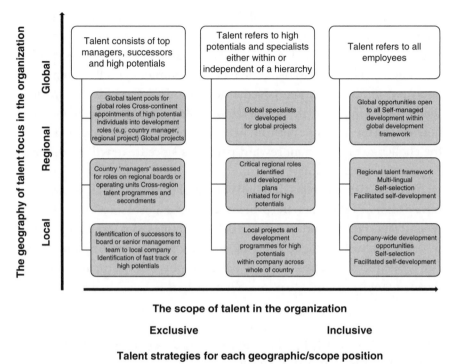

The scope of talent in the organization

Exclusive   **Inclusive**

Talent strategies for each geographic/scope position

Figure 4.1: Model of talent options based on traditional approaches.

to service the needs of the organization. At local level this could be a city, region or country; 'regionally' could mean north or south within a country or groupings such as Europe, the Middle East and Africa, the Americas and so on or globally managed through a group headquarters. Its key features will be succession management for top positions, assessment centres and development programmes for high-potential individuals. Other HR policies may involve reward and recognition: retention bonuses, attractive salary packages and so on. One-to-one executive coaching is increasingly an offering to this group. Where an organization takes a regional approach, talent management becomes slightly more complex. Similar programmes to the ones described in the local 'exclusive' approach are complicated by the need to reflect the regional perspective of the organization. For example, if the region is Europe, then top managers will be defined as typically the boards of directors of country organizations starting with 'country managers' and the first organizational line in each. High potentials will be defined as those who are able to move between countries and manage on a transnational basis. A variation on this theme will be where an organization is based around products, services or functions that span several countries in the region. Additional talent considerations here will be the ability to perform in different cultures, language skills and the challenge of consistent reward packages since there will be different emphases in each country.

The transnational considerations of regional talent strategies are multiplied significantly when the process takes on a global hue. The questions of language, culture and mobility will have implications. There is a worldwide shortage of managers who are able to grasp the implications of and perform effectively across a range of geographies. Talent management in those organizations that require such managers is a big challenge.

Talent refers to high potentials and specialists either within or independent of a hierarchy

A 'local' talent scenario can apply to the identification and development of a group of high potentials or specialists per se – regardless of any specific organizational position. The focus here is to ensure that the organization has a group of people with the knowledge, skills, attitudes and behaviours that can be transportable anywhere in the local area defined by the organization. There are two groups of people in this category. The first would be comfortable as a 'manager' in most functions. The emphasis is on developing cross-functional leadership and management skills and a good cultural/social fit to complement the perceived skill requirements. The second group will be specialists. In these cases talent management is based on ensuring a supply of accountants or technologists, for example, to satisfy local business needs today and in the future. The nature of the networked organization relies on the flexibility of the workforce to adapt to the 'shape' of the organization as it responds to business opportunity.

Project based or outsourcing companies will have this characteristic. One of the success criteria for such organizations will be a pool of employees who have specific technical skills or potential to work across the region, and the talent strategy will reflect this requirement. It will have a regional focus on those individuals who satisfy the needs of a cross-regional competency 'map'.

Such a philosophy can also apply on a global basis, although the challenge is multiplied significantly. An example of this would be the specific skills needed to set up and operate a manufacturing operation anywhere in the world. It is possible to identify and develop talent with appropriate technical or cultural skills to be able to do this on an ad hoc basis (e.g. set up a factory in, say, Wales and then move on to set up a factory in, say, China). Talent management will be focused on a few chosen individuals who can deliver this type of objective.

Talent refers to all employees

In this scenario, the employing organization has made the decision that the whole of the workforce has talent potential and will therefore establish a culture, processes and systems that are designed to ensure that the full potential of employees is realized. The characteristics of the talent strategy will be open competition for supervisory or management positions; equality of opportunity for learning, probably Web-based; and team-based reward structures. The culture will be one of inclusivity. Carrying on this model on a regional basis will be more difficult and will require skilful leadership. The multi-unit nature of the operation (across a region) means that the principles applied in the local operation will need to be applied with significant managerial expertise if expectations of inclusivity are to be met as it is applied in practice. For example, the open advertising and competition of all roles can work and is more cost effective on a single site. Once this is extended on a regional basis – and this may also mean across regional territories – the application becomes more difficult. Both culture and cost will play a part in how successfully such a system can be delivered. It is possible to adopt a position where all employees are regarded as having talent on a global basis, and opportunity for both job advancement and development are offered. Examples of this would include the service sector: hotels and restaurant chains (the McPassport is used by McDonald's to facilitate movement by its employees across Europe); consultancies or project-based organizations (e.g. architecture and urban infrastructure).

The matrix above highlights extremes on a continuum of talent definition from exclusive to inclusive and addresses what happens at the cross-points of geography and definition. Most organizations will have a talent strategy based on one of these cross-points or a combination of one or more.

An alternative is to simplify things further and present options for talent strategy to facilitate choices and transitions.

An inclusive/selective approach to talent

Whilst 'inclusivity' describes accurately the process by which the whole of the workforce is deemed to have talent and will be given the opportunity to develop, the term 'exclusive' can carry with it implications of elitism that does not always sit well with a diverse, multi-generational and multi-talented workforce. Exclusive is either something that is stylish, fashionable, rare and desirable or something that excludes others from participating. Too often, the latter is the perception or interpretation of exclusive talent strategies.

The pejorative nature of describing talented people as exclusive because they have been selected for development over and above that available to all is counterproductive. If the organization is to achieve a position whereby all employees have the opportunity to develop and most importantly *believe that they have the opportunity to develop*, then the language of engagement and the actions of engagement must match the intent of engagement.

In fact, 'exclusive' means that an individual or group of individuals have been selected for a specific reason. It may be that the shareholders (i.e. those who invest capital in the business and are looking for a return over and above that which they would receive in a bank deposit account) also expect to see that in the event of a CEO or executive departure (retirement, leaving for another opportunity) there is continuity of the strategy of the business and hence a continuing return on investment. Since not everyone has the ability or inclination to be a CEO, those who do have the ability will need to be identified and developed. This is not elitist. It is risk management for a share price sensitive position. It is known as 'succession management' and is a common feature of talent strategy. But describing those who have been selected as 'exclusive talent' can get in the way of delivering the objectives of talent management. Being chosen as a successor can lose its edge if the individual is regarded as elitist. There are no leaders without followers and followers don't want elitism if it is perceived as applying to those given unfair advantages to the chosen few. The 'exclusive' tag and mindset may give this impression.

If, however, there is a transparent, meritocratic process, then there will be engagement with those who have made it to these selected 'key' positions. Leadership and followership will be complementary. This isn't exclusivity but selectivity.

Similarly, there may be people in the workforce who have special technical skills that may be scarce on the open labour market. At the same time as ensuring succession to senior positions, the organization will also want to ensure continuity in its technical abilities. By these, we don't mean technology abilities, though these are important, but something much broader. Finance, production or marketing professionals, trained and skilled project managers or those with a historical knowledge of culture and change that will facilitate future change, are examples. This group may also have been described as 'exclusive' in the traditional definitions of talent, because they've been chosen for some specific training, coaching or mentoring.

But they aren't exclusive at all. They've been selected for unique differentiating skills that are critical for future success. It is not an exclusive group but a selective group.

Positioning talent in a global context: Five degrees of freedom

The organization has a choice about which definition, and hence strategy, it adopts for its talent management. The choice may be constrained by factors that limit how far it can go towards an inclusive approach, even though it may desire to do so. Or on the flipside, it may be totally committed to meritocracy and open processes, which may influence the development of a succession plan or the appointment of executives or managers.

Nevertheless, it's possible to synthesize the options into five key positions or degrees of freedom, as outlined in Figure 4.2.

The assumption behind this is that, because of the forces discussed at length above, an ideal position would be one whereby both inclusivity and selectivity are managed in harmony. This means moving towards position 5 in Figure 4.2. However, it is also recognized that organizations

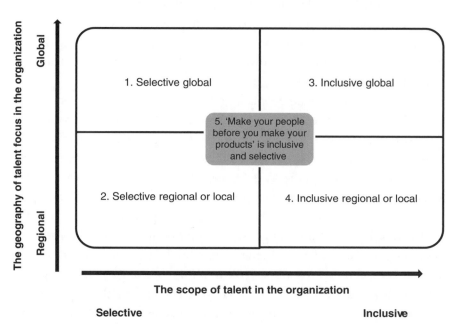

Figure 4.2: Five degrees of freedom: An alternative talent matrix.

will already have processes and systems in place that may be moving towards this position from their current approach. How to do so and achieve the objective of making your people before making your products is the challenge.

The key characteristics of each of the positions are summarized as follows:

1. Selective global

In this, the organization will have in place a global talent strategy for those individuals who are in share price sensitive positions, have scarce global technical skills or have demonstrated a performance and a willingness to be developed and considered for executive or managerial roles in the future.

The strategies that result from taking this position are important because of the worldwide shortage of those who are able to fulfil such global roles. It's vital for the future success of the organization that such people are attracted to and stay with the organization and are given global development opportunities. It's also critical to the success of the organization that the selection process for most of the positions identified is open and transparent.

This goes further than having assessment centres and all jobs being advertised on the company intranet. It means having an executive and management team with the nous, skills and above all self-confidence to ensure that the best and brightest of whatever gender or race are given the opportunity to be selected for the plans or programmes that are designed.

Those who are able to fill global leadership roles are scarce. It is critical that global organizations secure the services of such people if their objectives are to be achieved. And so the tools of talent that have been developed for such circumstances will be applied accordingly. We will talk in later chapters about such things as nine-box models, succession management and the implementation of global high-potential talent pools. These will be the critical methods for executing the global selective approach to talent.

2. Selective regional or local

The challenges that are faced by the global organization of ensuring the continuity of executive or managerial skills in the organizational hierarchy and technical skills regardless of hierarchy are equally important in regional and local organizations. Shareholder expectations don't differ and labour markets will still be tight. There will be variations from region to region and country to country but the principles will remain the same. These are to match supply and demand, strategy and scope for those roles in the organization identified as critical for business or continuity reasons.

If an organization is operating solely in a national or regional market, it should not believe the fallacy that its labour market is also local or regional. Those who are successful in selective roles (CEO, marketing director, project director and high potentials) are valuable people for organizations wherever they are in the world. In addition, the world is an open market for the attraction of such people. The selective local talent strategy has selective global implications for both recruitment and retention, and the need for labour market awareness to anticipate shortfalls or external opportunities for internal talent is paramount if appropriate talent strategies are to be designed.

The two selective examples in this matrix are familiar and have been the standard of talent management for the past twenty years. Brought about by the war for talent, organizations focused their efforts on a few key positions and developed or coached those identified for succession to such a level that they were able to step up to the plate when required to do so.

A few organizations have taken a different approach.

3. Inclusive global

At the other extreme on the talent continuum lies the inclusive approach. Global inclusivity is rare in the talent management field. There are barriers to mobility through language, personal circumstances and employment law. In addition, there may be challenges to delivering such an approach by internal organizational structures. However, if an organization can overcome some of these barriers then it is facing a global talent pool of people from whom it will be able to select those with the most appropriate knowledge, skills, attitudes and behaviours.

Hotel Groups such as Carlson Rezidor with over 30 000 employees (Radisson Blu, Park Inn, and Hotel Missoni) have 140 nationalities on the workforce and in any one hotel it is likely to see employees from across the world. The company has a philosophy to hire attitude and train for skills, has an objective of promotion from within and uses mentoring as well as a learning portal for development.

If the global organization can facilitate relatively free movement of talent around the globe, it will greatly increase the depth of its talent pool, and therefore give itself a competitive edge. In addition, the ability to offer opportunities to employees is a tremendous retention tool.

4. Inclusive regional or local

Where inclusivity is a characteristic of regional or local organizations, the delivery is one step removed from their global counterparts. But, whilst delivering an inclusive approach is more straightforward from a logistics point of view, it is equally challenging from a cultural point of view.

On the one hand, there needs to be a transparency of job or role fulfilment that requires a process and cultural underpinning. How are jobs or training and development opportunities communicated through the organization? Is the infrastructure in place to deliver the promise and are the executives and managers in regional or local organizations open to such a process? If these challenges can be overcome then there is a good possibility that a workforce will be not only engaged with the mission, vision and values but also committed to delivering over and above what is expected.

In addition, they will have the incentive and motivation to deliver their own potential to the full.

5. Inclusive/selective

The President of Anshan Iron and Steel Group Corporation in China noted that 'the current business environment has exposed weakness in our workforce strategy and limitations in our ability to compete on an international scale. Building an experienced and knowledgeable workforce is the most critical challenge we now face' (PwC, 2011). Ensuring an inclusive/selective approach to global talent management will help to reduce some of these limitations.

A strategic position on talent that allows an organization to develop the potential of all of its workforce whilst retaining the ability to fill key roles or those for which skills are scarce can be referred to as 'inclusive/ selective talent management'. The characteristics of this approach are consistent with the principles of making your people before making your products:

- The organization identifies the most senior roles for which continuity is essential from an outward-facing shareholder or key client perspective (CEO, client service director, product director, CIO).
- The organization then identifies the most senior roles that are critical for the continuity of internal projects and services (HR director, group project director).

These roles are the ones for which selectivity will apply.

Talent management at scale: The British National Health Service

Talent management is essential for the National Health Service (NHS). It is about risk management with regard to sustainably improving the health and wellbeing of the population, and ultimately saving lives. The challenge of managing talent is magnified by the significant scale and complexity of the NHS, being the fourth-largest organization in the world with a workforce of approximately 1.3 million people.

Workforce planning and talent development have evolved to ensure the right healthcare professionals, at the right place and the right time deliver high-quality care to the public. To enable this, the NHS partners with universities and further-education providers to commission education programmes based on its workforce planning predictions, investing significant resources to ensure that the workforce is highly skilled to deliver quality care to its patients.

The unique structure of the NHS consists of a series of interconnected healthcare organizations and services, each with evolving talent development needs, provides further challenges. Two national bodies – Health Education England, responsible for workforce planning and the educational and technical training of healthcare practitioners, and the NHS Leadership Academy, with its structured development programmes – are responsible for how the NHS develops the leadership skills and competences of its workforce. This demonstrates the holistic management of workforce development on a large scale.

Embracing an inclusive approach

All areas of the NHS have recognized that talent management is not exclusively related to those of 'specific value' but about embracing an inclusive approach to how it identifies and develops its talent to maximize the potential of every member of the workforce. It is about everyone.

This has been identified in approaches such as the inclusive Talent Management programme (iTM), which seeks to enable healthcare organizations to develop their talent management approaches inclusive of their entire workforce through supportive tools and guidance. The NHS Leadership Academy's national work on talent management is also identifying and developing tools designed to map talent at all levels of the workforce, recognizing that this is not something

(continued)

exclusive for leaders. In addition, Health Education England has identified a core work programme surrounding widening participation which seeks to target talent development at the support workforce. The majority of NHS organizations also have workforce development frameworks in place that enable a localized talent development of their workforce.

The NHS is always evolving. What is certain is that the NHS must continue to ensure that it has the right skilled healthcare practitioners, in the right place and at the right time to deliver high-quality care at the point it is needed. The NHS is continually demonstrating how it is possible to achieve and enhance a national approach to talent management and workforce planning of significant scale and complexity.

Adam J. Turner, MSc, MCIPD, PGDip (HRM), BSc (Hons), MInstLM
Adam specializes in talent and leadership development within Health Education England and has also undertaken national work leading on talent management with the NHS Leadership Academy.

Once these roles or positions have been identified, a process will be implemented whereby individuals are either selected or self selected and given the opportunity to demonstrate that they can do the job; or will be able to do the job at some future time if given development to do so.

The openness and perceived fairness of this process will be critical. This is not from a moral but from a business standpoint. Talent resides at all levels of the organization, and making sure that it surfaces and is converted to the creation of strong competitive positions for the organization is a critical objective. The inclusive/selective perspective will encourage the delivery of this.

However, such a process should take place in parallel with one which focuses on delivering a culture of opportunity and innovation within the whole of the organization and one in which sufficient resource is allocated to ensure that such opportunities can be realized. The challenge then comes about of identifying those individuals who are possibilities for the 'key roles' on the one hand and those individuals who have potential, aspiration and seem able to achieve higher positions than the ones they currently hold.

This part of the process deals with the selective part of the model.

However, this is just one manifestation of inclusive/selective. In addition, it will be important to make sure that all employees have the opportunity to develop their potential and fulfil their aspirations. As organizations implement their global strategy, this will be of critical importance. To reinforce this point, the CEO of Unilever has commented that 'as we shift eastward, we have to make sure that our corporate culture and operating model reflect the markets there. Trying to get that right is where I spend most of my time' (PwC, 2011).

Therefore, it will be necessary to make sure that those members of the workforce who aren't included in the selective group aren't excluded from development. More of this later.

This is a twin-track strategy of selectivity and inclusivity.

The talent management transition

It would be too idealistic to assume that the transition from an approach that is, say, exclusive to one that embraces the principles of making your people before making your products is a straightforward one. The complexity of the environment in which most global organizations work and their historical structure means that agreement to move towards selective/inclusive will require organizational crafting skills on the part of those responsible for talent.

The roadmap for crafting the transition will vary from organization to organization since the number of variables is large and the combinations too numerous. However, there are some steps that can be taken wherever the organization is in its evolution:

- Present labour market data that includes both quantitative analysis and qualitative (demographic) change should be given to senior executives. This will be the beginning of a process to seed the organization with the idea that things have changed and that a more inclusive approach is needed to complement the undoubtedly excellent succession and high potential work that has already been undertaken.

- Initiate a dialogue with the CEO about the necessity for change. Use information from the workforce plan to show where possible talent gaps will occur in future. There is enough labour market data to demonstrate that shortages will not just include specialist technology directors but sales people, engineers and contact centre workers.
- Use benchmarking to show how the organization compares with others but also use predictive analytics to show how advantage could be gained by adopting the 'making your people before making your products' philosophy.
- Engage the whole of the HR community in the new way of thinking and ensure that there is one voice when speaking of 'making your people'.
- Respect the history of the various parts of the organization and the probable different stages of their evolution. There are many different ways to get from point A to point B, as long as the organization gets there in the end.

So the talent process doesn't stop with improvements in the processes for selected roles. In the inclusive/selective organization, talent management will include all employees who have critical skills for the delivery of future strategy. This means additional inclusive talent processes, including:

- openness about performance and realism about potential;
- transparency in selection and promotion processes;
- space and support for self-development;
- an executive team and managers who have bought in to such a culture;
- an executive team and managers who don't hoard their high performers.

The onus is on the organization to ensure that all employees are given the opportunity to maximize their talents; and the onus is on the individual to ensure that they take all of the opportunities that are presented.

Chapter 5

Developing a global strategy for talent

Executive summary

- *There is a compelling case for aligning the talent strategy with the business strategy because maximizing the talent of individual employees is a unique source of competitive advantage.*
- *The characteristics of talent strategy are an agreed, organizational-wide definition; developing a pool of talent as a resource to meet identified needs; support from the highest level; activities that are developed with other HR policies and practices for a joined-up approach.*
- *Organizations should have a clear focus, HR practices that value people as a strategic resource and innovation in HR practice implementation.*
- *Talent strategy is the attraction, retention, reward, development and deployment of people in specific strategic positions or projects and the development of a culture of opportunity for all employees in order that the organization can achieve its business goals and objectives.*
- *The objective will be to match the talent supply with demand and ensure that there are people in the right place with the right skills to deliver the objectives and strategy.*
- *The business strategy, as well as being the determinant of talent strategy, can be derived from the value and contribution of the talent itself. Hence, it is the type of talent within the organization that could determine the business strategy, and not the other way round.*
- *Today's organization is likely to contain a very diverse set of people across geographies, which has the potential to impact on innovation in an unprecedented way.*
- *Reporting lines are less linear in this collaborative age and goals are shared across departments. The creation of new ideas and business opportunities by the making of connections and sharing knowledge is a more fluid process in a way that was difficult in strict hierarchical organizations.*

Global influences on talent strategy

On the one hand, focusing efforts and investment on pivotal roles could provide a major competitive advantage; on the other, businesses need to identify the key capabilities, competencies and positions before looking at the mix of talent required – the mix of local talent versus expats and permanent versus contingent employees (PwC, 2012). The achievement of effective strategies that deal with both the selective and inclusive is critical.

'The world is an open market for talented people' is seen as one of the principles by which making your people before making your products can be understood. In addition, there are other factors that need to be taken into account when developing a global strategy for talent:

- Regiocentricism: region and industry specific nature of talent management, i.e. some regions or industries offer more or less favourable conditions for the attraction and retention of talent. In addition, there is the ongoing challenge of the global vs local debate. Getting consistency of approach is often seen as a critical success factor between global and 'local' talent initiatives. Developing a strategic approach to talent will require an understanding of this point.
- The competences needed to deliver business objectives matched against insight about current talent and their aspirations and using

this to differentiate our organizations. This means identifying the employees and *skills* most critical to the organization and strategy, and determining what different groups, generations and individual employees want through personalized approaches.

- The recognition of the role of globally talented people to international success has coincided with shortages of international managers, the shift of competition for talent from national to regional or global levels, greater recognition by SMEs of the importance of talent, and hence a broadening of the competitive environment for talent, and an 'increase in mobility [which] is an influence on both the attraction and retention of talent' (Scullion and Collings, 2011).

- An employer brand or corporate reputation that facilitates the recruitment and retention of those eager to work in a global corporation with global opportunities.

- The challenge of developing 'global' managerial groups in transnational firms shouldn't be underestimated. Even within the narrow confines of Western Europe, different cultural interpretations have been shown to be problematic in identifying and developing talent (Boussebaa and Morgan, 2008).

The talent strategy will focus on which options are chosen and resources allocated. These factors will provide outside-in knowledge that will inform the process. However, it is also worth considering how strategy is defined and where talent strategy fits into the overall strategic direction of the organization.

Understanding talent strategy: Building a compelling case for talent

Agreeing a definition of talent that suits the organization at a point in its development is the first step. Developing a talent strategy to deliver the business objectives is the next. There is a compelling case for aligning the talent strategy with the business strategy.

The CIPD (2013a) notes that 'ensuring that the talent strategy is closely aligned with the corporate strategy must be a priority. Strategic analysis from the business perspective should feed into an HR forecast, which can help shape an organization's tailored approach to talent management'. This point has been reinforced because the need to identify, develop and retain top talent is a strategic issue.

The achievement of this objective has emerged as a major topic for international human resource management with a view to maximizing the talent of individual employees as a unique source of competitive advantage, which itself produces the challenges of getting the right skills in the right numbers to where they are needed, ensuring that knowledge and practices are disseminated throughout the organization and identifying and developing talent on a global basis. Indeed, having the right number of people at the right place at the right time and with the right skill sets are fundamental to both workforce planning and talent planning. Developing a talent strategy is key to this.

Characteristics of talent strategy

The characteristics of talent strategy include an agreed, organizational-wide definition, a strategic approach to talent management for developing a pool of talent as a resource to meet identified needs and support from the highest level but with engaged line managers who are committed to the objectives and processes of talent management activities that are developed with other HR policies and practices for a joined-up approach. Furthermore, organizations should have a focus, HR practices that value people as a strategic resource and effective HR practice implementation. In parallel with these, the need for measures of performance to be built into the talent strategy is also important.

From a business perspective it can be assumed that the strategy is about direction and scope, about the configuration of resources and about satisfying stakeholder demands over the longer term (Johnson, Scholes and Whittington, 2007).

Adapting this approach could lead to the definition of talent strategy as:

> Talent strategy is the attraction, retention, reward, development and deployment of people in specific strategic positions or projects *and* the development of a culture of opportunity for all employees in order that the organization can achieve its business goals and objectives.

The key here is building an approach to talent that is sustainable. Indeed, this may require a paradigm shift in the whole question of HR decision science resulting from the observation that 'HR and business leaders increasingly define organizational effectiveness beyond traditional financial outcomes to encompass sustainability – achieving success today without compromising the needs of the future. A common strategic human capital decision science can reveal pivotal talent under both traditional and sustainability-based definitions, and thus uncover important insights about the talent implications of the shifting definition of strategic success' (Boudreau and Ramstad, 2005).

In the same way as a business strategy, the talent strategy will set the direction, focus the effort, define how the organization goes about talent management and make sure there is consistency of message and action and enough resource to deliver.

Talent strategy at multiple levels

Strategies exist at several levels in any organization, ranging from the overall business (or group of businesses) through to business units or operations. The definition of strategy and the implications for talent strategy for each are as follows:

- *Corporate strategy* is concerned with the overall purpose and scope of the business to meet stakeholder expectations. This is a crucial level since it is heavily influenced by investors in the business and acts to guide strategic decision making throughout the business. Corporate strategy is often stated explicitly in a 'mission statement'. In this context, the corporate talent strategy will address the immediate issue of succession to key corporate roles but also determine the overall corporate approach. It is here where the concept of making your people before making your products needs to be embraced if it is to be disseminated throughout the company.

- *Business unit strategy* is concerned more with how a business competes successfully in a particular market. It concerns strategic decisions about choice of products, meeting the needs of customers, gaining advantage over competitors, exploiting or creating new opportunities, etc. At the business unit level, there will be the challenge of ensuring that there are enough selected people to fill executive or management positions and at the same time a company ethos that encourages and facilitates the development of all employees on the assumption of an inclusive approach.
- *Operational strategy* is concerned with how each part of the business is organized to deliver the corporate and business-unit level strategic direction. Operational strategy therefore focuses on issues of resources, processes, people, etc. (Johnson, Scholes and Whittington, 2007). Here the focus will be on ensuring that managerial, project or functional specialist talent supply meets demand. It will also be concerned with engaging the whole of the workforce to maximize both contribution and opportunity.

A talent strategy that is aligned to the organization's strategy will need to take account of the requirements at each level of the organization as follows:

- In the first instance the talent strategy will begin by analysing the organization's objectives and overall business strategy at a corporate level.
- The people requirements to deliver the strategy can then be identified with a specific reference to those the organization defines as talent. The objective will be to match the talent supply with demand and ensure people in the right place with the right skills to deliver the objectives and strategy.

- A similar process will take place at each level of strategy, i.e. corporate, business unit and operational.
- Any perceived gaps in people to fill key talent roles or a requirement for further knowledge or skills (such as that for international growth or the development of new products or services) will be filled with talent development activity.

Increasingly, HR analytics are being used as predictive tools to enhance this process, predicting the right skills, attitudes and behaviours of the 'ideal' employee or the return on investment of people initiatives or, more specifically, the return on investment in talent.

In addition to this selective approach, the talent strategy will also focus on delivering a culture of talent opportunity for all.

Talent strategy: The alignment of people to business

As we have seen from the above narrative and in response to the need for a fluid supply, a well-developed and tested talent management process has evolved. For many organizations, this begins with the belief in the need to align talent strategy with business strategy. The fundamentals of this approach are that once the objectives of an organization have been set the people requirements to deliver the strategy can be forecast and assessed against supply from both internal and external labour markets. At its best, talent strategy will anticipate the implications of business strategy and generate a pool of people in development who can fill business requirements. The process has an impact on a wide range of HR activities, such as succession management, employer branding, employee engagement, reward and next generation leadership development. In this approach an effective talent strategy would help organizations deal with highly volatile markets. Indeed, it has been argued that developing a talent strategy is at the heart of HR management and that 'making people your competitive advantage' is at the heart of business management (Lawler, 2008).

Diversity and inclusion at the London 2012 Olympic and Paralympic Games

Game changers

The London 2012 Olympic and Paralympic Games were many years in the planning and the diversity and inclusion work we led really started in earnest in 2008, four years out. We had 200 000 people to recruit in order to stage the Games. We wanted a diverse team. But the methods at our disposal, in order to achieve that diverse team, were all up for debate.

There are a set of compliance strategies, what I call 'Diversity 101', using quotas and compliance training to attempt to shift the needle. There are a set of corporate, social responsibility strategies, what I call 'Diversity 2.0', using unconscious bias training and so forth, again, trying to recruit a more diverse workforce than may otherwise be the case. But we tried something else. We aimed for systemic change, what I call 'Inclusion 3.0'. This involved game-changing tools, tools that helped achieve real inclusion, as opposed to decorating the tree 'with token diversity' and perpetuating the current paradigm. These are the paradigm-shifting methods that differentiate Inclusion 3.0 from Diversity 101 and 2.0 and offer the professional a new arsenal that can be employed to effect change.

The key methods used were:

We established talent pools

In order to achieve real inclusion, talent pools of people *different from you* need to be created. This is hard to achieve, as we are naturally inclined to hire in our own image. Building talent pools of diverse skill sets and diverse communities directly challenges the usual excuse for not hiring difference—i.e. lack of supply. It also helps future-proof the organization: the demand for labour tends to operate on shorter timelines than the cultivation and supply of it; having talent pools, embedded diversity in the recruitment process, saved costs and increased efficiency of time to hire.

(continued)

We established a guaranteed interview scheme for disabled people
This was merit-based, legal and ethical. It required pithy, accurate and specific job descriptions to be able to reject clearly unqualified candidates. However, I have yet to find a more effective intervention in terms of challenging the understandable cynicism and barriers that many disabled people face in the labour market, as well as capturing massively underutilized talent coupled with unlocked discretionary effort.

We conducted group interviews
There are two interventions we can make to correct potential interview bias. One is to have more than one person conducting the interview, so that different biases from different people can to some degree counteract each other. Better still, have more than one candidate, preferably a bundle, so that you can see skills (as opposed to experiences) play out in real time. We choose variety in bundles. When people are analysed in groups, their individual characteristics (e.g. gender) are less salient and their skill sets and how they interact with the group are more so.

We made use of benchmarking
Instead of quotas or other fixed, inflexible measures, benchmarking allows a better interaction with time-sensitive organizational realities. Teams can be benchmarked on their progress in terms of hiring to create a competitive dynamic and a market for diverse talent. Recruitment agencies should be benchmarked in order to calculate your return on investment. In all cases, peer review, instead of compliance quotas, is the driver. This is based on high-frequency real-time information sharing (monitoring), which not only maintains momentum and democratizes the workplace but also is by definition closer to the mission of the organization than compliance measures ever could be.

The ultimate game changer is attitude
The overall strategy was simple and effective. London 2012 demonstrated that social change is possible in an extremely resource-constrained commercial environment. But Inclusion 3.0 Game Changers do not require a sledgehammer. A quiet intervention is fine, as long as it is profound and strategic.

**Stephen Frost, Former Head of Diversity and Inclusion,
London Organizing Committee of the Olympic and Paralympic
Games 2007–2012, Head of Diversity and Inclusion at KPMG LLP**

Figure 5.1 shows how a talent strategy can evolve. The key assumptions are:

- Business objectives are set (shareholder value, market share, etc.) and from this a series of strategies are derived as to how the organization will achieve these objectives. Amongst these are finance, sales and marketing, and technology strategies.
- Once all of these have been agreed, the people strategy will be set, often using a workforce plan to identify the right people, in the right place at the right time and with the right level of skills.
- Within the people strategy will be the identification of key roles (CEO, marketing director), and the activities needed to ensure that the right people are in such positions. This could be the succession or executive development and is one part of the talent strategy.
- In addition, the need to ensure continuity in the knowledge, skills, attitudes and behaviours of other 'key roles' will lead to recruitment and attraction, retention or management/leadership development of those with high potential. This is the second part of the talent strategy.
- Also, the process of inclusivity will be addressed by making sure that there is both a culture of opportunity for all and processes by which

Figure 5.1: The alignment of talent strategy with business strategy.

employees can fulfil their ambition. This part of the talent strategy will be closely aligned to the overall people strategy and it is important that the two are 'joined up'.

- Finally, some measures of success will be identified to ensure that there is a return on investment in retention, executive and management development.

The talent strategy will need to take account of the inclusive/selective requirements of the organization. It will therefore ensure a supply of people to fill identified senior positions but at the same time ensure that the potential of all employees is maximized.

The process for developing a talent strategy

Figure 5.2 shows a possible process for talent strategy that is aligned with the business strategy. This is based on a four-stage model of gathering hard and soft data, converting this into information, using the information to inform intelligence and offering insight based on the analysis. The key components are:

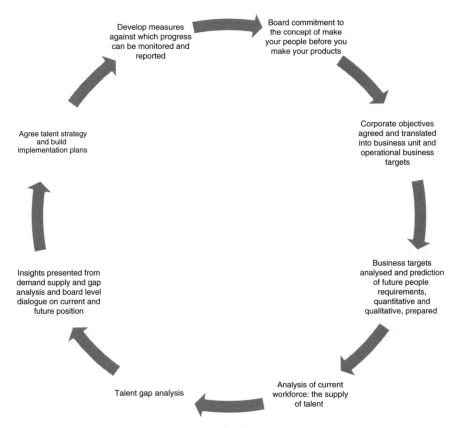

Figure 5.2: The process for developing a talent strategy.

Building board commitment

Making your people before making your products goes beyond the traditional approach and therefore requires that the board will take the subject beyond the boundaries of succession. Hence, a strong point of view with a business focus will need to be presented and accepted by the board if progress is to be made.

The role of the CEO in this regard will be critical. This is covered in a later chapter. But the insight provided by the HR or talent director will be the enabling factor. These insights will include the effect of labour market dynamics on the ability of the organization to attract talent, predictive analytics about the effect of talent initiatives on both tangible and intangible company assets as well as the status of succession plans.

Corporate objectives and business unit targets

On the assumption that talent strategy will be aligned to business strategy, the first part of the process is really to understand the business objectives and then translate them into talent objectives. Business objectives could be high-level corporate ones (such as double shareholder value in three years) or more specific, based on geography (e.g. expand in India) or markets (e.g. grow customer base with a particular product). Each business objective will have an implication for the types and numbers of talent needed and will therefore need to be clarified.

The development of a global talent strategy will require input at three levels:

- Corporate: What are the talent needs for board or group level employees? How will talent flow throughout the regions, countries or companies covered by the corporate strategy? How can the culture be developed to ensure freedom of movement and opportunity? What are the implications for the management of such a process?
- Business unit: The talent strategy for the business unit should be set within the same context as that for the corporation as a whole. Hence, if it is important that talent moves between the units of the company, how can an individual business unit deal with the requirement – how

can the 'loss' of key skills to another country or company be countered by gains? What is the process for making this happen?

■ Operational level: The operationalizing of talent strategy to local or departmental level is, like the implementation of any other strategy, one of the biggest challenges. As Rumelt (2011) so insightfully puts it: 'a good strategy has coherence, co-ordinating actions, policies and resources to accomplish an important end. Many organisations, most of the time, don't have this'.

A key source at this point will be the intelligence gleaned from the strategic workforce plan.

Assessing the current talent supply and potential

Having thus prepared an estimate of demand, the second step will be to analyse existing supply. Which of the current workforce are able to fill selected positions in the short or medium term? Which of the current workforce have shown themselves to be prepared to develop in the longer term? But this area goes beyond the succession and high potential processes implied in this narrative. In addition, the talent strategy here will look for specific skills of behaviours across the workforce and those who are willing to convert these into actions, products or services that will enhance the competitive position of the organization. This group of talented people will be as critical for the long term as those in selective positions.

Talent gap analysis

In the same way as a workforce plan, gap analysis can be undertaken at this point. This will provide intelligence on such things as: Where are the talent shortages or abundances highlighted by the previous analysis?

Where does short-term effort need to go (attracting people for specific continuity posts)? Where does longer-term effort need to be placed (skills development or cultural change)?

Talent gap analysis will require external information to help in developing a picture of labour market supply as well as internal information that comes from matching the talent demand against the business strategy.

Insights from talent analysis

The information gathering that arises from the above processes will provide the basis for strategic options. However, this is no longer about the presentation of talent spreadsheets or nine-box models. The board and senior executives of the organization will be looking for insight from the people professionals. For talent this means demonstrating how the deployment of talent can enhance the company's competitive position and how talent analytics and the subsequent actions can transform the business opportunity. Insight is a deep and profound knowledge. Talent insight is deep and profound knowledge of how talented people will create prosperity for the organization.

- As a result of this discussion, the CEO and executive team will review their options. These may be at the strategic level – about talent and competitive advantage, talent and culture change and the consequences of making people before making products – or at the operational level – for talent development, reward or specific actions for specific individuals. Critical to this will be that the ownership of making your people before making your products resides with the CEO not HR or the talent director. Pull together all of the information on demand, supply and proposals and present to the board for discussion/agreement.
- The series of measures will be agreed against which progress in implementing the talent strategy will be assessed. The plan will be to

present such information as part of the normal operating review process and in the same timeframe/reporting schedule as sales or financial performance.

Preparing a talent strategy

The dialogue that has taken place at board level is the precursor to the go-ahead to develop a talent strategy and the allocation of resource to execute the strategy. Talent strategy will be aligned with business objectives and will consist of:

- A set of objectives against which the strategy is being designed, e.g. have successors to the top 15 posts in the organization or ensure that all employees have access to development tools on the corporate intranet.
- The process by which these objectives are going to be achieved including attraction, retention and development.
- The management development interventions or engagement that will be required to ensure line managers buy into the ethos and practice of make your people before you make your products.
- A set of milestones against which objectives will be assessed and a timeline for implementation and review of the talent strategy.
- An organization-wide communication and engagement to suit the demographic make-up of the workforce, face-to-face, line manager briefings and social media.
- A set of measures against which all aspects of the talent strategy can be assessed.

The progress of the talent strategy will then be presented back to the board and executive committee and crafted to do more of the things that are working well, to fix things that aren't and to add things that seem to be relevant through experience but weren't included in the original concept.

The above strategic process is based on the alignment of the talent strategy with the business strategy.

Talent management: The alignment of business to people

In addition to the approach of alignment and fulfilment outlined above, in which the talent strategy is aligned to the business strategy, a different perspective is emerging. In this, the business strategy, as well as being the determinant of talent strategy, can be derived from the value and contribution of the talent itself. Hence, it is the type of talent within the organization that could determine business strategy and not the other way round.

This has come about because of the changing nature of work and the working environment. Today's organization is likely to contain a very diverse set of people across geographies. This mix has the potential for innovation in an unprecedented way. Reporting lines are 'less linear in this collaborative age and goals are shared across departments' (Waller, 2013). But not only reporting lines: ideas as well and the creation of new business opportunities by sharing knowledge and making connections in a way that was difficult in strict hierarchical organizations.

In this scenario, one of the organization's employees, possibly by working in collaboration with others around the world and at any level or in any node, would identify a business opportunity that could be created using the unique talents within the company but that has not been built into the 'business as usual' strategy; this might be a new product or service, an improved process or a new approach to customer relationships. The company decides to go ahead with the project and hence additional revenue streams are created that were not originally part of the strategic plan. In this case the business has evolved because talented people took initiatives, confidently and independent of business as usual. Such a case was exemplified by Google, whose willingness to allocate free time to its employees to undertake their own personal projects or in collaboration with others has led to considerable business benefits.

Such an approach is not just about a culture of innovation determining new products or services. A further example is where the company's talent in mergers and acquisitions is superior to that of its competitors. Hence, the strategic option to adopt M&A as a way of growing the business is a competitive advantage. It will therefore determine the strategic approach (e.g. M&A trumps organic growth because the company has people who are able to deliver the benefits better than their competitors). In these examples it is talent that has determined the direction and strategy of the company. The business strategy has been aligned to the company's talent and the conventional view of strategic alignment has been reversed.

Huselid and Becker (2011) put forward the view that a focus on capability first and foremost could be a source of value creation through differentiation. This is expressed diagrammatically in Figure 5.3. In this approach, the business strategy follows the talent that resides in the organization, and from this new revenue streams arise. The strategic competences possessed by individuals or groups of individuals allow the organization to build a strategy around the competence.

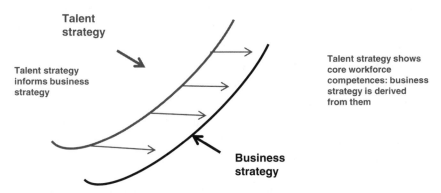

Figure 5.3: Using the talent of individuals to develop the business strategy.

Moving to inclusive selective: The role of talent specialist

The development of a strategy for talent will require that talent professionals or those with specific talent responsibility have credibility to persuade business executives of the efficacy of their proposals and how they can contribute to the development of the competitive advantage of the organization.

It is necessary to combine the ability to talent spot for selected positions whilst at the same time ensuring that an organizational culture develops that facilitates and encourages the emergence of talent at any level. The new talent specialist has to combine both roles. In fact, this fits into the emerging role of the HR profession as a whole.

The role is changing. Evolving from the work of David Ulrich in the 1990s, new competences and responsibilities have emerged, including:

- Acting as a strategic positioner by understanding the social, technological, economic, political, environmental and demographic trends facing the organization and knowing specific expectations of customers, investors, regulators, and communities, and then building internal HR responses that align with these external requirements. If talent strategy is to succeed then those responsible will have to achieve credibility with business leaders. They will do so by having a dialogue around the strategic agenda and how talent can support the delivery of business goals (Ulrich *et al.*, 2013).
- This means becoming a 'credible activist' and knowing the business context, the critical success factors for the business and being able to engage in business discussions.
- Finally, the success of the strategy dialogue will be enhanced if those responsible for talent and talent management can offer an integrated approach to HR management.

The contribution of talent management has to go beyond the tactical supply of selective positions, although this activity is important. Instead, it should be a strategic contribution, based on the assumption that people are a source of competitive advantage and that there are business benefits to making your people before making your products.

Talent strategy: Achieving coherence

The development of a coherent strategic response for talent will be dependent on business credibility on the part of those responsible for its delivery. And most of all it will require insight about talent, insight about the organization and insight about how the two fit together to deliver competitive advantage.

The following are some critical factors in developing a talent strategy that will facilitate this:

- There is clarity of understanding about the business objectives and business strategy. Those responsible for delivering the talent strategy will therefore need business insight as well as people insight. And most importantly they will need to be seen as credible in the eyes of business managers. After all, it is the business manager who ultimately owns the delivery of the talent strategy.
- The talent strategy is understood to be a priority by the CEO and executive team. To achieve this, those responsible for talent will have to present their case in the same way as any other functional specialist, such as technology or marketing. This means demonstrating a return on talent investment, the use of predictive analytics in demonstrating the value added of talent investment or the value destruction on not having a focus on talent. They will be business people when dealing with the executive team as much as being 'people' people.
- It's necessary to put the case that talent can no longer be regarded as an exclusive concept but applies to the majority of the organization. Talent strategy satisfies the need to be selective and inclusive. This is as much about culture as it is about process.

These critical success factors extend the scope and responsibility of those responsible for talent in the organization. They now become strategic positioners, credible activists and capability builders (Ulrich *et al.*, 2013).

Chapter 6

The CEO as the 'owner' of the talent strategy

Executive summary

- *The role of the CEO has evolved over the past decade as talent management has gone beyond the responsibility of a single department or function to an organization-wide issue with a long-term impact.*
- *It is critical to the achievement of the CEO's obligations to the organization's stakeholders that there is a flow of talent to each level or network node and that every employee has the opportunity to maximize their contribution to their own and the company's success.*
- *The CEO will need to have the insight and understanding about the importance of encouraging the development of talent at all levels.*
- *This means a CEO who is committed to the promotion of talent throughout the organization will be open minded and tolerant of people's ambiguities and ideas.*
- *The CEO will know what's going on with 'selective' talent in the organization and will be informed about their progress and opportunities throughout. He or she will cherish not only the talent in the selective group but also the talent at all levels.*
- *The CEO should promote talent mobility, building experience and increasing organizational flexibility, whilst also acting as a role model for talent development.*
- *This means a culture from the top by which all employees are regarded as talented and making sure that line managers understand that they should facilitate the progress of members of their teams who have aspirations for new roles and opportunities.*
- *A critical role of the CEO is as a human capital developer.*

The basic qualities for 'assured managerial success'

It has been argued that the CEO is the owner of the strategy, but this is tautological. By definition, the CEO is the owner of all strategy. It isn't ownership per se but the type of ownership. If making your people before making your products is to succeed, the CEO and leadership team's ownership will need to be a full-on commitment. How the CEO and other executives articulate and demonstrate support will be the difference between success and failure.

Talent is the top priority for many CEOs. This is because competition for talent is intensifying and so talent will be represented more in organizational strategy. The impact of talent on major business decisions was emphasized by the CEO of Manpower, who advised other CEOs to 'accelerate how they access, mobilize and optimize talent to remain competitive in the face of talent shortages, margin compression and economic uncertainty'(ManpowerGroup Press Release, 2013).

The role of the CEO has evolved over the past decade as talent management has become less of a simple managerial matter dealt with by a department and more of a huge problem with an enormous impact on a firm's sustainability. As a result, many organizations have raised the profile of talent and have sought to develop a clear point of view about how they regard and manage talent and 'a clear model of talent management that is shared throughout the organisation'. The success of these objectives will in part be determined by the active participation of the CEO. His or her leadership in the creation of a selective inclusive approach to talent will be of critical importance (Hatum, 2010).

There are different interpretations of what such a statement means and it is worthwhile investigating these further if the 'make your people before you make your products' principles are to be implemented effectively.

It is critical to the achievement of the CEO's obligations to the organization's stakeholders that there is a flow of talent to each level or network node and that every employee has the opportunity to maximize their contribution to their own and the company's success. If both of these factors are satisfied then the chances of delivering an organization's objectives will be improved. There will be a convergence of the interests of multiple stakeholders.

A culture of performance *and* opportunity

This requires the creation of a culture that favours both the highest levels of performance and the highest levels of opportunity. The CEO will require leadership qualities that would be recognized by most students of the subject, such as charisma, innovation, energy, enthusiasm, dependability and honesty. But it will also require the CEO to have insight and understanding about the importance of encouraging the development of talent at all levels.

Henry Mintzberg (2011) addresses this subject and adds to the definition of the characteristics of effective leaders by including other attributes. These are of particular relevance to the talent savvy CEO:

> A CEO who is committed to the promotion of talent throughout the organisation will be 'open minded and tolerant of people ambiguities and ideas.' It is not sufficient to recruit and develop against a static fixed set of organisational competences. These are important of course and have certainly been created in alignment with the organisation's business strategy. But these may not always reflect rapid change in markets or stakeholder demands. It is important therefore that the organisation has a culture of innovation and talented people who are willing and able to put forward new ideas. The CEO will not only set the culture by which such things happen but will encourage the identification and attraction of people who are able to do so.

IMD and 'the role of the CEO in talent strategy'

CEOs are in the talent business. They must be able to spot it, attract it, develop it and retain it. Even with complex HR systems to manage talent acquisition, development and deployment, the CEO remains the ultimate custodian of the company's talent pool. Three must-dos dictate the CEO's effectiveness in this role.

Define talent broadly

When leaders talk about business talent, generally they refer to senior executives and those marked as high potentials for senior executive roles. But this focus on talent management can be restrictive. The critical task is to ensure that the firm has the right people in 'mission-critical roles' in its value chain.

Additional categories of mission-critical employees include the great individual contributors, knowledge workers and specialists who work with their intellects and creative capabilities, and the many unsung heroes – in middle management and on the frontline – who are not destined for the higher reaches. Instead, they are essential in maintaining the effectiveness of the business system in its key details. Getting the best out of these pools of pivotal employees is essential to the firm's performance. The CEO must spotlight the importance of their contributions – and support the various HR systems necessary to develop and retain them.

Build on talent

The second talent task for CEOs is to get the most out of the talent at their disposal – helping people be successful and ensuring that talent rises and flows into the value-creating areas of the business. People should know that they are on top management's radar – but not develop unrealistic career expectations that can generate frustration or a sense of entitlement.

(continued)

Talent management also requires the CEO to encourage managers and specialists who themselves are not bound for the top but have a record of bringing talent through and releasing it to the organization. So, it helps if the CEO devises methods to ensure that managers not only do not sit on their best people but also, critically, do provide them with development opportunities.

Look beyond talent
In the 'war for talent' it is easy to be wowed by smarts and to discount 'fit'. The CEO's core contribution in this regard is to make sure that in their recruiting activities the firm's managers probe beyond raw talent and ensure good fit. Fit with the job, fit with the team, fit with the firm's values and its evolving needs and, indeed, fit with the CEO as well as the immediate boss. Leaders are often conscious of the need to recruit people different from themselves. But while diversity of perspective may be important, differences in values can spell trouble. The full cost of on/off-boarding high-quality talent is very high. It's best to ensure fit before entry.

Therefore, when hiring a 'misfit', the onus is on the manager doing the hiring to set expectations and ensure that others already in the firm understand, value and absorb the different things that the newcomer will be bringing. CEOs must also alert managers not to oversell the job or the firm. While it can be tempting to paint very rosy pictures to attract star candidates, this tactic can quickly lead to disillusionment on both sides. Fit cuts both ways.

The comments above reflect the feelings and thoughts of those CEO's from a wide range of companies who recently attended the annual IMD CEO Round Table meeting.

Preston C. Bottger, Professor of Leadership, IMD
Jean-Louis Barsoux, Research Fellow, IMD
IMD is a leading business school located in Lausanne, Switzerland. Its main focus is on developing global leaders through high-impact executive education. Its vision is to 'be the best in the world at developing successful leaders – individuals, teams and organizations'.

- A critical quality of the CEO in the 'make your people before you make your products' philosophy is that he or she is both connected and informed. The CEO will know what's going on with the 'selective' talent in the organization and will be informed about their progress. But he or she will go beyond the few in this category and have an awareness of talent development at large. The CEO will have an idea of the talent issues and opportunities in each area. He or she will cherish not only the talent in the selective group but also talent at all levels.
- A reflective and insightful CEO will encourage executives and managers to have a similar outlook. In turn this will be transmitted to the kind of people who are selected for the talent pools or the selective processes. There will be a trickle-down (or trickle-through-the-network) effect inspired by the outlook of the organization's leader. This doesn't mean that everyone in the organization is reflective and insightful – though this has clear advantages – it means that those chosen for selective roles have been chosen with insight; and the culture of opportunity is developed with reflection on its advantages.
- Finally, the CEO will have the courage to challenge the status quo in terms of those who are chosen for selective roles and the overall approach to talent management for inclusivity.

The implementation of these principles is important if the CEO is to provide the pivotal role in encouraging inclusivity in the approach to talent as well as ensuring that the leadership and managerial cadre has a sufficiently large pool of talent on which to draw. And the evidence as to how this works in practice will be investigated in the next section.

How the world's most admired companies manage talented people

The CEOs of large multi-national organizations face a wide variety of challenges, including those of growth, productivity, risk management, tightening corporate governance, innovation and, increasingly, competing for talent (Mascarenhas, 2009). Those who do well in these areas will enhance the reputation of the companies that they lead.

One of the external indicators of this reputation is the ranking in such annual surveys as Britain's Most Admired Companies (in UK business publication *Management Today*), America's Most Admired Companies and the World's Most Admired Companies (*Fortune* magazine). Often, corporate recognition in such surveys can count towards building the employer brand.

The surveys are conducted annually and each company represented is assessed in up to nine categories that have remained fairly constant over the 20 years or so of the surveys' history. In the UK these are financial soundness, use of corporate assets, value as a long-term investment, quality of management, quality of products and services, innovation, quality of marketing, corporate, social and environmental responsibility, and the ability to attract and retain talented people. Companies that have been the most prolific winners of these categories include Tesco, Diageo, Shell and BSkyB. Those recognized for their ability to attract and develop talent include BASF, GlaxoSmithKline, Balfour Beatty, Kingfisher and Rolls-Royce.

In the USA, *Fortune*'s annual survey has identified Apple, Google, Coca-Cola, Starbucks, IBM, Disney, Southwest Airlines and Berkshire Hathaway for their abilities in the talent sphere.

When research was undertaken into what made such companies mavens in the field, a range of characteristics of talent management were identified (Brown and Turner, 2008). The role of the CEO was critical in all respects and it is worth considering them in more detail.

Talent is regarded as a strategic priority

There are strategic implications for regarding talent as 'top talent'. Share price and hence the value of the organization can be affected by the perception that there is strong and reliable succession in place at board and executive team level. However, there is also a view that the whole workforce has strategic value and hence needs the attention of the CEO. Examples of this range from the technology or design start-up dependent upon its creative employees to deliver applications, to the global manufacturing organization dependent on its operational workforce to produce at lowest cost and highest quality. In both cases the workforce is strategic insomuch as their performance will deliver strategy.

Hence, caring for both types of employee, the selective and inclusive, is a strategic priority and making your people before making your products relies on success in both. There was some evidence that talent in most admired companies was regarded as a strategic priority as well as an operational necessity.

One study concluded that there were critical areas in which the CEO could shape the organization to ensure both perspectives, which included (ChiefExecutive.net, 2013):

- Refocusing the organization away from talent management to managing talent. This meant a 'business-centric, outside-in view of the capabilities needed to maximize talent performance' which were 'tied directly to measures of market success'.
- Developing agility in individuals at all levels of the organization. To achieve this would require investment in training including coaching and action-learning programmes. Furthermore, the CEO should 'promote talent mobility to build experience with change and increase the organizational flexibility of talent deployment'.
- Focusing on critical roles and performance throughout the whole organization which would 'require an expansion of succession planning focus and capabilities in many organizations. Define key roles wherever they exist in the organization, not just at the top. Once completed, focus on the critical skills needed for these roles'.

The role of the CEO is critical in ensuring that these actions can be implemented. To do so will require a cultural acceptance that these are valuable activities, resources to make sure that they happen and feedback to make sure that they are improved.

CEO's recognize that getting talent right adds value to the bottom line

Warren Buffett is one of the world's most successful (and richest) businessmen. He has managed Berkshire Hathaway for nearly 50 years and in that time the 'per share book value' has grown from $19 to $114,214 (Berkshire Hathaway, 2012). In 2012, Buffett's legendary letter to shareholders noted that the company's 'Big Four' investments – American Express, Coca-Cola, IBM and Wells Fargo – had performed well and that ownership interest in each of these companies increased during the year. It also noted that 'the four companies possess marvellous businesses and are run by managers who are both talented and shareholder-oriented'. Buffett sees a relationship between talent and business success. He should know.

And yet there is still work to do on the part of people professionals to provide the evidence that such a perspective is a robust one and can be supported by evidence.

The most admired companies in the world try to ensure that investments in talent management are related as much as possible to the achievement of business results. There is recognition that good performance in one will have a knock-on effect to performance in the other. Chief executives in these organizations understand that excellence in talent identification, attraction and development have implications for the bottom line. Hence, a key role of the CEO is to choose the talent that will make sure that his or her business units are led in the right way but also to ensure that there is a culture of development and encouragement for all employees to maximize their potential.

And more than this. With the advent of big data and workforce analytics, the CEO can support efforts to bring the reporting of people practice and performance to the forefront by providing technical resource to put in place an infrastructure whereby such data can be gathered. The CEO has the ability to provide the platform that accommodates workforce analytics, the culture that ensures its acceptance and the leadership to facilitate it.

Talent-focused CEO's are aware of their organization's talent position

If the principle of making your people before making your products is to succeed then the CEO will need to be heavily involved in talent and talent management at all levels. PepsiCo's CEO has written that 'talented people are vital to our continued success, and we continuously invest in our associates, giving them the tools and training to succeed' (Nooyi, 2012). In a similar vein, when Lenovo India's managing director 'is not meeting customers and business partners, his focus is on talent: coaching, team-building and making the right pitch for the right people. "Talent management today tops my agenda and role," he says' (Sengupta and Mukherjee, 2011). This is recognition from the CEO that 'people and teams are what go into making a successful organisation'. The reason for so much focus is that 'it is becoming increasingly difficult to get good talent which matches the company's culture, has execution skills and understands the business' (Sengupta and Mukherjee, 2011).

There is active involvement on the part of the CEO in talent management in the most admired companies in the world: 'given its importance, talent management and strategy is increasingly driven from the top. CEOs and their peers oversee talent management strategy rather than delegating it to HR departments. HR, in turn, is responsible for supporting the strategy and executing it' (Nikravan, 2012). In this type of environment 'CEOs and their talent managers create that culture, they're not only creating capability and potential for the organization, they're creating an opportunity for every individual to grow' (Nikravan, 2012).

The role of the CEO to succeed could be summarized as follows:

- To ensure that he or she has active regular discussions about selective talent, being involved in their deployment and development and having an input to their progress.
- Precipitating a culture from the top by which all employees are regarded as talented and have the opportunity to fulfil their potential. This means making sure that line managers understand that they should

facilitate progress of members of their teams who have aspirations for new roles and opportunities.

- Acting as a role model for talent development and mentoring and coaching others to do so as well.

Talent management goes way beyond the responsibility of talent departments or line managers alone. It is a strategic issue and the CEO will be actively involved in its evolution, will enquire about progress and will act as a champion of talented people wherever they are in the organization.

The CEO regards talent retention as important as talent attraction

As well as contributing to a corporate reputation that attracts good people, the CEO has a crucial role in making sure that, once on board, they stay with the organization. This is becoming a pressing issue.

A report from leading European Business School IMD notes that the attraction and retention of talent 'is the top concern for more than 60% of employers ... In the business world, where holding onto your best people translates into competitive advantage and the related financial aftermath, this is certainly cause for concern' (Mancesti, 2012). The CEO can make a significant difference in the retention of talent.

In the first place, the CEO can create an environment in which those with talent are given oxygen to perform well by creating opportunities to demonstrate their skills. This is a cultural issue in which the CEO can have a direct influence. Delegating talent management to line managers won't be enough. Some line managers may hoard their talent and shield them from the rest of the organization. The CEO has the overview of the whole organization that can prevent this from happening (together with the HR community responsible for talent management).

Second, it is important that all employees are engaged with the strategy and direction of the organization. It isn't enough to assume this is the case just because workforce turnover is down by a percentage point or two. The CEO will have a key role to play in ensuring what could be called 'engagement vigilance' (i.e. that engagement isn't judged by the annual employee attitude survey but is an ongoing process of management that is the norm) is built into the culture and, indeed, built into the objectives of managers. The CEO will set the standard by which this assumption is fulfilled by personal behaviour to ensure engagement and by ensuring that the organization's performance management systems are effective.

The best CEOs work hard to retain their talented people. They recognize that the efforts to attract people to the organization through the employer brand or employee value proposition can be wasted unless there is vigilance to keep the talented employees once they are on board. In a global organization this is difficult. The spread of geographies will mean that much of the retention work will have to be devolved to local leadership. In this case the CEO will have the twin objectives of acting as role model for retention by inquisitiveness and providing the reporting infrastructure that ensures the question of retention transcends the level of conversation that comes about because turnover is too high. This isn't a quantitative debate alone. It is also qualitative. It is about whether leaders recognize and are active in keeping talented people. The CEO can influence this outlook as much as any other area of management.

Both internal and external candidates are considered

In the most admired organizations, the CEO encourages a culture of internal development as well as the recruitment of people from outside. This could be called a healthy mix but the constitution of this mix is completely dependent on the context of the organization (i.e. there is no magic formula for levels of turnover or length of stay with the company). Nevertheless a PwC report (2012) notes that 'CEOs are more focused on recruiting local talent and developing/promoting from within', and this seems to be a growing trend (especially given the likelihood of talent shortages because of those changes outlined in earlier chapters).

How does this work in practice?

In the first place there is the question of insight and understanding the role which is to be filled. In his study of multi-unit leadership, Edger (2012) draws attention to the process of portfolio talent matching which ensures that the unit manager has knowledge skills and behaviours that 'fit' a particular unit or site and cites both Sainsbury's and Greene King as examples of organizations that have processes for so doing. The main criterion for success in this matching was deep knowledge or insight on the part of the leaders of each unit. The role of the leader was to understand the internal candidates for such roles and to make sure that the fit was relevant to the specific needs of the unit. The advantage of this approach is that it gives visibility to roles for which a match today and in future will be required and for which internal talent can be developed; though, of course, it may be necessary to recruit from outside to fill roles, especially where a new project or market development is taking place.

But where people were brought in from outside, the most admired companies had a policy of hiring the 'very best people' with no compromises.

The role of the CEO in ensuring a healthy mix of internal and external candidates for posts in the organization can only be successfully delivered if the CEO applies the inquisitiveness that appears to be a feature of leading talent-focused executives. Such a characteristic can come from having a culture of awareness of the necessity for so doing, and this is one of the key purposes of the culture that is perpetuated by the CEO throughout the organization.

They invested in branding the company as a leading employer of talent

The final point that came out of the studies of most admired organizations was that the CEO understood the value of having a reputation for talent and making sure that this was perpetuated throughout external labour markets. There are several ways in which the CEO can facilitate this objective:

- First, to provide investment into the employer brand. If making your people before making your products is to deliver success then the attraction and retention of the right people with the right skills will be as critical as any other business objective. Hence, the same principle that applies to the product marketing spend should also be applied to the employer branding spend (though there will be a significant difference in the value of the two since advertising products and services will be one of the critical activities for revenue generation).
- Second, to make sure that senior managers in the organization understand their contribution to the employer brand by their actions.
- Third, to facilitate a culture whereby all employees become advocates of the company, its products and its services. The employer brand, e.g. this is a great place to work, will converge with the product brand, e.g. we delight customers with what we make.

The concepts of how to develop an employer brand and its associate, the employee value proposition, will be covered in later chapters. This section emphasizes that the employer brand is as much the responsibility of the CEO as the product or service brand is. In leading organizations there is a strong executive focus on the former as well as the latter.

Making your people before making your products will be a paradigm shift for many organizations. There will be both strategic and operational implications of this refocus. The strength of the CEO's commitment to this point of view will determine its success or failure.

The talent leadership code

In Dave Ulrich's view of the 'leadership code', there are five important criteria for leadership success. In addition to being a strategist and executor and from being able to answer the question of personal proficiency (am I ready to lead?) two further attributes of the CEO are particularly relevant to the 'making your people before making your products' philosophy:

- Human capital development concerns the sustainability of the organization through people. What kind of talent do we need? How should they be organized and managed? How can we persuade good people to join and stay?
- Being a talent manager deals with the question 'Who goes with us?' and is about building long-term talent advantage.

It is critical that the CEO has the vision to be able to dedicate enough time to these two areas in order to build a long-term model of people in the organization that will deliver advantages for the organization's stakeholders: shareholders, customers and employees.

The success of the CEO in achieving this will be measured through a range of deliverables. Of prime importance to the effective CEO will be whether he or she has achieved business objectives such as profitability, shareholder value and market share. But there are some softer measures that may reflect the commitment to making your people before making your products:

- The amount of airtime people issues are given at executive committee or board meetings. If they are appendices to the main agenda then it is unlikely that the organization will be able to perpetuate a 'make your people before making your products' culture. A benchmark could be 20% of the meeting should concern people-related issues. Surely this leaves plenty of time for strategy, sales, orders, debtors, stock and cash?
- Whether robust talent-related objectives are built into the organization's performance management systems.
- Whether measures of employee attitudes include talent metrics relating to progress, satisfaction and retention.
- Do regular meetings take place with those in the selective group and in the succession plan for senior executive roles?

- How visits to operating units across the world are used in engaging talent, two-way conversations that will give the CEO an impression of potential and attending leadership programmes as an observer/commentator.
- Receiving feedback on internally sponsored business-related projects.
- Engaging through social media or 'town hall' meetings.

The role of the CEO in ensuring that there is a philosophy of making your people before making your products will determine whether the principles are implemented. The role of people professionals is to make sure that he or she has sufficient evidence that this is the case. The act of faith that was a feature of much of talent management should now be supplemented by acts of business sustainability.

Chapter 7

Coordination and coherence in implementation

Executive summary

- As the concept of talent passes from the exclusive fringe of HR management to its core, the expectation on the delivery of benefits will increase.
- One of the challenges in HR management in general and talent management in particular will be to ensure that the tools by which the ideas of talent are delivered are integrated with the tools of management of the organization as a whole with measurable outputs.
- This means ensuring that there is a joined-up approach to talent and management from the setting of strategy right through to the evaluation of the output.
- Success from the talent strategy will come from creating advantages for the organization that are credible, discernible and measurable.
- Coherence in point of view; coherence in delivery and coordinated policies and actions will be critical to the success of the strategy.
- To answer some of the fundamental questions about the impact of the strategy, talent managers will have to move from merely providing data to providing value-adding insights.
- Analytics must produce insight that is relevant to provide the CEO with information that will make a difference to what the organization is trying to achieve.
- The success of making your people before making your products will depend on an integration of all elements of the organizational value chain from the identification of skills to the recruitment of people with those skills to their development and maximization of potential.

Talent management and performance

Gaining recognition within the organization about the value and necessity of talent management, engaging the CEO as a champion, ensuring that talent receives extended time at executive and board meetings and having 'sign off' for a talent strategy are the beginnings of the 'make your people before you make your products' process.

Investment in people 'uses up resources in order to bring about lasting improvements in productivity, worker well-being or social performance through changes in the functioning of the organisation' (Tomer, 2006). And yet the quantitative justification of such desirable outcomes remains an area of contention.

Academic debate about the impact of HR management on business performance has been going on for over 20 years and yet there is still scepticism. Theoretical ambiguity and empirical invalidity are often cited as reasons for a lack of resolution. And yet there is evidence of a consistent relationship between effective HR management practices and performance. The strength of this relationship is hard to predict for a number of reasons, including interpretations of what is meant by performance and how the different practices of HR management implementation affect outputs, but relationship there is. The effectiveness of implementation will be one factor that will permeate through to the eventual outcome. And so when looking at the tools of talent management it is not enough to marvel at the beauty of their design. Instead, the quality of how they are applied and the capture of their effects should have equal prominence.

Furthermore, in a global context the tools of talent management will be subject to paradoxical challenges that will not normally be present in purely national contexts. These could well include the tensions between western and eastern cultures, those of advanced or transitional economies, the ongoing debate about global or local solutions to talent problems and the practices of the multi-national as they are applied to national environments (Warner, 2009).

Such challenges require both insightful talent strategies and excellence in operational delivery.

Creating identifiable advantages

As the concept of talent passes from the fringe of HR management to its core, the expectation on the delivery of benefits will increase. If the idea of making your people before making your products is to be sustained there will have to be identifiable advantages for the organization.

So, one of the challenges in HR management in general and talent management in particular will be to ensure that the tools by which the ideas of talent are delivered are integrated with the tools of management of the organization as a whole with measurable outputs. This means ensuring that there is a joined-up approach to talent and management from the setting of strategy right through to the evaluation of the output. Such a process won't be straightforward as 'the gap between good strategy and the jumble of things people label strategy has grown over the years' (Rumelt, 2011).

Critical to effectiveness will be the finesse with which the concept of making your people before making your products is delivered. Research has shown that an organization's general managers will internalize HR management practices better based on the level of knowledge and 'professional experience of the subsidiary HR manager' (Bjorkman *et al.*, 2011).

This means that the delivery of a global talent strategy will depend not only on having an outstanding strategy but also on excellence in delivery of the strategy, that is global insight and local application (Bjorkman *et al.*, 2011) which goes beyond excellence in talent management tools and techniques and includes the active involvement of leaders and managers at all levels of the organization.

European Talent for Tomorrow at Panasonic

Panasonic is a global organization made up of over 500 companies, with close to 290 000 employees. Although the organization is best known for its consumer products, such as televisions, it actually produces a vast array of products – some 15 000 – that, as well as appliances for the home, include eco and industrial products such as aircraft and automotive electronic parts.

Significant global events both economically and environmentally have created enormous challenges for Panasonic, and hence the quality and calibre of its leaders is more critical than ever before in its hundred-year history.

Against this backdrop, Panasonic Europe introduced a two-year programme for its emerging, next generation of leaders which has two main aims: to cultivate tomorrow's leaders and to retain them. Any business facing the challenges of the last ten years knows that retaining talent is not just about remuneration. The defining elements of Talent for Tomorrow is that it is self-nominating, has a three-stage rigorous selection process and the applicants have to achieve the support of not just their line manager but also their HR manager and the managing director for their part of the business. It also has significant budgetary implications for their business.

Once on the programme the delegates are contracted to complete the two years of development, which also has to fit into their daily

(continued)

schedule. Interestingly, despite the contractual and time implications, this programme attracts unprecedented interest and is fully supported by the senior management population. Why? Because the aims of the programme are directly aligned with the needs of the business.

The delegates embark on a number of modules that are delivered through subject matter experts or through experiential opportunities. They complete a corporate social responsibility project and undertake an overseas secondment. The delegates obtain practical knowledge in areas such as project management, leadership skills, communication skills, business finance, culture, intensive Panasonic business philosophy training and fundamental management skills. The participants improve their skills in areas such as leading teams, communicating effectively, influencing, working with external organizations, innovation and creativity, building multi-functional relationships and adjusting quickly to new challenges and new environments.

Clearly, just offering this traditional model of leadership alone is not going to create sufficient impact. Probably the most significant element of this development has been the introduction of a new way of learning. The concept of a learning journey with an extended learning experience through pre-work and post-work has created the opportunity for additional topics to be introduced, ranging from neuroscience, emotional intelligence and understanding one's own and others' energy levels to implementing mentoring and coaching. The programme is also now tangibly measured with a robust assessment process.

The combination of all of the above has meant that Talent for Tomorrow is not for the faint-hearted. The result has been successful for Panasonic Europe with a network of people aligned in the company's purpose and ready to be tomorrow's leaders.

Patty Grant, European Learning and Development Manager
Richard Mills, Director UKHR and European Talent Management

Critical success factors in implementing talent strategy

The goals of talent management and its relationship to making your people before making your products won't be achieved unless:

- There are advantages for the organization that are credible, discernible and measurable.
- Senior executives in the organization buy into and commit resources to the approach.
- Managers within the organization see advantages for themselves and their areas of responsibility by prioritizing people over other factors.
- Employees believe in the approach and that it will enhance their sense of meaning and fulfilment.

As important as any of these issues for both credibility and sustainability will be how this is delivered in practice. The tools of talent management aren't just used when there is a high-level departure or a particularly poor set of employee attitude survey results. They are dynamic and strategic on the one hand and delivered in real time for operational excellence on the other. In addition, it has been shown that 'a good strategy has coherence, coordinating actions, policies and resources so as to accomplish an important end' (Rumelt, 2011). How to achieve these goals will determine the success of 'making your people before making your products'.

Achieving coherence in application and delivery

Since most complex organizations spread resources amongst projects or departments, there is a real danger that the 'make your people before you make your products' approach will be diluted as it moves from idea to practice. Creating a coherence between idea, strategy and execution will be critical to success. There are two important considerations here:

Coherence in the point of view

The first is to achieve what could be called 'coherence in point of view'. In practice, this means having a clear understanding that making your people before making your products is the accepted way in which the organization is led and managed. To do so will require an understanding about what the concept means. This will be achieved by having clarity about the selective/inclusive approach to talent management (i.e. everyone is regarded as having talent and there will be an organizational culture that facilitates opportunity for people to achieve their ambitions); at the same time, there is a need for selective roles to have additional emphasis placed on them. Notwithstanding the CEO succession, there will be a range of positions for which selection will be necessary at some point (not everyone in the short term can become technology platform director or head up the three-year strategy for growth in China).

The communication of this point of view and the organization-wide engagement of its message will be challenging because, if misunderstood, it can look like lip service to inclusivity whilst maintaining exclusivity. The way this will be dispelled will be by action over time. Beginning with the CEO leading by example, it will cascade throughout the organization:

- Successors will be fairly chosen and succession planning smooth and transparent.
- There will be unpredicted appointments in place of favourites because enlightened managers will adopt the view of looking outside-in as well as inside only.
- There will be opportunities for development and skills enhancement at all levels.
- It will be accepted that great ideas don't necessarily come from executives or managers but from anyone at any time.

- Achievement will be celebrated at all levels that will be genuine.
- Cross-functional projects will be excellent because there will be no barriers to talent mobility, and organization-wide knowledge sharing will be the norm.

These are the hallmarks of an organization that has embraced the 'make your people before you make your products' philosophy. Coherence of point of view will facilitate the approach. Success in achieving the organization's goals will cement the process in place.

Coherence in delivery

The second aspect of coherence will be that of delivery. This will require the balancing of natural internal competition to get there first or to show more benefits than others against the need to make the idea one that is accepted enthusiastically throughout the organization. The answer is not some mega-strategic master plan (that will almost certainly fail because it is unable to respond to changing market or environmental forces) but a crafted approach by which the principles are agreed but there is flexibility in delivery and application.

As the idea of making your people before making your products gains acceptance and credibility, there will be new approaches and ideas that can be used to enhance delivery. The challenge in large multi-nationals is to make sure that there aren't a thousand variants which become too complex to negate any advantage.

One way of making sure that this coherence is achieved as the concept is rolled out is to coordinate actions and policies within and without the HR or talent management function.

Coordinating actions and policies

Coordinating actions across the organization to operationalize the 'make your people before you make your products' philosophy will require implementation skills and focus that go beyond the philosophical excitement that can accompany the 'make your people before making your products' philosophy. In fact, implementing such a 'project' will be as difficult as gaining buy-in in the first place.

Coordinating actions are steps that are coordinated with one another to work together in accomplishing the guiding policy. Implementing a talent strategy will therefore require:

- The right level of resource allocation. Strategy setting is about choices between various approaches designed to achieve success for the organization. But once these choices have been made there should be resource to ensure their delivery. This will inevitably be problematic in the idea of making your people before making your products. On the one hand, the usual methodologies by which strategic choices are made such as return on investment and return on capital employed are not well developed in the people arena. In spite of brave attempts to create measures for return on investment in talent (ROIT) or return on human capital (ROHC) there is a persistent lack of belief on the efficacy of such measures. Hence, the HR or talent director's business case for investment in the approach will almost certainly be less refined (and accepted) than that of, say, the marketing, finance or technology director. Two things have to happen to reverse this. First, people professionals need to sharpen their act in terms of people metrics. The act of faith in people development investment is not sustainable. Second, those making investment decisions should be prepared to offer support in developing the business case for making your people before making your products. This means that the finance specialist will provide technical know-how, and technology directors should provide the technology platform on which the necessary information about people can be collected and analysed.
- Second, there really needs to be agreement of consistent policies across the organization in respect of making your people before making your products. In global organizations this is likely to be problematic. There are some obvious barriers to reward rationalization, e.g. in different parts of the globe; the basis of a bonus in one country may be anathema to another; the approach to flexible working, so well accepted in

one part of the organization, is anathema to managers in another; and the idea of development opportunities for all may be seen as expensive and unnecessary. The context of the organization will inform how much compromise is allowed in these areas. However, it is likely that this will remain a conundrum.

- The third aspect of coordinating action is to have consistency in approach. What this means is that if a nine-box model for talent evaluation in selective posts is agreed, tested for its global relevance and proven in its application then the nine-box talent model is used. Unless the business model is for total devolution of accountability, it's no use having a nine-box model used in the US, a 16-box model used in the UK and a four-box model used in Hong Kong. Nor does it add to the idea of global buy-in to the 'make your people before you make your products' philosophy if graphology is used for executive selection in one country and not in others or if development is available for all in one department but others are not so committed. Making your people before making your products applies universally. It is intended to complement the selective approach to some roles or positions with an inclusive approach to all. The way to achieve this is by having coordinated actions and policies. The way to undermine it is by having fragmentation in application and selective implementation.

Developing a coherent approach to the implementation of strategy and having coordinated actions and policies will be facilitated by the allocation of resources to make them work.

Ensuring that sufficient resources are allocated

The precise level and amount of resources that an organization will need to convert the idea of making your people before making your products work in practice will be dependent upon the specific context of the organization. The type of organization structure (hierarchy, network, project), how much of an inclusive or exclusive culture prevails in the current environment and the level of commitment on the part of the CEO and executive team will each have an impact.

But 'if a chain must not fail there is no point in strengthening some of the links' (Rumelt, 2011). And so it won't be any use having great ideas and policies if these are going to break down through a lack of resources overall or in a specific area. For example, the organization decides to give all employees the opportunity for self-development but doesn't have a sufficiently friendly and accessible website to allow this through e-learning, or the bringing together of the high potentials from around the world falls down because local units don't have the travel budget. These seem to be trivial items in the greater scheme of things but are the reality of implementation. The question is: 'How much resource should be allocated, who should own the resource and how should the cost-benefit analyses be reported?'

Expert commentators, such as the CIPD, SHRM and Jac Fitz Enz, have given advice on using metrics for impact that may help support the case for securing resources. A recommended process is to:

- Identify where HR can make a strategic impact.
- Select appropriate metrics from which organizational insights can be drawn.
- Communicate insights from metrics for maximum impact.

Even with this guidance, the issue of metrics has dogged the HR community for some time and it needs to be addressed if the justification for resource allocation is to be achieved in a way that is business focused.

People management, big data and workforce analytics

There have been many attempts to build HR metrics so that they can be used to add quantitative weight to the case for investment in people, with mixed results. Amongst the methodologies put forward are (Wakeman, 2013):

- **Employee Value** = Current Performance (How am I doing today?) + Future Potential (Am I ready for what's next?) − (3×) Emotional Expensiveness (Am I worth it?).

- **Human Capital ROI** = Revenue − (Operating Expenses − [Compensation + Benefit Costs]) ÷ (Compensation + Benefit costs).
- **Return on Investment in Talent** = Total Benefit of Investment in Talent − Total Costs of Delivering Talent Programmes or Initiatives × 100.

Add these to the usual ways in which people performance is reported – labour turnover, revenue per employee, diversity percentages of the total workforce and so on – and a picture emerges of HR reporting that is at best rudimentary (when compared with other functions and disciplines) and at worst unacceptable in the modern organization.

But there is evidence that this is changing rapidly with the emergence of big data and workforce analytics and so it is worth looking at these in more detail in order to develop the case for resource allocation. There has been exponential progress in the application of data to support HR decisions. If harnessed, the outputs from this can be used in support of the overall business case in the quest for resource allocation.

Talent analytics and the 'datafication' of HR

The fundamental questions being addressed by talent management are 'Does the organization have the people who will take a key business unit, or the organization, from where it is today to where it needs to be tomorrow?' and 'What do business leaders need to know to be confident that people investments made today will pay off tomorrow?' Dealing with these will require that talent managers move from providing data to providing insight. The advent of big data and the growth of talent analytics are the opportunities to make this move.

The opportunity to develop the business case for making your people before making your products has been greatly enhanced by the emergence of the phenomenon of big data, which refers to the massive amount of information that is available both within an organization and outside of it. IBM has defined this across four dimensions: volume, velocity, variety and veracity. The company argues that the availability of such is possibly game changing from a business perspective. It may well be in the sphere of people management.

In support of the use of big data in business decision making, McKinsey has shown that there are five broad ways in which using big data can create value (Manyika *et al.*, 2011):

- Big data can unlock significant value by making information transparent and usable.
- As organizations create and store more transactional data in digital form, they can collect more accurate and detailed performance information.
- Big data allows ever-narrower segmentation of customers and therefore much more precisely tailored products or services.
- Sophisticated analytics can substantially improve decision making.
- Big data can be used to improve the development of the next generation of products and services.

And these assumptions have been developed further from a people perspective by *Forbes*, which argues that big data's greatest HR value may well be as a predictive tool (Biro, 2013):

- Analysing the skills and attributes of high performers, big data allows organizations to build a template for future hires. HR and leaders can learn what to look for with incredible precision.
- Big data is democratic, supporting a meritocracy and enabling companies to make smarter decisions. Google has an entire HR team devoted to 'people analytics', which measures qualities such as social skills, flexibility, emotional intelligence, initiative, attitude (negative or positive; aka 'good fit' vs 'bad fit') and perseverance.
- Big data is a great people detective. It's unbiased and discovers talent. The right algorithms can pinpoint hidden potential by harvesting and then filtering reams of information to deliver a star in the making.

From a talent management perspective, big data can be used both strategically and operationally. An information revolution is taking place in which providing evidence-based insights will be important for HR. A point confirmed in *The Atlantic*, which notes: 'dedicated analytics teams in the human-resources departments of not only huge corporations such as Google, HP, Intel, General Motors, and Procter & Gamble, to name just a few, but also companies like McKee Foods, the Tennessee-based maker of Little Debbie snack cakes' (Peck, 2013).

Predictive analytics

The availability of big data per se will not be enough and it is the application of insight to the data that will make the difference. Hence, the use of predictive analytics may revolutionize the way HR professionals report people (and their own) performance.

Boudreau (2012) goes so far as to say that predictive analytics will impact significantly on the future of talent management, citing Google's use of a formula that predicts the probability that each employee will leave, allowing the company to 'get inside people's heads even before they know they might leave'. In addition, such analytics may reveal 'when employees are ready for learning opportunities, likely to benefit from a stretch assignment or ready to contribute to a new project'. He concludes that 'talent management and HR leaders might do well to get into the "habit" of considering how predictive analytics implications that face marketers today may be a harbinger of the future of employer'.

There are a number of ways in which talent analytics can deliver what is required (Burke, 2013):

- In the first place the analytics must produce insight that is relevant. Statistics about historical turnover levels are interesting. The question is whether they can be used to provide insight to the ways in which talent is managed and deployed. If they can, all well and good. If not, then talent analytics will have to change to provide the CEO with insights that will make a difference to what the organization is trying to achieve.
- The second point is about impact. In this respect talent analytics should address 'the need to move up from describing a current state to predicting where talent leaders want to be tomorrow' (Burke, 2013).

Both of which will need good sources of data that are not as well developed as could be. There are ways in which this can be addressed, and building an analytical capability for talent management will require:

- Data that is accessible and of a high quality. This will be a challenge because that quality of data available to the people professional is often poor caused by 'fragmented systems, processes, and capabilities' (Harris, Craig and Light, 2011). To overcome this, effort needs to be put into ensuring that there is consistency in the available data (by improving HRIS) and an agreement by all units worldwide to analyse and report in the same way. If these twin strategies are successful, it will allow the organization to 'compare internal groups, benchmark externally, and track causal relationships between human capital investments and performance outcomes. In order to manage talent strategically, organizations need to use human capital metrics that can guide strategic decisions and actions, and not rely solely on backward-looking measures that simply report the past' (Harris, Craig and Light, 2011). HR will then be in a position to predict instead of merely report historical data, and this will filter through to a better understanding of the implications of change on performance. This will allow a better focus on the investment required for talent and the amount of resource allocated.
- A strategic perspective on information. As Harris *et al.* conclude: 'to take advantage of analytics, you need the integration of data, analyses and processes throughout the enterprise. Too often, HR analytics are localized and one-off operations. A disciplined and methodical approach to analysing, forecasting, predicting and optimizing global HR processes, capabilities and outcomes will improve the impact of talent, and of the HR function, on the business' (Harris, Craig and Light, 2011). This goes beyond justifying the sending of high potential sales people on a training course and justifying it because sales went up after they came back. Such an analysis may be important in the tactical cost of training but less so in the wider strategic case that is being made for making

your people before making your products. So a strategic overview will be required to show the impact of all people initiatives on the organization's performance.

- We have already noted the importance of the backing of the CEO and executive team. The success of the application of predictive analytics to the big data available in the organization will require the buy-in, support and advocacy of the CEO and the executive team. For many organizations, considering people issues will for the first time be undertaken in the same way as for functional projects such as investment in new technologies or products and services. This is a paradigm shift after many years of HR not being able to present its business case in such a way. It goes without saying that such credibility will not only come about by soothing words about people being the greatest asset but also from hard evidence that they are. Predictive analytics with the support and belief of the executive team may bring about this step function in the reporting of business impact by people professionals.

It goes without saying that this is a shift not only for the CEO but also on the part of people professionals, and the acquisition of analytical skills within the HR community will be a necessity.

There is a revolution taking place within HR in terms of how it analyses and reports data and this will filter through to how it applies the analytics from this data in the field of talent management. The many tried-and-tested tools of talent management can now be applied with laser-like precision to the areas in which there is most benefit, and there will be information to back up the levels of investment required to do so. In particular, applying information in this way should ensure a better integration of talent management with HR management and, more importantly, with the general management of the organization.

The success of making your people before making your products will depend on an integration of all elements of the organizational value chain from the identification of skills to the recruitment of people with those skills to their development and the maximization of their potential.

At this stage the approach to making your people before making your products will be at the point of acceptance by the executives of the organization because insights will have been offered, a business case produced and agreed and the approach to talent strategy outlined with associated resource requirements. The next stage will be the most difficult since all of the ideas promulgated and debated will now be put into action through implementation.

There are several strands of activity here, including identifying and attracting talent, how talent is developed and managed, retention and measuring the outputs of the talent strategy.

The following chapters explain how these activities are executed in global organizations.

Chapter 8

Identifying talent

Executive summary

- *The strategic overview for the identification of talent is the strategic workforce plan. This will have as its objective the delivery of the right people in the right place at the right time and with the right skills. Talent identification is at the heart of each of these key targets.*
- *The pool from which talent can be selected will be larger if the organization has a culture of innovation and success in bringing in and nurturing its people.*
- *Where talent management is a selective process, identifying talent will be concerned with creating a pool of people who can fill identified positions in both the short and longer terms.*
- *Where talent is seen in an inclusive way, the identification process is concerned with getting the right cultural and skills fit for the organization as a whole.*
- *Where talent management is inclusive/selective, identification will embrace both activities.*
- *High potential talent reviews, leadership competency profiles in multi-national enterprises and the nine-box talent model continue to be used.*
- *The best talent pools are those that embrace a diverse range of talent across gender or ethnicity.*
- *One of the challenges facing those looking to identify talent is the need to ensure that a global perspective is taken. This means having reliable information across international boundaries.*

Identifying talent from outside whilst developing internal potential to the full

At the height of the talent wars, US business journal *Fast Company* outlined the principles of effective talent management. Amongst these was the need to recruit talent continuously and to develop people to their full potential. In both cases the identification of talent was critical (*Fast Company*, 2000). Simply filling jobs wasn't the issue for talent identification. 'It's getting the best candidates who are the best fit at the right price. That requires a more sophisticated, managed approach' (Cappelli, 2011).

But it isn't easy to do so. David Clutterbuck in *The Talent Wave* (2012) raises doubts about the efficacy of traditional talent identification systems, such as assessment centres, for three reasons. First, talent can emerge as well as be 'selected'; second, talent involves 'aptitude and application' and so 'people of equal potential who have not been given the opportunity to gain the practice hours tend to be seen as less talented'; and, thirdly, there can be bias in perceptions about talent. His solution is to identify people with key characteristics, including assisting the development of others, a willingness and ambition to take on greater responsibilities and a high motivation to learn new things.

Where HR professionals can get this right, the impact can be significant. Huselid, Jackson and Schuler (1997) evaluated the impact of HR manager capabilities on HR management effectiveness and its impact on corporate financial performance. In the 293 US firms, 'effectiveness was associated with capabilities and attributes of HR staff ... relationships between HR management effectiveness and productivity, cash flow, and market value'. There are business benefits to good people practice, and identifying talent is one such area.

Talent identification includes behaviours as well as knowledge and skills

For some organizations, having the knack of identifying and bringing in the right people is a key differentiator. American health giant Walgreens with revenues of $72 billion and 240 000 employees has long been regarded as an exemplar of external talent selection. Indeed, its founder, Cork Walgreen, was considered a genius for picking the right people to hire. But the culture of the organization extends to letting internal talent flourish as well since Walgreens gives 'its employees a creative outlet for revenue-generating workplace ideas, while creating value for shareholders and a valuable experience for customers' (Walgreen's, 2012). In one case, identifying external talent was a critical success factor; in another, the ability to identify internal talent and creating an environment where it could flourish.

These points reinforce the view that talent identification is about technical skills and abilities on the one hand and the right attitudes and behaviours on the other. This principle applies as much to the CEO as to the frontline customer service worker.

Making your people before making your products does not imply a simple assumption that everyone has talent and therefore everyone can do any job. Instead, it requires that the employer identifies and attracts people who undoubtedly have talent but are prepared to apply that talent and learn how to improve it. At the same time it requires employees who are willing to be 'made', 'grown' or developed.

The talent pool benefits from a culture of innovation

The pool from which talent can be selected will be larger if the organization has a culture of innovation and success in bringing in and nurturing their people. Such a culture will eventually be translated into perceptions of the organization through the employer brand. A reputation for talent becomes a self-fulfilling advantage for both attraction and retention.

Previously, we have raised the positive reasons for an ongoing dialogue at board or executive team level during the strategy setting process and this will have generated information about specific roles and insight about the talent needed to deliver the culture of innovation and success. Hence, setting the talent strategy will create an understanding on the part of the organization about both the quantity and the quality of talent that is needed to deliver the business strategy or to create new business opportunities. Identifying who and where those people are and when they will be available is the next step in the process.

In the first place, the strategic workforce plan will provide the information for identifying the type of talent needed for longer-term business success. On the one hand, the talent objective could be specific: 'We intend to grow our business in China and need a new chief executive with a track record of developing new markets'. Or it could be more general: 'We need people at all levels with a strong customer service ethos'. Further refinement can be achieved through segmenting the workforce, thereby coming up with groupings of people or skills that are required in the present and future. These two elements form the demand side of the talent identification equation. The supply of people comes about by a combination of performance and potential on the one hand and the traditional measures of talent and behaviours such as willingness to learn, willingness to adapt, being able to see the bigger picture or having skills and an outlook for the organization's future direction on the other. Supply measures include performance management, assessment processes, competency profiling and talent reviews. The succession plan, of course, is the process whereby those with potential selective positions will be identified. Talent identification is done at both strategic and operational levels (Figure 8.1).

- Where talent management is a selective process, identifying talent will be concerned with creating a pool of people who can fill identified positions in both the short and the longer terms.
- Where the definition of talent is inclusive, the identification process is concerned with getting the right cultural and skills fit for the organization as a whole.
- Where talent management is inclusive/selective, identification will embrace both activities.

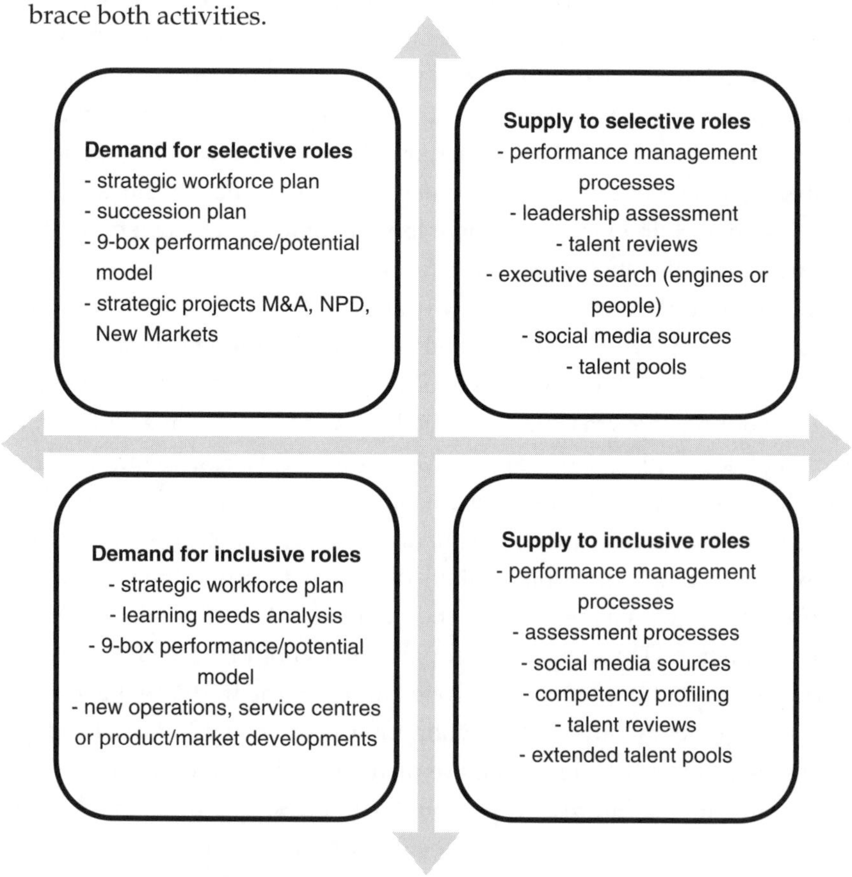

Demand for selective roles
- strategic workforce plan
- succession plan
- 9-box performance/potential model
- strategic projects M&A, NPD, New Markets

Supply to selective roles
- performance management processes
- leadership assessment
- talent reviews
- executive search (engines or people)
- social media sources
- talent pools

Demand for inclusive roles
- strategic workforce plan
- learning needs analysis
- 9-box performance/potential model
- new operations, service centres or product/market developments

Supply to inclusive roles
- performance management processes
- assessment processes
- social media sources
- competency profiling
- talent reviews
- extended talent pools

Figure 8.1: Information sources for talent identification process.

Hence, the identification of talent requires a broadly-based approach with a wide sweep of the external market and detailed understanding of the internal organization, its structure and its culture.

Rio Tinto: Talent at the grass roots

Rio Tinto is a leading global mining and metals company, employing 67 000 people working in more than 40 countries across six continents. The group's businesses include open-pit and underground mines, mills, refineries, smelters and power stations as well as a number of research and service facilities. The group also owns and operates infrastructure that takes its products to its customers, including railways, ports and ships.

The group was founded 140 years ago and over its history has developed an approach to working with national and local governments and local community stakeholders in the areas where it operates or plans to operate, which has profound impacts on the way that talent is identified, nurtured and developed at local level, in line with our commitment to sustainable development, which is integrated into everything we do. This means that talent development at Rio Tinto is far more extensive than ensuring a ready-now supply of candidates can be prepared to fill the most senior executive roles at corporate level.

Many of the world's most attractive sources of natural resources are located in remote territories, often times in countries where the skills required to plan for their extraction and delivery to customers are not available locally. In seeking to gain and maintain a licence to operate, it is always the group's intention to bring shared value to the communities, regions and countries in which it works, and this therefore means the creation of a workforce capable of both operating and leading its operations on the ground, whether in the developed economies of Australia, Canada and the USA or in newly emerging countries such as Mongolia, Madagascar, Mozambique, Guinea and Peru. Before Rio Tinto enters a new territory, a critically important aspect of planning and preparing for operational

(continued)

readiness is to assess the availability of local talent and/or the investment required to develop local capability to support the foundation and growth of a new operation. This involves the establishment of local apprenticeship schemes, the identification of school students for sponsorship onto university degree programmes and local management and executive development programmes to attract key in-country and global diaspora talent to consider employment with Rio Tinto in their home country.

In order to embed a culture of talent development at the grass-roots level, the ownership for identification and development of people is increasingly seen as an accountability of line management. While there are many global leadership programmes that are designed to provide development for key transition stages through our talent pipeline, this is increasingly supplemented by localized complementary initiatives, coaching programmes and the open provision of technology-enabled learning for all employees, wherever they work, so that individual employees are empowered to drive their own development to a greater extent than has been the case. The group's diversity and inclusion programmes also focus on ensuring that an all-inclusive approach is taken to identifying and developing talent from within the organization, with a particular focus on ensuring that the senior leadership population is representative of the diversity of the markets in which it operates.

Fiona Whitworth, Group Adviser, Performance and Talent Management

Balancing the identification of internal talent with bringing in new faces

Most organizations will face the dilemma of how and when to bring in new people. The reasons for this may be the development of new products or services, launching in new markets or the natural ebbs and flows of large workforces, retirements, promotions, strategic realignments and so on.

Organizations such as Unilever nurture home-grown talent whilst at the same time attracting people from outside the organization. The CEO is actively involved in such decisions and the company is flexible enough to change if one particular approach is not working. Whilst Google is held as an exemplar in both the identification of its talent and, once selected, getting them to create business opportunities. The company notes that it has been 'keeping the pipeline of innovation going by tapping its employees and letting ideas percolate up ... the company has a relatively small group of employees – more than 30 000 workers ... it is trying to create an arena where people can be brought together in surprising ways to innovate ... We try to have as many channels for expression as we can, recognizing that different people, and different ideas, will percolate up in different ways' (He, 2013).

Identifying talent people both within and outside of the organization can be achieved through a variety of methods.

Talent identification begins with the outputs of the strategic workforce plan

The strategic overview for the identification of talent is the strategic workforce plan. This will have as its objective the delivery of the right people in the right place at the right time and with the right skills. Talent identification is at the heart of each of these key targets.

The identification of talent can be regarded at two levels. First, there is the selective talent that may be needed for leadership or specialist roles; then, there is the identification of talent throughout the organization. The former may be brought about by talent management processes; the latter by a culture of talent opportunity.

Typical outputs of the strategic workforce plan that will be used in the talent management process include:

- Quantitative information: numbers of people required, where and when.
- Qualitative information: current and future skills requirements, information about the geographic mix envisaged in the business in future and the implications for knowledge, attitudes and behaviours.

Those responsible for talent will be required to provide insight on top of this information since workforce planning is nowadays more than a numbers game. What are the implications of the plan for competitive advantage? Can we do more with our people to deliver a strategic edge? What is the impact on our culture of the vision of our future business and how will this impact on the kind of people we need? Each of these points has an implication for people management in general and talent management in particular.

Talent identification through segmentation

Increasingly, the use of workforce analytics allows a perspective that was previously unavailable to talent managers. Multi-unit enterprises applied the concept in talent pool segmentation, though there were a number of challenges in so doing (McDonnell and Hickey, 2011).

The case for segmentation in the area of talent management is enhanced by the increasing application of predictive analytics. Several factors have combined to change the picture making it possible to embed workforce segmentation into people management programmes. On the one hand, globalization has accentuated differences that emerge across the workforce. On the other, technology is making it possible to move work across groups in remote locations. New analytical tools and an abundance of workforce data are available to help understand both current and prospective employees 'and the value they can deliver to the organization from a more granular perspective' (Jesuthasan, 2013).

Companies now realize that to attract and retain talent and to achieve maximum value across geographies 'they need to look at the distinct segments that make up their workforce' determine how those segments deliver value to the organization and 'what those segments value from the organization in return' (Jesuthasan, 2013).

The high potential talent review

The high potential talent review is one way of identifying those people who may be a good fit for some of the selective roles, but it has wider objectives, including (Hanson, 2011):

- gauging the status of the organization's talent pipeline, particularly for selective roles;
- the opportunity to assess individual development opportunities;
- the alignment of career interests with opportunities for development;
- identifying high potentials for more senior-level roles;
- identifying short-term successor candidates for most-critical roles.

The succession planning process is used to identify those within the selective group who have the potential, aptitude and motivation to be considered for senior roles. The CIPD (2011b) notes that in an international context getting the global consistency/local relevance balance right is a critical objective together with 'recognising and clearly articulating the financial value of global talent. In both cases, the role of HR professionals is to provide insights across the organisation'.

This will involve those people who have been identified as being able to take on new responsibilities immediately, and those scheduled for development in the longer term.

The leadership assessment process

The selective aspect of the 'make your people before you make your products' philosophy is often supported by leadership assessment exercises. The purpose of these is to identify those who are, or will be, able to fulfil the organization's leadership roles in future.

ArcelorMittal, the world's leading steel and mining company, has a variety of objectives for its leadership assessment that would be echoed in other global organizations and these include:

- to provide development opportunities for individuals;
- to limit potential business risks to the organization, i.e. to ensure future leaders are identified and developed;
- to gain a greater understanding of leadership potential throughout the whole organization;
- to make sure that there are opportunities to speed up personal development and effectiveness;
- to improve succession planning, promotions and recruitment for selective roles;
- to enhance team effectiveness and diversity management;
- to give a strategic overview of the organization's development needs.

The succession process in global organizations

In the global inclusive/selective model, those roles identified for selection will normally be part of the succession management process. This will be done at three levels:

- At a corporate level there will be a need to identify talent across the whole organization; this is normally done in conjunction with talent identification at the regional or local level. The objective here is to achieve a helicopter view of the whole organization in order to determine the key selected posts around the world, the current supply to match the demand in these posts and the identification of the individuals or particular competences needed for these posts. The output of this will be a corporate talent plan matching demand and supply, identifying hot spots where there are shortages and identifying the kind of people who will fill these roles. The decision then will be about identifying internal candidates for the roles or to identify potential outside people.

- In addition to selective roles, the corporate succession plan will also identify individuals who are already shaping up to fill more senior roles and, most importantly, whether the organizations within the group are able to demonstrate that they are creating opportunities for all employees to aspire to new roles or projects. The global perspective also means that such factors as cultural fit can be used in the identification process.
- At the business unit level the succession plan has three objectives:
  - To ensure that people are identified who can fill senior executive positions in the short term for risk management and in the medium to long term to ensure strategic continuity.
  - To ensure that the corporation as a whole has identified executives and managers who are able to fulfil roles in other units or divisions and are given the opportunity to do so.
  - To ensure that the culture of the unit facilitates the encouragement of talent at all levels. This could be through having a culture of opportunity or through enlightened managers who recognize that part of their role is the development of the talents of all employees.
- Finally, at the operational level, the succession plan will ensure that the demands for executives and managers within departments or projects are satisfied by a supply of people through their performance or demonstrable attitudes and behaviours.

Succession planning will be most effective against the following principles:

- When it is set against the context of the business: how will it contribute to the realization of goals and objectives?
- When there is clear understanding of the key roles for which succession is needed.
- It has the support of the CEO and ownership of the succession process.

- When it is incorporated into the HR cycle so that it becomes an integrated part of the organization's people management.
- Clarity about who takes responsibility to evaluate whether they are the right people with the right skills/experiences.

The process of succession planning could be criticized for being too rigid. It's important therefore to ensure that the forum at which succession issues are discussed (e.g. a talent review board) recognizes that its role is more than the sign-off of an annual plan (though this is important). It is about providing a flow of people who can take on bigger roles worldwide. This demands an added dynamism to the process that may not be met by a fixed structure. Succession planning becomes succession management that has a strategic element whilst at the same time meets operational requirements.

Talent identification through competency profiles

There is an increasing use of leadership competency profiles in multi-national enterprises. Amongst the competences such things as having a global mindset; being able to communicate effectively across the organization's geographical boundaries; and working with different cultures, cultural fit and managing uncertainty and global complexity.

The importance of recognizing the addition of cultural variations in the development of competency profiles shouldn't be underestimated. In the Chinese privately owned enterprise, *guanxi* was an important criterion for talent identification. *Guanxi* refers to a network of informal interpersonal relationships established for the purpose of conducting business activities throughout China and East Asia. The Chinese *guanxi* is more complicated than any kind of Western interpersonal relationships, because *guanxi* is based on long-term orientation and mutual trust. Research has shown that the 'social network is important for some talents in the posts that need to communicate with governments, or need to develop more projects' (Zhang and Bright, 2012). *Guanxi* is therefore an important requirement for managerial talent in some Chinese organizations.

The point about the inclusion of cultural considerations in competency profiles was made in Chris Edger's studies of multi-unit leaders in both the UK and internationally. He concludes that:

> At a more strategic level it is not unusual for companies to appoint country of origin directors who form a bridge between the home company and local subsidiary. Through such mechanisms the international multi-unit firm can achieve a balance between ensuring central control and consistency whilst addressing the nuances of the local market.
>
> **(Edger, 2012)**

The competency profile in this scenario would include such bridging skills in addition to those business qualities normally regarded for leadership positions.

Identifying talent using the nine-box talent model

In spite of numerous accounts of its demise, the nine-box model remains in robust health. This enduring tool of talent management was based on a McKinsey and GE methodology conceived during the 1970s as a way of helping corporations to decide into which business units they should invest their money. Over time the potential for such an approach to the management of investment in talent was recognized and the model began to be applied in organizations around the world.

The nine-box talent model is a well-established matrix that allows an organization to assess readiness in delivering talent normally for selective roles. The two axes are based on performance and potential, and an example is included at Figure 8.2.

Some have questioned the model because of the subjectivity of some of its applications. How can anyone assess potential, for example? Or performance can vary from month to month or from year to year. Nonetheless, the model has endured the criticisms to which it has been subjected. As a way of calibrating the decisions of the managers who gather around the table to plot the future of those identified as 'talent' in the organization, the nine-box grid is a useful model.

POTENTIAL

VALUABLE SPECIALIST **High Performance, Low Potential** Far Exceeds Performance Expectations Capable of assuming a new role Highly competent Acts as role model	**EMERGING POTENTIAL** **High Performance, Medium Potential** Far Exceeds Performance Expectations Capable of growing into a more complex role Could advance to the next level Highly competent Acts as role model	**TOP TALENT** **High Performance, High Potential** Far Exceeds Performance Potential to grow into a role with broader responsibility Could advance one level within two years Highly competent in current role Acts as role model
EMERGING SPECIALIST **Medium Performance, Low Potential** Meets Performance Expectations Capable of assuming positions at the same level of complexity Competent in current role Reliable performer	**SOLID CONTRIBUTOR** **Medium Performance, Medium Potential** Meets Performance Expectations Capable of growing into a more complex role Could advance to the next level Competent in current role Core to the business, consistent performance results.	**RISING STAR** **Medium Performance, High Potential** Meets Performance Expectations Potential to grow into a role with much broader responsibilities This person could advance into a role at least one level Competent in role Core to the business, consistent performance results
UNDERPERFORMER **Low Performance, Low Potential** Below Performance Expectations Lacks competence in current role If no improvement displayed, leaving the organization may be appropriate	**VARIABLE PERFORMANCE** **Low Performance, Medium Potential** Below Performance Expectations Inconsistent performance Lacks competence in current role. May still be new to position Improved performance is necessary	**NEW TO ROLE** **Low Performance, High Potential** Too Early to Assess Performance Adapting to a new role Could take on greater responsibilities Possible successful results once this person matures in their new role

PERFORMANCE (vertical axis)

Figure 8.2: The nine-box talent model.

The vertical axis is about performance and will normally be tied in with the organization's performance management system; the horizontal axis is about potential and is based on line manager views, assessment centres or psychometrics or abilities demonstrated in a strategic or other project. Whilst performance can be objective (or at least as objective as performance management systems can be), the potential assessment can lend itself to a whole range of biases if not managed in the right way.

The objective is that once an individual has been identified and allocated a place on the grid a number of developmental actions can follow.

There have been modifications to the model, either increasing or decreasing the number of boxes, but the approach is essentially the same.

The advantages are:

- It provides a strategic overview of the whole workforce.
- It provides a framework for a structured debate on the subject of talent for areas such as succession planning, leadership development and employee engagement.
- It is straightforward and can be embraced by all managers.
- The outcome allows for the focused targeting of development expenditures and provides a cost-effective solution.

The disadvantages are:

- The definitions of performance and potential can be subjective.
- It can be too rigid in its application.
- It is reliant on the assessment of managers who may not have the full day-to-day, real-time performance as perceived by others, such as subordinates.

The nine-box talent model is a convenient way to structure a range of disparate career conversations into a relatively coherent whole. Its simplicity has made it one of the most enduring of tools in the talent management toolbox.

Creating talent pools

A common practice in the talent management process is the use of talent pools as a means of gathering together groups of individuals of similar grade or status (senior managers, middle managers, etc.) who have been identified as having the potential to advance in the organization. The establishment of a talent pool has the advantages of:

- ensuring that there are sufficient people with the right behaviours and level of training to fill positions throughout the organization's hierarchy and thereby enhance the achievement of the business's objectives;

- allowing a consistent approach to leadership or management development in which the organization's competency requirements and cultural point of view can be communicated and 'taught';
- giving a sharp focus to development activity that can be controlled and measured;
- being cost-effective since there are economies of scale by a broad-based approach.

The challenges of such an approach such as 'ensuring appropriate segmentation and responding to changing individual circumstances' can be dealt with by ensuring that there is 'careful planning, communication and stakeholder management' (Yarnall, 2011).

In the selective process, groups of individuals will be identified as having the potential to move to more senior positions. These groups will be for positions at various levels. The types of talent pool will include:

- business unit leaders who are seen as future chief executives;
- managers who are seen as future executives;
- those who are able to provide innovation and new thinking;
- those with the knowledge, skills and cultural nous for international assignments.

The best pools are those which embrace a diverse range of talent across gender or ethnicity.

A study of the creation of talent pools in multi-national corporations found that 'the decision to include an employee in a corporate talent pool is a two-stage decision process in which mostly experience-based (on-line) performance appraisal evaluations are used as an input in largely cognition-based (off-line) managerial decision making' (Makela, Bjorkman and Ehrnrooth, 2010). As a result, inclusion in the talent pool 'is determined not only by performance appraisal evaluations, but also a number of factors that influence the decision making in the second stage of the talent identification process including cultural factors; the relationship between the individual and the decision makers; and the position of the person in question' (Makela, Bjorkman and Ehrnrooth, 2010).

Talent identification: Using performance review data effectively across international boundaries

One of the challenges facing those looking to identify talent is the need to ensure that a global perspective is taken. In an inclusive/selective model of making your people before making your products, this means that having reliable information across international boundaries is of prime importance.

Tools such as the nine-box talent model that are sometimes criticized for their bias in the assessment of potential at least give a structure around which talent identification can be made. This is particularly useful in the selective part of the process for those on a fast track or succession plan. But they will only provide half of the story.

In addition, data about performance (again criticized for its bias and for the failure of line managers in completing the process) is critical. Hence, effective performance reviews go hand in hand with talent identification. To achieve this requires open and honest relationships and a consultative organizational culture. If both are in place then internal talent can be identified more easily.

The identification of talent outside of the organization comes from those responsible having market intelligence at a macro-level (where is the best source for automotive engineers, contact centre workers or green energy specialists, for example?) and specific information about the organizations in which they are likely to work.

It's necessary to have both insights in place to achieve the organization's goals.

Chapter 9

Attracting talent at all levels

Executive summary

- *There are three levels of attraction in global organizations: 'corporate', at a specific regional level or the local business unit, 'subsidiary' or 'company'.*
- *The employer brand is becoming an increasingly important tool in the presentation of a market proposition for talent at each of these levels; an organization will have an employer brand whether it likes it or not.*
- *The employer brand consists of the attributes that make working for the organization different or particularly attractive as a whole and the adaptations for the levels below the corporation.*
- *It should connect values, people strategy and HR policies and be intrinsically linked to a company brand.*
- *The employer brand is one way of differentiation in tight labour markets.*
- *Social media is increasingly used as a way of communicating internally and connecting with existing employees, as a channel for learning and development or as a powerful medium by which the employer brand can be projected to the outside world.*
- *The employee value proposition turns these into results that are both tangible (such as reward) and intangible (such as opportunity).*
- *In creating a meaningful EVP, therefore, the organization will want to know: What do existing employees find in the company that makes them want to stay? What do potential employees outside of the company look for in an employer and how does our organization meet these needs? What is it that differentiates us from other organizations as an employer?*

Attracting talent: The operational foundation

YouTube presentations by Apple, Ernst & Young and Google, amongst others, are intended to demonstrate the values and culture of the organizations and the benefits of working there. Attracting talent in competitive global markets requires an employer brand that resonates across generations and geographies; distinctive global, regional and local EVPs; and a well-thought-through use of social media as a resourcing tool that can convey the key messages in real time to a global talent community.

Whilst identification was an important first step, attracting talent is the second.

Talented people can be identified either on a specific basis (a person for a role or the organization) or on a generic one (groups of people for projects or new operations). In addition, the type of talent that would be able to flourish in the 'make your people before you make your products' environment would also be specified through competency profiles and attitudinal or behavioural analyses. Predictive analytics for the optimization of skills and attitude combinations will increasingly be applied at this point.

So on paper there are specifications for the talent that is needed for the organization to deliver its business goals. The challenge of attracting them to the organization follows from this. This part of the 'make your people before you make your products' process is a critical operational step.

The employer brand

An organization will have an employer brand whether it likes it or not. It will be perceived in the labour market as being of a particular kind or type shaped by the opinions of those who work for it, want to work for it or used to work for it. Increasingly, these opinions will be through social media. So there are two choices. First, to create, shape, develop and track the brand, or, second, to let it happen accidentally (Right Management, 2005). Given the criticality of attracting and retaining people, and the importance of how the organization is perceived in this process, the first option appears to be one that should be followed.

Employer branding specialists Universum (2013) surveyed over 200 000 students to find out about perceptions of the most attractive employers. In addition to Google and Microsoft, and consultancies PwC, Deloitte, Bain and BCG, notable names included Ernst & Young, BMW, IKEA and Nestlé. Whilst the Employer Branding Institute ranked Tata and Canon amongst Asia's best employer brands.

This is why the employer brand is becoming an increasingly important tool in the presentation of a market proposition for talent. This is especially true for international organisations because it affects such important issues as talent management and employee engagement. Nevertheless, there are particular and unique 'wicked problems' that make the challenge of employer branding in global organizations particularly difficult. As well as cultural differences between the various parts of the organization around the world there are also the 'contradictory logics underpinning innovation' (Martin, Gollan and Grigg, 2011). It will also be a critical feature of projecting the meaning of the 'make your people before you make your products' philosophy to external labour markets and other potential stakeholders.

The employer brand is a way for organizations to differentiate themselves in competitive labour markets. Consistency in employer image is a critical part in this process. It is increasingly being seen as a differentiator across the world from Zhejiang in China, where it had a 'key role in intentions to accept a job offer, and as a mediator and a key variable in the initial recruitment' (Jiang and Iles, 2011), to Russia, where companies with employer brands 'gained a number of economic advantages due to lower rates of staff turnover and higher rates of HR investments in training and development activities of employees' and that 'internal recruitment practices, internal training programs and highly efficient incentive activities were widespread and employees were actively involved in the decision-making and management processes' (Kucherov and Zavyalova, 2012).

Characteristics of the employer brand

The employer brand is 'a set of attributes and qualities, often intangible, that makes an organization distinctive, promises a particular kind of employment experience, and appeals to those people who will thrive and perform best in its culture' (Barrow and Mosley, 2005). It is the 'package of functional, economic and psychological benefits provided by employment and identified with the employing company' (Barrow and Mosley, 2005). Its role is to provide coherence with the objective of improving processes such as recruitment and retention.

In building the employer brand a holistic approach will be required 'by seeking to ensure that every people management touch-point is aligned with the brand ethos of the organisation' (Mosley, 2007).

It should connect an organization's values, people strategy and HR policies and be intrinsically linked to a company brand. It is normally associated with a single organization, but there is also the possibility of having industry-wide employer brands. The intense competition for talent in the engineering sector at the beginning of this century, for example, meant that some industries were struggling to find and attract candidates for engineering roles. And so greater emphasis was placed on 'brands' of industries as well as organizations as elements in attracting talent (Wallace, Lings and Cameron, 2012).

The employer brand has relevance to both the global and regional/local context. In India, for example, 'the dramatic changes in the workforce trends and the immense competition in the labour market have made it imperative for companies to develop strategies to differentiate themselves; the panacea to this problem is employer branding. Employer branding undoubtedly is a significant precept of modern management, one that offers a fine blending of the science of marketing with the art of enlightened human relations management. It is also one of the strongest bulwarks ever against the scourge of unbridled employee attrition' (Kapoor, 2010).

The employer brand consists of the attributes that make working for the organization different or particularly attractive, including:

- competitive compensation
- attractive working conditions
- managers who develop, engage and support their employees
- good communication
- a supportive culture for progression and development.

The reason that there is so much interest in developing the employer brand is because it gives the organization an opportunity to forge the link between the corporate brand, the people strategy and how this is articulated in practice. The employer brand is one way of differentiating in tight labour markets. In addition, organizations are increasingly recognizing that there is a trend 'towards organizations taking a more integrated internal/external approach to employer brand development and management', as they try to create 'an employee value proposition that could provide a central reference point for both its employee engagement strategy and recruitment communication' (Kunerth and Mosley, 2011).

Dewhurst, Harris and Heywood (2012) note that 'while there's no substitute for development programs that will help emerging-market recruits rise, global organizations need to strengthen other aspects of their employer brands to succeed in the talent marketplace in these countries'.

And in all markets, companies are likely to find that many young, aspiring managers view being part of a broader cause and contributing to their country's overall economic development as increasingly important. Articulating a company's contribution to that development is likewise an increasingly important component of any employer brand.

Employer brands are at least as much about retention and engagement as they are about recruitment. As one leading HR professional puts it: 'people will leave your organisation as surely as night follows day. If the brand is doing its job, they'll be fewer in number, fewer still will leave prematurely' (Roberts, 2008). Nonetheless, the employer brand is an investment that, like most other aspects of talent management, demonstrates a rate of return.

As it has matured as an aspect of HRM and talent management, the approach to employer brand management 'takes a more holistic approach to shaping the culture of the organisation, by seeking to ensure that every people management touch-point is aligned with the brand ethos of the organisation. In providing a robust mechanism for aligning employees' brand experience with the desired customer brand experience, and a common platform for marketing and HR, employer brand management represents a significant evolution in the quest for corporate brand integrity' (Mosley, 2007).

The employer brand and the corporate brand

There is a link between the employer brand and corporate reputation. The two are mutually reinforcing and are important to both attraction and retention.

Those organizations with good corporate reputations demonstrated people management that created a culture of excellence. The employer brand is part of the proposition to attract the type of employees necessary to ensure excellence in the development of the company's products and services. There is support for the assertion that organizations with better reputations attract more applicants, and could select higher-quality applicants. The link between the corporate brand, the employer brand and the ability to attract and retain talented people is not purely conjectural but a reality.

As organizations move towards becoming an employer of choice, offering a good range of development opportunities could enhance the employer brand. Furthermore, person–organization fit research showed that women and ethnic minorities in particular would be attracted to an organization that had a commitment and policies for diversity management.

An important part of people management is concerned with the employer brand, which in turn is closely related to the corporate brand. Evidence shows that there are advantages for organizations that spend time on both areas, and that the role of the people or HR professional will increasingly embrace this activity. Making your people before making your products can be a powerful message in both attracting and retaining talent across the organization.

The employer brand and organizational values

But the employer brand isn't just an outward-facing tool for attracting talent. In the hotel sector, for example, it is seen as much more of a way in which the organization's values are demonstrated internally as well. This means that success comes from employees making the brand come alive:

> 'employees must be committed to demonstrating the brand values ... each time a customer interacts with the brand ... employees' brand commitment is defined as the extent to which employees experience a sense of identification and involvement with the brand values of the company they work for'
> **(Kimpakorn and Tocquer, 2009).**

Hitachi: Making globalization of talent management a reality

Hitachi Europe Ltd – headquartered in Maidenhead in the UK and a subsidiary of Hitachi Ltd and its subsidiary companies – offers a broad range of information and telecommunication systems; power (including nuclear); rail systems; digital media products; industrial components;

air conditioning; manufacturing systems and procurement and sourcing with operations throughout 12 countries across Europe, the Middle
East and Africa. Hitachi's main focus is on its social innovation business: delivering innovations that answer society's challenges.

The challenge
Hitachi is a complex organization with 320 000 staff in 900 companies
globally, each of which operates relatively independently. Hitachi's
challenge was to introduce consistent processes, policies and systems
to create a global best-practice approach to talent management. This
initiative was led by Corporate HR in Tokyo working closely with HR in
the regional head offices, including Europe.

Facing the challenge
Starting in 2011, Hitachi developed a roadmap to identify the changes
required to create a clear competitive edge through the attraction,
development, deployment and retention of talent. It started with the
basics that already existed in many of the group companies but were
inconsistently applied across the group. It soon became clear that
the challenge was not just the development of the new approaches
but their implementation across many diverse businesses in a culture
where there would be no mandate for change. This meant that while
developing new approaches HR needed to focus on change management and influencing the key stakeholders to engage with them if they
were to succeed.

The engagement strategy was a partnership between HR colleagues
in Tokyo communicating with parent companies and the regional head
offices interacting with the businesses in their regions. This included
inviting them to be part of the decision making process and piloting
change in some cases as well as running regular conferences, training and other events to keep them informed and involved. Building

(continued)

strong relationships with the main influencers and demonstrating how change could benefit the businesses were the two keys to the success of this strategy.

The programme of change started with implementing a global database as a source of consistent employee data to support management decision making. Mercer job grading and market data were introduced for all management and professional roles to create an understanding of how roles differed and to make it easier to identify development roles and other opportunities. A global performance management system was piloted to measure performance in a consistent way and a global careers site was launched to give Hitachi staff better visibility of job vacancies and encourage movement between group companies. The first global employee survey was run in September 2013 to measure engagement and identify best practices and opportunities for improvement. These tools, combined with new global assignment policies, are seen as the foundations for global talent management but are just the start of the journey.

By early 2014 the database contained details of 250 000 employees, over 80% of management roles were graded using the Mercer system and 140 000 staff had responded to the employee survey. The performance management system was launched to 35 000 staff and 400 roles were advertised on the careers site. Progress had been rapid and the new approaches were becoming 'business as usual'. With the right strategies in place to engage employees and implement effective change, Hitachi is confident that the global approach to talent management will have tangible business results: from reduced recruitment costs to improved integration and ultimately increased revenue and profit generation.

Stephen Pierce, HR Director, Hitachi Europe
Christine Cooke, Learning and Development Manager, Hitachi Europe

In building the employer brand the following should be taken into account:

Attractiveness

How relevant is the brand in attracting and retaining a broad range of employees? Does it embody a sense of community and is it a 'great place to work'? Does it offer opportunities for development and a sense of corporate, social and environmental responsibility and social justice?

Accuracy: Consistency between the employer brand and the employer experience

In marketing terms 'your brand is the promise you keep'. Furthermore, the brand 'is not what you say it is. It's what they say it is'. It is no different in respect of the employer brand. Does the actuality of the brand meet the espoused values of the brand as reflected in the company website? The argument that 'you'll never know till you get there' is now defunct and has been seen off by social networking sites that can communicate employee attitudes in real time 24 hours per day. If an organization says that people are its greatest asset then they had better be.

Awareness

The third element of employer brand building is to ensure awareness. This is where marketing skills converge with those of HR in that the tools to develop awareness have long been used in delivering the organization's message to its external customers. The same principles may be used in developing the employer brand. Clearly, social networking sites are paramount in building employer brand awareness. Having the skills to articulate the brand values through such sites and then being able to do so are new skills within the HR function. Nonetheless, they are essential to ensuring that the brand is not only attractive and accurate but also seen by those to whom such things matter: employees and potential employees (Moroko and Uncles, 2008).

Differentiation

Why should an employee continue to work for or be attracted to one company as opposed to another? Where there is choice, there needs to be differentiation. The employer brand should embody why it is that this organization is different from its competitors as an employer and developer of talented people.

Culture and values

The employer brand should embody culture ('the way we do things around here') and values ('these are the things in which we believe'). There are two important points here: first, how to put culture and values into words; second, how to make sure the culture and value language are acted out in the organization.

Relevance

Finally, there is the question of relevance. An employer brand isn't a static instrument for attracting and retaining people but a dynamic one that should evolve with time. The employer brand is a way of building an emotional bond. It's important to understand exactly what this means in the 21st century because this may be different to that of the 20th. (There are exceptions to this, of course. L'Oréal's 'because I'm worth it' was written in 1973.) For the employer brand this means understanding today and tomorrow rather than yesterday and today. The employee attitude survey is one source of information about what employees want; market research through partnerships with agencies is another. But the best source is by gathering data from social networking sites and synthesizing this into both information and insight for incorporation into the employer branding process.

Those organizations that have a strong employer brand will have an advantage in a competitive labour market and can help to reduce recruitment costs as well as increasing employee retention. There is now a compelling case for devoting time and resource to the development of the employer brand. Making your people before making your products will depend on having people who are fully engaged with the values of the brand.

The employee value proposition

The employer brand is an important part of attracting and retaining talented people. It will embody the values and reflect the culture of the organization. The challenges facing global organizations concern the homogeneous nature of the employer brand and how it fits in to a heterogeneous world.

One way of 'flexing' some of the propositions is through the development of an EVP which is a compelling offer and includes financial benefits through the reward system and (as importantly) non-financial benefits including the approach to ethics through corporate, social and environmental responsibility; the level of diversity and inclusion; and the organization's approach to work, life, career and development opportunities. Whilst the employer brand describes the organization's attractiveness to current and potential employees, the EVP turns these into results that are both tangible (such as reward) and intangible (such as opportunity).

Towers Watson (2012) found that when the EVP was clearly articulated and communicated employees were able to get a better understanding of the 'give and get' of a career at their organization, along with the value – both extrinsic and intrinsic – of staying.

A definition of the EVP is 'the collective array of programs that an organization offers in exchange for employment' (Towers Watson, 2012). It includes reward and recognition, career development and considerations such as the organization's culture.

The EVP in a global context

As with so many aspects of talent management, the development of an EVP will depend on the context of the organization. From a global perspective, this often means consistency between countries, engagement across cultures and sustainability over time.

Three case studies of French organizational expansion in Asia reflect this point. In response to the reality that multi-national corporations are struggling to attract and retain Asian professionals because 'young Asians prefer local companies to Western multinationals', the implementation of talent management programmes was a common response and formed part of the EVP in the region. The reputation for being able to offer such developmental opportunities in a global context was seen as an attractive part of the approach. But evidence shows that there was an escalation of HR responses as the competition for talent grew and the proposition evolved 'from the developmental approach (with a training program) at Alstom, then the broader scope of Danone's policies (attraction, retention and development) and, lastly, a more all-encompassing and consistent HR policy at L'oréal that covers development, career management and compensation' (Dejoux and Thevenet, 2012).

McDonald's developed an employee value proposition after surveying the values of 10 000 employees in 55 countries and was able to build the responses into themes which went to make up the EVP. The themes were 'People and Culture', 'Flexibility and Variety' and 'Development and Opportunity'. Recognizing that there would be country variants to some of these, the company nevertheless insisted that the basic elements were consistent across all countries so that over time they would 'leave their mark'.

Creating a meaningful EVP

The process followed by McDonald's and others is based on gaining insight into the views of employees and matching these against information about the labour requirements from the external market. In creating a meaningful EVP, therefore, the organization will want to know what existing employees find in the company that makes them want to stay, what potential employees outside of the company look for in an employer, how the organization meets these needs and what differentiates it from other organizations as an employer.

The EVP can then be developed using this information and will include hard elements such as reward, working hours or location and training commitment together with more intangible propositions about the working environment and friendliness. This information can then be used as a sense check to establish whether the EVP is aligned to the corporate strategy and differentiates the organization in the eyes of existing and potential employees.

Examples of EVPs abound and there are many variants as to what are their constituent parts (although reward features in all). It is possible to group these into three main areas, as shown in Figure 9.1.

Having developed the employer brand and the EVP, the onus is on the organization to make sure that these are consistently 'managed' and delivered.

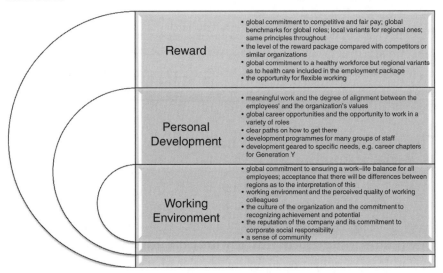

Figure 9.1: Employee Value Proposition for a global employer.

MAKE YOUR PEOPLE BEFORE YOU MAKE YOUR PRODUCTS

Measures that reflect the employer–employee relationship and the EVP

A challenge facing those responsible for developing the EVP is to assess how effective this is and build an evidence-based approach. In this respect, the Corporate Leadership Council proposed four possible metrics (2002):

- The Offer-Fit Index
  - This index measures employee satisfaction against the attributes of the EVP (weighted in accordance with the employee's career decisions).
- The Employee Commitment Index
  - Which is the strength of the employee's attachment to the organization.
- The Employee Engagement Index
  - This is a measure of how engaged the employee is with his or her day-to-day job.
- The Employee Retention Index
  - Which is a measure of turnover risk.

Predictive analytics can be applied here to develop models that not only reflect historical data but also give an idea of possible outcomes. Furthermore, social media is increasingly being used by prospective employees to work out what it might be like to work for particular organizations.

The creation of a digital narrative through social media

The rise of social media has had a revolutionary impact on how talented people are engaged with and attracted to an organization. Recognizing that their policies and practices are likely to be different from country to country and from organization to organization, harnessing the power of social media can be a powerful driving force for attracting talent. A 2012 European study found that over 40% of respondents highlighted social media as a source of recruitment and a majority believed that using social media or professional networks was an important source of quality candidates (Turner, 2012). Both sets of indicators are likely to increase significantly and the creation of a 'digital narrative' for potential employees is essential.

Social media can be used as a way of communicating internally and connecting with existing employees, as a channel for learning and development or as a powerful medium via which the employer brand can be projected to the outside world. It can be used to develop 'social professional networks' or professional communities and increasingly as a recruitment tool.

In the latter case it can attract people who are looking for jobs but, most importantly, the information contained within social media sites can be used for direct search.

As well being hailed as putting an end to one-way conversations and as the future of recruiting, social media can be a powerful contributor to ensuring that the employer brand reaches the community quickly. The benefits for global organizations have been described as 'investment in social capital' (Huy and Shipilov, 2012) that lead to:

- Helping 'emotionally attuned executives see where their company needs nurturing. It reduces the power distance and helps executives build and maintain human bonds with a large group of employees more efficiently'.
- Allowing employees to 'identify themselves more readily with an organization and can provide them with varied nonfinancial rewards'.
- Since 'employees join communities to experience authenticity, pride, attachment and fun', social media can help to 'build pillars of emotional capital more effectively'.

A factor will be to make sure that the right medium is used for the right purpose, and, as the UK's *People Management* (2013) magazine urges, 'choose your platform carefully'. LinkedIn, as platform of choice for recruiters, has a different role to play than Facebook with its one billion members or Twitter's 140-character sound bites. These, as well as Tumblr's creative following, Google's own social network and the value of video through YouTube, are all possibilities in disseminating the values encapsulated through the employer brand.

Building a social media strategy for attracting talent will be helped by having clarity of objectives and outcomes. The Conference Board's *Brave New World* report (Neal, 2013) highlights a range of considerations:

- What are your social recruiting objectives?
- What opportunities are you trying to create?
- What problems are you trying to solve?
- To which audience is your social media campaign being targeted?
- What does success look like?

Having raised these questions, other considerations include which platform is best, what the legal considerations are and the capacity of the organization to manage and deal with the responses.

Attracting talent: Social organization and support

The employer brand and the EVP articulate the cultural values and policies that will appeal to talent overall and can be adapted to specific segments or groups. But words, websites and awards will be irrelevant unless they are converted into practice. And so it has been argued that the modern organization needs a form of management that is socially responsive which may include initiatives to balance work and family demands; leave entitlements, disability benefits, entertainment and fitness, gratuities; sickness and accident premiums or employee assistance programmes (Scott-Ladd *et al.*, 2010).

The argument in favour of such support is the recognition that organizational benefits will not only create a motivated workforce with positive business outcomes but also have a positive impact on society at large. The inclusion of corporate social responsibility statements and progress reviews in the annual reports and accounts of many organizations is testament to this recognition. It is an attractive message to most people and extremely attractive to some.

Attracting talent to specific roles or units

The first part of the talent attraction challenge was to develop the employer brand and the EVPs in such a way that they were integrated into the overall values and culture of the organization on the one hand and were of relevance to potential and existing employees on the other. A measure of their success, of course, would be that embodied on attraction and retention rates.

Attraction to selective global roles

The global shortage of the types of talent that would fill selective roles has been outlined in previous chapters. Surveys such as those by the ManpowerGroup have explained the shortages, whilst consultancies such as BCG have explained the consequences. Attracting to selective roles therefore should be seen as a strategic imperative that goes beyond having headhunters on retainer just in case a senior level departure occurs.

Attraction to selective roles will have a number of elements. In the first place there will be clarity about the overall proposition that would appeal to people in this category and this will be a mix of reward, development and profile and, increasingly, diversity, corporate responsibility and family friendliness; second, an employer brand which states that this would be a great place to work if you are looking for excitement, satisfaction and a career enhancing move; and, third, it will provide a route to market by which such propositions can be communicated.

In addition to search agencies there is an increasing use of social network applications which will source those whose public profiles suit a particular post. Networking events and global or regional conferences are two other ways in which selective talent can be attracted (in the latter case through projecting the organization's achievements in case study format).

Attraction to selective regional or local roles that are able to adapt to different cultural environments

The principles that apply to global attraction will also be relevant to regional or local roles, although there will be some variation. For example, how is the employer brand translated into local markets? Does it carry the same weight from one region to another or are modifications necessary? And having considered this there will be the question of how relevant social media is in recruitment in these markets: is it the same strength as others or will alternative methods be needed, such as traditional face-to-face methods of attraction?

High potential people who have the capability to undertake a variety of global or regional roles

The definition of high potentials falls into two types and there may be different ways of attraction for each:

- The first is the graduate output of the world's universities. Competition to pick the best is intense and so the organization will have to demonstrate its unique differentiators to graduates who are seen as having the potential to achieve selective roles.
- The second group are those high potentials who have already made progress in their careers and may be looking for their second or third post.

In the case of graduate recruitment, the use of social media will be essential for making the initial attraction. But this will only be the first stage. Incentives to join may include bearing the cost of further education (indeed, there is a trend towards recruiting high potentials before they go to university with the attraction of paying university fees for the most exceptional), attractive reward packages that exceed those of competitors and gimmicks such as new computers or tablets (even for attending interviews in the case of specialist technology roles).

For the second or third post high potential, the challenge of attraction is more difficult because these talented people are dispersed and possibly invisible to those seeking their services. It is here that the employer brand can be used to back up social media campaigns with a message targeted specifically at this group.

Specialists with global skills

Specialists with global skills are the hardest group of all to attract. They will already be well rewarded and, in the case of the employer who understands the value of their skills, locked in with longer-term incentives (monetary or qualitative, such as further education and development). There has to be a unique reason for leaving the shelter of the current employer to the unknown. Such reasons may include a larger role or more responsibility, a more recognizable employer brand that will bode well for future career moves or more money or additional financial benefits. Then there may be issues about longer-term contracts, a better and more attractive working location, better work–life balance policies or assistance with moving or housing support.

It is likely that there will not be a common denominator to attracting those with global specialist roles and so a standard package would seem to be out of the question. Instead, tailored packages from a menu of potential benefits will almost certainly be necessary and at this point talent management goes beyond leadership development into reward strategy.

Employees who are able to work in a multi-cultural environment in a variety of business units around the world

Away from the selective roles, the modern workforce is as mobile as it has probably ever been. Examples from business sectors as diverse as hotel and leisure and skilled trades such as building on large-scale projects (Olympic stadia, nuclear reactors, wind turbines, oil and gas) show that there is a growing number of employees who are able and enthused by the challenge of multi-cultural environments. Attracting such talented people is as essential as the recruitment of the CEO under the principles of making your people before making your products, and so the talent strategy will have to build in processes that are able to do so. Once again, social media has global reach; the employer brand is particularly relevant and word of mouth can be a powerful attraction tool if there is incentive for those doing the talking to persuade those doing the listening.

The EVP exists along a continuum

The EVP is an all-encompassing statement of the culture and policies that make the organization an attractive place to work. As organizations have evolved to the highly competitive circumstances of the market for talented people so too has the proposition. At one end of the continuum, the EVP will reflect employee development opportunities with attractive reward packages; at the other end, they will be more comprehensive and include a wider range of benefits. There is a trend towards segmenting the target market for talent and building flexibility into the component parts of the EVP, depending on which segment is being targeted and which 'bundles of HR practices' have the most attraction verging on the individualization of employment practices (Horwitz *et al.*, 2003).

Furthermore, there is increasing recognition to develop propositions that offer customization depending on the type of talent being targeted. For example, organizations 'that recognize and respond to the need to reshape how work gets done and how careers are built will achieve a competitive advantage by attracting and retaining valuable female talent. Organizations should shift their focus from an emphasis on face time to an emphasis on results, giving employees more control over how, when, and where they work. They also need to move away from the traditional career model that emphasizes full-time, continuous employment and instead embrace arc-of-the-career flexibility that allows women to adopt a protean orientation, managing their own careers in order to align them with their personal values' (Cabrera, 2009).

In order to make your people before you make your products an organization will need the type of people who have the outlook and mindset that sees a convergence of interests between the individual's objectives and those of the organization. This is a significant challenge because as well as attracting skills the organization will have to attract attitude and behaviour. All against the backdrop of tough labour markets epitomized by shortage.

The process of attraction therefore goes way beyond placing advertising or drawing up short lists of potential targets based on headhunter insight. These are important but only part of the process. In addition, the organization will have to develop a reputation over time of being a great place to work and then convert that reputation into practice.

This goes beyond having good HR policies or talent programmes. It is an organization-wide commitment on the part of the leaders and managers to create a culture of opportunity, fairness and most of all meaning at work and to articulate this into values that will go to form the EVP and then ensure that this is projected to the market through the employer brand.

Chapter 10

Developing the whole workforce

Executive summary

- *Making your people before making your products has, at its heart, the need to develop all employees to achieve their full potential.*
- *'Flat' organizations, remote nodal networks, project-based structures, matrix management and self-managed teams rely for their success not only on transformational visionaries or efficient transactional leaders but also on skilled team members at every level.*
- *The two-dimensional development challenge of performance and potential becomes three-dimensional in global organizations with the addition of time and space.*
- *The challenge of global development is to ensure a convergence of the needs of individuals (selective and inclusive) in a way that enhances the culture of the organization, whilst at the same time contributing to the achievement of the overall strategic goals. This is alignment on a grand scale.*
- *Leadership meta-competences to be developed include Understanding the big picture; Attitude and approach, Leadership as a driving force (e.g. inspiring others, building trust and delegating), Communication, Innovation and creativity, Leading change and Teamwork and followership.*
- *Competences that are more inclusive are cross-border or functional team working and being able to work in culturally diverse environments.*
- *In the modern global organization a strategy for developing the whole workforce is likely to be crafted as the environment changes, new opportunities arise or priorities alter.*
- *The deliverables of a development strategy will be a supply of leaders with the skills to create competitive advantage and a workforce that can function effectively in diverse, rapidly moving environments.*

A new management mentality in global organizations

When French communications giant Alcatel grew its business to over 700 international operations, it was faced with the challenge common to many global organizations: how much emphasis to place on the 'centre' and how much to decentralize to local units. Here was the paradoxical situation of wanting independence and giving the best chance of responding to regional market demands on the one hand whilst at the same time hoping that cross-unit collaboration would result in world-beating innovation on the other. To manage these dichotomies Alcatel realized it needed a new approach, 'one that would reflect a keener understanding of countries ... of the individual operations that it had acquired ... balancing the needs of local independence and system interdependence' (Mendenhall *et al.*, 2008). The solution was the development of a cadre of global leaders to deal with these new challenges.

Ensuring that there is a supply of executives and high potential employees who create and deliver strategy to secure regional or global growth is a priority development activity. Leadership programmes, secondments or expatriate appointments are some of the most common methods. But the position in most organizations during global competition is that the traditional focus of development needs to be expanded to embrace a whole workforce development approach.

Whole workforce development

'Flat' organizations, remote nodal networks, project-based structures, matrix management and self-managed teams rely for their success not only on transformational visionaries or efficient transactional leaders (the merits of each often feature on leadership programmes) but also on skilled team members at every level. To achieve this, the skills, capabilities and performance of every member of the workforce will need to be aligned with business strategies. Whole workforce development addresses this challenge by creating an environment that satisfies remedial needs (i.e. it fills skills gaps that could have been shown up in, say, the succession management or employee engagement process), but it is also inclusive in that it seeks to develop beyond the immediate. By this we mean that everyone is regarded as having development potential regardless of where they fit into the organization.

The provision of an effective combination of global and local expertise is also important with the main objective of having employees with the right skills at the right time in their careers who can be ready to take on a range of roles. The practical challenge is to recognize the different skills needed in different markets which match with career opportunities (Ernst & Young, 2012).

It could be argued that competitive advantage through talent management can be achieved in global organizations because of the access to global talent which local competitors do not have. This theoretical position needs to be firmed up through workforce development because of the need to develop people to stay rather than the fear of developing people who subsequently leave.

Development in a global context therefore has two functions:

- First, it means taking care of the developmental needs of those in selective positions. Global selective roles require people who are hyper-sensitive to the needs of others, are able to bring diverse groups of people together, have courage and are prepared to take risks, excel in negotiation and mediation skills and have 'deep cultural knowledge and strength in mobilizing networks of community resources' (Tobin, 2013) A factor that makes this even more of a challenge is that the cultural differences are so varied between countries that what is relevant and important to understand in one country may well be different in another country (Mitchell, 2013). Three dimensions in this context means excellent performance, high potential and both sensitivity to, and ability to engage with, a range of international cultures.

- The second function is development for those in inclusive positions. It means having opportunities for all individuals to maximize their own potential in pursuit of the organization's goals. The challenge of global development is to ensure a convergence of the needs of individuals (selective and inclusive) in a way that enhances the culture of the organization, whilst at the same time contributing to the achievement of the overall strategic goals. This is alignment on a grand scale.

Making your people before making your products has, at its heart, the need to develop the totality of the workforce. It means giving everyone the chance to achieve their full potential. This is based on the belief that they will apply that potential to the achievement of the organization's goals as well as their own. A fully engaged workforce that is developed to its maximum capability is a powerful competitive force. Development benefits individuals and teams, organizations and society (Aguinis and Kraiger, 2009).

Development in three dimensions

The well-defined development programmes that have evolved over fifty years to equip leaders and managers, honing strategic perceptions and the engagement of people, require additional content if they are to be fit for purpose for this period of globalization.

Thus, technical skills, understanding and working effectively in the organization's processes and the behavioural requirements of working in cross-functional teams remain important, but they increasingly require the skills needed to build relationships with people from different backgrounds, across a wide range of functional areas and geographies and in different time zones. The impact of these 'soft' issues shouldn't be underestimated. Hence, as in the attraction of talent, the two-dimensional criteria of performance and potential become three-dimensional with the addition of time and space.

As organizations plan ahead for global expansion there will be issues of culture, language, process and operational skills that transcend any one business unit or level in the organizational hierarchy or node in the network or matrix. It is not just at the most senior levels where employees working globally need political intelligence and a high level of understanding of what will be appropriate in the circumstances. Anyone working in a global project team or supply chain will also have this perspective.

The question of generic or technical competences

The competences within this capability are both technical and generic. Technical competency embraces the knowledge and behaviours that people must have to perform effectively at work; the technical attributes that they may need to fulfil a role or a job and demonstrable performance outputs that satisfy a set of standards. This competence includes such requirements as 'the ability to prepare a profit and loss account', 'the ability to write code', 'working knowledge of Mandarin' or 'having an understanding of American law'.

Generic competency includes those things that transcend any specific role and may be initiative, creativity, flexibility, open-mindedness, self-reliance or self-confidence.

Global organizations will need to decide how much development effort goes into each of these areas. Do we focus on building a superbly technical workforce on the assumption that knowledge and skills will carry the day or do we focus on generic skills based on the assumption that a team built on cooperation and good human relations will work round any performance obstacles?

There is evidence for both points of view. On the one hand, the over-riding factors leading to effective performance were mainly technical cred-ibility and the ability to use systems and processes to meet performance standards. Traditional talent development processes such as training are extremely effective at imparting technical competences. But, on the other, organizations operating globally may also require skills in behavioural char-acteristics amongst the workforce such as 'able to work in teams', 'encour-ages diversity and listens to alternative viewpoints' or 'is prepared to go the extra mile for customers'. In this respect the term 'generic competences' emphasizes a range of important qualities and capabilities including prob-lem solving and analytical skills, communication skills, teamwork compe-tences and 'skills to identify access and manage knowledge' (Garavan and Carbery, 2012). Generic competences also include 'personal attributes such as imagination, creativity and intellectual rigour and personal values such as persistence, integrity and tolerance' (Garavan and Carbery, 2012).

The ability to work in and with different cultures, the ability to work in cross-functional or geography teams and the ability to manage uncer-tainty caused by different time zones or decision making processes may also feature as generic competences for those in global organizations.

So it's possible to conclude that the competences to be addressed by devel-opment in global organizations are made up of a mixture of both the technical and the generic. One study concluded that employers who operate in a global labour market now seek employees who possess not only a high level of spe-cific job-related skills but also a high level of generic competences which can be applied across a wide range of jobs (Young and Chapman, 2010).

A further consideration is the depth of knowledge to accompany the development of a competence.

Hedgehogs, foxes and career success

Vikram Mansharamani (2012), Yale University lecturer and author, has a viewpoint based on Greek poet Archilochus' famous statement that 'the fox knows many things, but the hedgehog knows one big thing' and went on to draw attention to Isaiah Berlin's 1953 essay *The Fox and the Hedge-hog*, which compares hedgehogs that 'relate everything to a single, central vision' to foxes who 'pursue many ends connected … if at all, only in some de facto way'. Mansharamani's argument is that career hedgehogs have come to dominate many professions, including academia, medicine, finance and law. Specialists with deep expertise have ruled the roost.

The observation that 'specialists toil within a singular tradition and apply formulaic solutions to situations that are rarely well-defined' (Mansharamani, 2012) contributed to the conclusion. This would have adverse effects on the economy because a collection of specialists means a less flexible labor force, and retraining in technological developments means constantly shifting human resource needs. Generalists on the other hand are better at navigating uncertainty and the trend therefore is to go for employees skilled in numerous functions because they are 'more valuable as management can dynamically adjust their roles. Many forward-looking companies are specifically mandating multi-functional experience as a requirement for career progress' (Mansharamani, 2012). The upshot of this is that 'individuals should manage their careers around obtaining a diversity of geographic and functional experiences. Professionals armed with the analytical capabilities (e.g. basic statistical skills, critical reasoning) developed via these experiences will fare particularly well when competing against others more focused on domain-specific skill development' (Mansharamani, 2012). This comes down on the side of the generic fox.

Nonetheless, it is highly likely that both types of person will work in and flourish across the globe given the different cultures that will exist. Thus, whole workforce development will have a broad focus on technical and generic competences not only for its global leadership or selective roles but also for its workforce as a whole.

A complex developmental picture is beginning to emerge. It is both broad and deep, and crosses time and space. The outputs required to satisfy the many competing demands from such considerations will be at both the strategic and operational levels. They will require 'solutions' that create outstanding global leaders on the one hand and a highly developed global workforce on the other.

The competences and meta-competences of global leadership or selective roles

In a global context, the degree of importance to each generic leadership competency is of particular note. Being able to communicate and engage with a workforce, for example, is important across leadership groups. But doing so in an international context is more complex because barriers of language, time and space will impede the global leader who is not able to respond to these global nuances (Mendenhall *et al.*, 2008). The benefits of recognizing this and building a sustainable approach to development at leadership level are both strategic (the ability to do the right things) and operational (the ability to do things right). There are benefits for both. There was a positive relationship between authentic leadership and supervisor-rated performance in a study of organizations in China, Kenya and the USA, for example (Walumbwa *et al.*, 2008).

It's possible to represent leadership competences at three levels. The first is the individual leader's core personality; the second is his or her personal values; the third concerns the individual's leadership behaviours and skills. This last level consists of what are described as meta-competences. These include:

- understanding the big picture
- attitude and approach
- leadership as a driving force (e.g. inspiring others, building trust and delegating)
- communication
- innovation and creativity
- leading change
- teamwork and followership.

This taxonomy of leadership implies that some things can be developed and that some things are fixed at an early stage in life. Leadership development should focus on those things that can be fine-tuned 'for greater efficiency and greater potential contribution' (Tubbs and Schultz, 2006).

From selective roles (i.e. developing those in leadership or management positions), generic competences include such behavioural attributes as communication skills, the ability to manage people and teams effectively and problem solving. In a global context the ability to manage in different cultures and thrive on uncertainty would be of additional value. In addition, the well-trodden leadership research path invariably produces a list of behavioural competences such as charisma, vision, decisiveness, inspirational communication, honesty and integrity, and analytical and creative thinking. Goffee and Jones' (2006) excellent perspective on leadership asks the question 'Why should anyone be led by you?' and concludes that leadership is situational, leadership is non-hierarchical, leadership is relational – there are no leaders without followers. They urge leaders to 'be yourself more with skill', create a community, be authentic and generate enthusiasm.

A study of best practice in leadership and succession planning found that 'organizations effectively integrate leadership development and succession planning systems by fully utilizing managerial personnel in developing the organization's mentor network, identifying and codifying high potential employees, developing high potentials via project-based learning experiences and manager-facilitated workshops, establishing a flexible and fluid succession planning process, creating organization-wide forums for exposing high-potential employees to multiple stakeholders, and establishing a supportive organizational culture' (Groves, 2007).

Nevertheless, findings showed that managers in the early stages of their careers place more emphasis on technical rather than generic competences. As a consequence, this can have an impact on leadership performance rather than functional. Hence, development should therefore be both technical and behavioural.

A focus of traditional leadership development has been very much on the leader rather than leadership (Uhl-Bien, 2003). This means that often there is too much emphasis on those who have been formally appointed to senior positions. Another perspective is that leadership is something that can happen at any level, whether from those appointed to formal roles or those who undertake leadership behaviours demanded by a specific set of circumstances regardless of their roles. In global organizations, where formal control may reside a good distance away, there's a case for leaders who both understand 'corporate' requirements and are able to interpret these and apply them to regional or local contexts.

Competences for the whole global workforce

The characteristics of the global organization will influence the types of competency required. For example, it is likely that most employees will have to be proficient in working in diverse work contexts. This means having a focus on generic skills, a trend that has been evolving over recent years.

Groves (2007) argues that 'the new workplace places emphasis on skills that go beyond the technical and include a full spectrum of soft skills. Talented employees are expected to display these generic competences in combinations that meet the demands of a unique and continually changing work environment ... it suggests that on-going talent development processes need to be flexible, adaptable, and capable of scalability and in tune with the evolving context. As a consequence, talent development must increasingly be work-based in order to develop capabilities to cope with the temporality or dynamism of work context'.

The question of how people develop is as germane to the development of the whole workforce as the why of delivering business objectives. Understanding how can inform the types of development activity that can be implemented.

A number of models have been proposed to explain how people learn. The 70:20:10 model (Lombardo and Eichinger, 1996), later amended by Ulrich and Smallwood to 50:30:20, asserts that a large part of development takes place through on-the-job training: 20 or 30% through formal learning experiences and 10 or 20% through life experiences. These findings point to work-based development or on-the-job training as priorities.

The Bersin model refers to four levels ranging from level one (no formal training) through to level four (a combination of training programmes, coaching, performance support and assessment, knowledge sharing and a culture of learning). The whole workforce model would target level four and ensure that managers have the skills and incentive to deliver in an environment whereby all employees recognize the benefits from owning their own development and doing something about it. Organizations that have done so had some common characteristics (Leverone, 2013):

- They put a priority on career development: match the skills, styles and preferences of your staff against the needs of specific roles and business requirements.
- Initiated career conversations: managers act as a coach to their team.
- Promoted transparency: ensure information of internal vacancies is readily available.
- Encouraged 'big picture' thinking: ensure managers do not hoard their talent and consider a way to reward managers who recognize that talent belongs to the company and not their own unit.
- Cross trained: enhance the skills of your staff and keep critical knowledge in house.
- Supported internal networking.

Furthermore, organizations that recognize cultural differences and the (language) barriers to achieving a common understanding have taken these points to heart in their quest for whole workforce development, for example Goldman Sachs in Japan, which introduced a programme to help local staff interact more effectively with staff around the world, and Panasonic, which gives its employees at all levels exposure to different parts of the business and involvement in cross-border projects.

Creating a development strategy for global organizations

A learning and talent development strategy has been defined as 'a tailored, organisation-wide talent management strategy that provides a focus for investment in human capital and places the subject high on the corporate agenda' (CIPD, 2013a). A global inclusive/selective development strategy will be a whole workforce approach. It's possible to look at the creation of a strategy for talent development at three levels.

- In the first place investment in talent development will have to have clarity about its purpose and objectives. This will be at corporate level, for example an organization-wide leadership programme, executive coaching for potential successors or all-employee programmes on diversity and cross-cultural working.
- Second, development in the 'make your people before you make your products' philosophy means development for all. On the one hand, there will be leadership development but, on the other, there will be investment in platforms for all employees to both articulate and have the opportunity to achieve their career aspirations.
- At the third level, and important because of the complexity of global talent development, there will need to be coordinating actions to deliver a coherent approach and measures to track progress and benefits.

Figure 10.1 shows the characteristics of development at each of these levels.

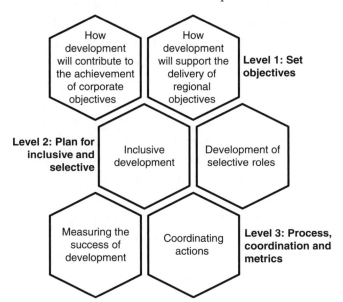

Figure 10.1: A model for whole workforce development.

Objectives: What is the organization trying to achieve through whole workforce development?

The inclusive philosophy towards development is not based on altruism, although it will certainly bring satisfaction to many. Its prime purpose is to ensure that the workforce has the necessary knowledge, skills and attitudes to deliver the organization's objectives. However, as well as reflecting longer-term business aims, the development strategy should also address operational realities and constraints. In addition, it would be culture sensitive and built in a way that reflects and maximizes the advantages of a diverse workforce. Amongst the development target segments will be:

- People to the most senior leadership or managerial positions to satisfy the needs of the succession plan in the long term (and hence the demands of shareholders looking for continuity and ongoing success). This development can also include rotating those identified as high potential through corporate HQ as exemplified by Bertelsmann. The organization brings a number of their high-performing employees from their emerging markets to spend two years at the corporate centre to give them exposure to the kinds of functional and geographical issues they could expect to face whilst at the same time as being given real work assignments. When they return to the local market they are much more familiar with the strategy and direction of their company, have developed a wider internal network and have had exposure to many senior leaders (Dewhurst, Harris and Heywood, 2012).
- Those who have been signposted to new global expansion projects in the medium term, developing new markets, launching new products, and identifying and integrating mergers and acquisitions.
- Those who are ready now to take up new posts; a development project is the way in which they are introduced to leadership or managerial positions.

The content of development can cover a broad range of subjects such as:

- Leadership or executive development through formal business training or coaching. Whilst at Panasonic a number of programmes were organized by the corporate HQ and held primarily at its HR development centre in Osaka. Leadership development should be comprehensive and systematically integrated into the organizational culture in order to produce leaders who can deal adequately with organizational challenges (Amagoh, 2009).
- Management training through formal business courses, or projects and assignments.
- Cultural or organizational awareness for all employees across all parts of the organization.
- Technical or systems skills for all employees across the world to ensure consistent application.
- Career or personal development plans for all to ensure a transparent and inclusive talent management approach and a means of creating opportunity.

The assumption here is that talent development is an investment for the future, so an organization may train for future skills even during an economic downturn therefore taking more of a longer-term view. This is likely to be a 'corporate' decision and hence viewed as part of the overall development process. In addition, development can also support the organization's corporate responsibility or citizenship.

This is not a fixed process and the development strategy must be kept up to date as the business environment changes and as information is gathered on the effectiveness of developmental interventions. This is of particular interest at the regional level and so the umbrella of corporate level objectives is likely to have underneath a range of developmental objectives that can be adapted to regional units. The development strategy will have to recognize the need to balance global and regional needs. To be successful here will require a deep understanding of cultural differences and sensitivities.

Key principles of a development strategy

Some of the principles in this set of objectives could be:

- Expenditure on learning and training should show measurable benefits. These can be tangible commercial benefits or the intangibility of an engaged workforce (and indirect business improvement since the engagement of employees in a continuous learning journey will often lead to their feeling more committed and more likely to stay with the organization).
- Learning can be directed towards key business priorities.
- Learning and development should also be linked to individual career aspirations.
- Learning is a cost to the business that, though it delivers benefits in terms of productivity, should be delivered efficiently and effectively.

An important part of learning to lead is through experience. Hence, leadership development should contain formal programmes as well as experiential learning. Experience can be gained through assignments or projects, and some would argue that these should be at the core of executive development. Such assignments could include strategic projects or start-ups.

Best-practice organizations integrate leadership development and succession planning through mentoring, understanding the needs of their high-potential employees, project-based learning, an effective succession planning process, organization-wide fora to identify high-potential employees and give them the chance to work with multiple stakeholders and establish a supportive organizational culture.

Development for selective roles

Global organizations are increasingly mindful of research to support their quest for the best approach to development for leadership and other selective roles. This is to ensure a reasonable supply of internal resource to fill selective roles during periods of global expansion or organizational change. Amongst the ideas are:

- Experiential learning through encouraging mobility in the senior positions and giving development through international assignments (Deloitte, 2011). Indeed, action learning was considered a vital element of executive development.
- Co-constructed coaching involving 'a highly informed active partner in the leadership learning process' which provides a 'critically reflexive dialogue' can complement or even be used as an alternative to executive coaching which is more non-directive (Kempster and Iszatt-White, 2013).
- The development of 'responsible global business leaders' and projects such as 'Project Ulysses' (supported by the 2007–2013 Culture programme of the European Commission) – which involved sending participants to developing countries to work in cross-sector partnerships with NGOs, social entrepreneurs and international organizations – was found to be beneficial in six areas: responsible mindset, ethical literacy, cultural intelligence, global mindset, self-development and community building. The development of competency and awareness in these areas was helped by a number of processes, including 'resolving cultural and ethical paradoxes; constructing a new life-world, that is, developing a new perspective of self and the world; and making sense of the emotions experienced while on assignment' (Pless, Maak and Stahl, 2013).
- Management education that includes 'reflective practices that develop awareness, the will to manage, and what some call "heart and soul"; systems thinking, integration, and understanding of how to work effectively in today's globalized world, and application of these attributes to understanding and implementing the broad responsibilities, purposes, and (ethical) values associated with businesses and other organizations' (Waddock and Lozano, 2013).

Much of the evidence points towards combining several development experiences for those either already in or moving into selective or leadership roles. Figure 10.2 shows a few of the permutations that are possible in taking this holistic view.

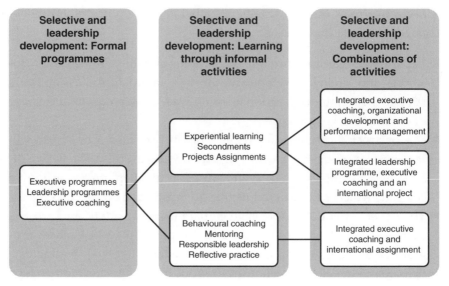

Figure 10.2: Formal, informal and combined development for selective/leadership roles.

Development for inclusive roles

There has been a social shift in learning. It is now more about interaction than instruction and has to address the different learning styles of a multi-generational workforce and the different approaches that will be demanded across cultures (CIPD/Cornerstone, 2013). Increasingly, and of particular relevance to inclusive roles as part of whole workforce development, there will be an integration between coaching, organizational development and performance management, recognizing that experiential learning is critical to building capability and confidence.

This has implications for development per se and its ultimate impact on careers as a whole. Indeed, it has been argued that a new, more adaptive model of career progression has emerged. This replaces the typical career ladder in which progress in the organization was upwards via a series of fixed steps. In the new model the steps have been replaced by a lattice which allows an individual to move in many directions between a set and a subset. In this structure it is possible to move faster or slower and to change direction at certain points. For such a model to work, career building has to be a shared responsibility and adaptable over time. It requires trade-offs and choices which will lead to better planning, better decisions and greater satisfaction. This involves career customization on a large scale. Indeed, Benko and Weisberg (2007) call it 'mass career customisation'.

High potential at Merlin Entertainments

Merlin Entertainments plc is the second-largest entertainments company in the world. Merlin runs over 100 attractions in 22 countries across four continents. It owns and operates global iconic brands such as; Alton Towers, LEGOLAND, Madame Tussauds and the EDF Energy London Eye. The company, which listed on the London Stock Exchange in November 2013, is headquartered in Poole, UK and employs 22 000 staff worldwide.

Global talent challenge

With ambitious expansion plans to open at least six to eight attractions a year, a LEGOLAND park every two years and develop resort accommodation and second gates, Merlin faces a challenge to identify, recruit, hire and retain strong talent across multiple brands and diverse cultures. To support this growth, the company's HR strategy concentrates on the ability to supply the business with the right calibre of people, at the right time.

The Merlin high-potential development programme

Merlin's Hi-Po development programme was created to provide targeted development to leaders considered potential successors to the senior leadership team. Each participant would gain insight and clarity on their core strengths and focus on an individual plan to address their development needs.

The first incarnation of the programme, while considered successful, highlighted some improvement areas for subsequent programmes.

(continued)

It became apparent that the nomination process for the programme needed to be less 'gut feel' and more robust, supported by evidence regarding the participant's performance and potential. Similarly, the process also needed to consider the motivation of potential participants and whether such a programme was aligned with their career aspirations.

Improvements to the second programme predominantly centred on an enhanced nomination process, through which the group HR team supported the validation process alongside the divisional leadership teams. Once a provisional selection had taken place, the potential delegate was then invited to meet with the group HR director and managing director to discuss their development and career aspirations.

The success of Merlin continually developing its Hi-Po population can be evidenced through increased promotions within key talent areas, such as group finance, to individual cases of people promoted through several grades in a short time. Overall, the programme has strengthened Merlin's plans for viable successors for its most senior leadership roles to support its future growth strategy.

Tea Colaianni, Group HR Director

Hence, the whole workforce approach to development should see this in the context of development that gives not only specific skills but also attitudes and behaviours towards change and adaptability for future roles. Thus, the development of learning environments that offer employees diverse forms of participation will foster learning at work. These may include:

- opportunities for engaging in multiple communities of practice;
- access to a multi-dimensional approach to the acquisition of expertise;
- the opportunity to pursue knowledge-based courses relating to work.

Where organizations offer expansive learning environments there is a better chance for the integration of personal and organizational development (Fuller and Unwin, 2004).

The role of e-learning in whole workforce development

The technology revolution in e-learning, which has gone through rapid and unprecedented changes, has serious and positive implications for developing the global workforce. It is changing the way that people learn and develop. This applies not only to education providers (36 000 enrolled for Harvard's first massive online course) but also to organizations that wish to develop their own content because of:

- speed of dissemination of learning 'content' around the world;
- consistency of learning messages and points;
- depth of subject matter that can be offered;
- breadth of dissemination of subject matter;
- diversity of subjects that can be covered, from induction and technical through to health and safety training as well as massive open online courses (MOOCS).

The diversity of e-learning approaches allows flexibility. Micro learning, for example, is aimed at new ways of responding to the growing need of lifelong learning for members of society, such as knowledge workers. This can cover a single topic, limited in length, available on different devices and accessible at all times to suit individual learner preferences.

Examples of global companies implementing e-learning into their development interventions include:

- Unilever, which offers learning programmes in more than 20 languages to nearly 130 000 employees in over 100 countries. It has 7600 e-learning modules and its Learning Academy provides career skill maps for all its functions.

- Hewlett-Packard, which has nearly 93% of its training in virtual courses and self-directed online courses, allowing flexible access so that employees can log on at any time to 10 000 modules. In 2011, HP aligned these programmes to its business priorities (technical 68%, sales 21%, professional skills 7% and leadership 4%). HP has also introduced about 30 learning communities so that colleagues on a global basis can interact using a global platform so as to share experiences, access to podcasts, tools and presentations.
- Toyota, which has developed an educational system based on OJT which it sees as essential for the development of its employees and transfer of knowledge.
- Siemens, which sees training and lifelong learning as a sustainable investment giving its staff at all levels the chance to fully develop their potential.

Once again, combining the advantages of e-learning with other types of development activity is of particular relevance for global organizations.

Combining formal and informal learning interventions for inclusive roles is shown in Figure 10.3.

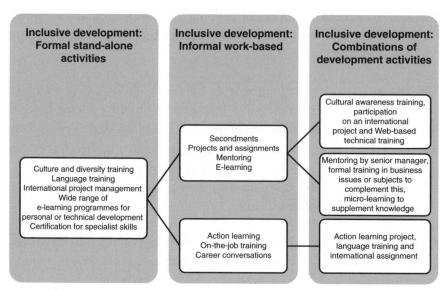

Figure 10.3: Formal, informal and combined development for inclusive roles.

Process, coordination and metrics

The coherence of strategic intent and action that was discussed in earlier chapters will also be in evidence when dealing with whole workforce development. Having clarity of development objectives at corporate, business unit and operational levels will be accompanied by a well-thought-through action plan and a structured approach to how resources are allocated. In addition, robust metrics should be developed to track the progress of development activity.

The Conference Board (2013) advocates a particular approach to strategic talent management that will facilitate this implementation. This can be adapted specifically for whole workforce development as follows:

A strategic-thinking orientation

Any development activity will require a strategic approach. This means aligning whole workforce development behind business objectives. For example, if the organization has plans to expand its business in Asia Pacific, it will need leaders and executives who understand and are proficient in regional culture and business methods (knowledge), understand the specific implementation issues in the region (assignment) and have been able to learn from others with experience (coaching or mentoring). Combining these development activities into a holistic development plan will address the leadership resourcing issue not only in an operational sense (say one year) but over a longer 'strategic' timeframe (three to five years).

But a strategic-thinking orientation will include the whole workforce. The developmental needs for regional growth therefore will mean a workforce that understands the objectives of the strategy (engagement with the business), the different ways of doing business in new areas (cultural and diversity training), will be able to work within a new set of supply chain processes (technical or systems training) and be mindful of the needs of others in remote teams (team effectiveness). A combination of these interventions will be the development in a whole workforce approach.

Finally, it's important that there is a systematic approach to all of these activities. Whilst ad hoc interventions may solve today's logjam, they won't necessarily satisfy the need for forward, holistic thinking.

A results-driven focus

The emphasis on alignment of talent strategy to business strategy is a feature of making your people before making your products. The assumption is that a motivated and engaged workforce forms the foundation on which all other strategies are built. The reasons for so doing are to move towards a convergence of personal and business goals.

The development strategy should follow this mantra. The objective is to make employees who can deliver business objectives. A results-driven focus complements the personal agenda.

Building leverage and connections across the organization

It's important that development is not a siloed, stand-alone activity. There is an opportunity in whole workforce development to connect business units and individuals. In this respect the very process of development can be used to 'build social capital' across the business.

At corporate level, well-managed and well-thought-through development activity in selective positions (secondments and assignments for example) can act as a bridge between geographic and ultimately cultural and personal boundaries. At an inclusive level, cross-business developmental activity can create a workforce better able to understand the needs of global operation. In both cases development means development of knowledge and skills on the one hand and behaviour, attitudes and culture on the other.

In the modern global organization a strategy for developing the whole workforce is likely to be crafted as the environment changes, new opportunities arise or priorities alter. Nevertheless, development is not merely a function that supports business needs but one that increasingly drives business performance. Its focus is the whole of the organization; its deliverables will be a supply of leaders with the skills to create competitive advantage and a workforce that can function effectively in diverse, rapidly-changing environments.

To achieve these goals, those who lead, manage and work within the organization will need a mindset that respects diversity, allows innovation and is both inclusive and consultative.

Chapter 11

Managing talent in an age of transparency

Executive summary

- *Good management is good talent management.*
- *Employees expect their managers to be open and transparent with them. This will affect motivation, engagement and retention.*
- *A sunao mind means to see things as they really are and to make decisions without any bias or prejudice.*
- *Managers should be open to listen to the opinions of others as well as using their own experience and judgement.*
- *Management teams need to be open in encouraging their staff to try new things and to speak their mind.*
- *Everyone develops in a different way and it will be important for a manager to have an open mind as to the right intervention which will best support their team member.*
- *When recruiting for a new member of staff the manager should be open-minded as to the best person for the role and avoid the temptation to select someone who is similar to themselves.*
- *To recognize that people from different cultures will respond differently and having a sunao mind will be essential for a manager to recognize talent.*

Good management is good talent management

There is a greater expectation on the part of employees about where their careers could be taking them and a greater onus on the organization in general and line managers in particular to have transparent, open discussions about this. An additional benefit of such openness will be improved motivation, engagement and retention. As the implementers of talent strategy, therefore, line managers are responsible for managing performance and identifying talent in their areas. Such an assumption is important in the 'make your people before you make your products' philosophy.

The challenge is brought into even greater focus when management takes place in an environment of cultural diversity. An acceptable management style in one country may not travel well across geographies. An awareness of this point is important for the success of management in general and talent management in particular. Having an open or 'sunao' mind and being flexible in approach can be the difference between engaging and alienating a diverse, multi-cultural workforce.

In addition to the technical competences to do the job, such characteristics as transparent communications, being open-minded and tackling problems head on are amongst the recognized attributes of effective line managers. Others include (Hoyte and Newman, 2008; Toegel and Barsoux, 2013; Wilson, Lenssen and Hind 2006):

- respect for employees at all levels;
- honesty and trustworthiness;
- commitment to the growth and development of the team;
- challenging to unethical behaviour;
- being honest and open;
- a willingness to act on criticism whether it's internal or external;
- not being complacent and assuming things can't be improved;
- being open to new ideas and challenging others to adopt new ways of thinking;
- having the courage to confront situations.

In essence, good management is good talent management and there are indications as to what this means in practice. Extensive research by the CIPD for its *Talent Strategy, Management and Measurement* (Tansley *et al.*, 2007) report concluded that talent management should be linked to performance management, be joined up with reward practice and be closely related to other key human resource practices. Case studies of Standard Chartered Bank which advocated 'conversations that count' and Google which balanced formal and flexible systems demonstrated that line managers were critical to the success of any talent strategy. There is a solid body of evidence about the strong relationships between the two factors.

Managing in complex situations

Yet, whilst managers may have the theoretical tools, backed by decades of research, to go about their daily work, they often find themselves surrounded by complexity and ambiguity. In such situations, previous training will only provide some, and not all, of the answers. One way to overcome these problems is for managers to have an outlook that allows them to go beyond the scope of their experiences to date, to have a mindfulness that allows them to use new sources of information in how they achieve their objectives. Where they are able to demonstrate this, 'results indicate that managerial mindfulness has positive effects on reputational effectiveness and work-unit performance when the situations are characterized by high role ambiguity, but the positive relationship disappears when role ambiguity is low' (Han and Zhang, 2011).

An approach that encapsulates this principle is that advocated and epitomized by Konosuke Matsushita, founder of Panasonic. He emphasized the importance of having a sunao mind. This is 'the level of the human mind where it becomes free, transparent, and able to think and able to decide without any prejudice ... it allows us to see things as they really are' (Matsushita, 1988). In other words, this is having an 'untrapped' mind.

The relevance of this approach comes about because of the need for a distinct approach to knowledge creation and management that goes beyond being explicit and documented as a prerequisite for action. Instead, knowledge arises because of the action. This is learning by doing in which knowledge doesn't reside within a single member of the team but comes about from contributions by many. The solution isn't always a process of 'knowledge creation, application, performance' (Chia, 2003). Although this is still relevant in some situations, other avenues are also followed. In Matsushita's words:

> If we are trapped by considerations of self-interest, we are apt to view things as we want them to be, not as they really are. The basis of our judgment will not be what is right, but what pleases us. In order to grasp reality correctly and make sound judgments, we must strive to evaluate things objectively, free from value judgments and preconceptions. The untrapped mind (sunao mind) is capable of transcending all concern for profit and loss, ideology, power, and social status. It is an uncluttered mind that can see white as white, yellow as yellow.

Sunao in practice: Panasonic's action-learning teams

In Panasonic's action-learning teams, 'there is framing and reframing of the problem, and every team member must be objective, have an open mind, and remain unbiased. Through questions, the problem can be framed and reframed as the group practices *sunao* mind in accepting each other's interpretation of the perceived problem. With greater clarity of the real problem, a more effective action or decision thus emerges from the team to help in solving the problem' (Marquardt, 2011). The essence of sunao is the adaptation of thinking and behaviour in response to the changing environment and in the willingness and aptitude to learn. For leaders and managers, who play a critical role in the management of talent – both selective and inclusive – sunao is an additional consideration to complement those skills outlined in earlier discussions.

Matsushita (1978) wrote of the importance of sunao and its contribution to collective wisdom, in essence to seek the views of others in order to make an objective and well-considered decision. 'It can be frequently observed that damaging decisions are made by leaders who have based their decision on their own limited knowledge or possibly wrongly influenced by their inner-circle'. Sunao is a concept that views organizational life, in an open and constructive way. Such an approach will require people to be free from the adherence to having narrow views. This quality facilitates a view that is free from prejudice.

Panasonic's implementation of sunao mind

Sunao was an integral part of the success criteria for Panasonic's line managers. The approach was actively encouraged and developed with the belief that it would help them to understand the importance of listening to employees and the achievement of collective wisdom.

Matsushita (1978) believed that managers 'must humbly listen to what is said by consumers and employees'. Having a sunao mind allowed a manager to see the 'true state of affairs. Based on this insight they will then be able to determine what does and does not need to happen'. He was concerned about managers who invariably believed they were right or who believed that they were more important and as a result did not listen to others' opinions. He feared that they would try to manage based on their own limited knowledge, which might ultimately lead to poor decision making.

Instead, there should be a spirit of tolerance and compassion, and these qualities would allow managers to manage in a way that realized the full potential of all employees. A sunao mind also makes it easier for a manager to be flexible and versatile in adapting to any circumstances and to look at issues with a fresh perspective. One of the eight Global Leadership Competencies of Panasonic is 'Information seeking and Sunao Mind'. The expectation was that a Panasonic leader needed to find ways to understand relevant information about the industry, market trends, competitor activities and customer needs. Based on such information, they would be encouraged to take appropriate decisions. To be able to do so, however, would require a sunao mind so that they would not be influenced or have a bias based on their previous experiences.

A sunao mind influenced all aspects of development from global general management to customer service in Europe to R&D in Vietnam. This even extended to mergers and acquisitions undertaken by Panasonic where sunao was applied to enhance the chances of retaining talent within the acquired organizations. In the spirit of collective wisdom and having a sunao mind to their capabilities, they often went on to play key roles in the Panasonic group (Unoki, 2013).

Other studies of multi-national organizations have shown that there are implications for managerial practice when implementing sunao, not least of which are those of culture, communication and trust (e.g. Crossman and Noma, 2013).

Sunao as a critical leadership skill

Many organizations refer to the importance of having an open mind and being transparent with their employees and it is often referred to in value and mission statements. The fundamental difference of having a sunao mind is that it goes beyond being open and transparent as a principle to an open mindset as a culture whereby all issues are looked at in a different perspective. This applies to decision making at several levels and throughout the organization but is particularly relevant in the management of talent.

Global talent management at Ernst & Young

EY is a global leader in assurance, tax, transaction and advisory services. The insights and quality services we deliver help build trust and confidence in the capital markets and in economies the world over. We develop outstanding leaders who team up to deliver on our promises to all of our stakeholders. In so doing, we play a critical role in building a better working world for our people, for our clients and for our communities.

Our target aspiration is to have more female partners and many more women in business leadership positions. Whilst women currently represent almost half of graduate hires, only 9% represent partner hires. Despite slightly higher attrition rates for men, women's promotion rates are lower than men's and recent research in the professional services sector suggests it takes women three times longer than their male counterparts to make partner.

We realized five years ago that our ambitious targets could not be achieved without deliberate intervention in three areas: supporting women develop their careers, educating the broader organization and holding leadership accountable. As our largest and most diverse area (81000 people across 93 countries), Europe, Middle East, India and Africa (EMEIA) provides an interesting case study.

In addition to locally driven networking and mentoring initiatives, we offer three EMEIA-wide training interventions. The first helps our female managers to develop their networks and discuss the issues they face in progressing their career. The second, delivered in partnership with Cranfield School of Management, brings together high potential female senior managers from across EMEIA to develop self-confidence, an authentic leadership style and an understanding of the inherent differences in typical male/female career strategies. The third is targeted specifically at female partner candidates from across the region and focuses primarily on personal brand and impact.

Running formal learning interventions for women heightened our awareness of the need to educate everyone, especially our leaders, about typical gender differences and how to avoid unconscious bias. Key messages and organizational learning from our women's programmes are shared regularly with our partners. Web-based learning on unconscious bias is also required for all partners and managers, which has increased understanding and stimulated debate on hiring and promoting. All collateral supporting the employee lifecycle has been reviewed to ensure inclusive language.

By far the most impactful initiative has been the engagement of senior leadership, setting the tone at the top and ensuring that each leader takes responsibility for the influential role they play in establishing a culture that values difference. Critical to this has been the strategic use of data to drive debate and change and, over time, broaden the lens used to identify future leaders. Regular leadership pipeline reviews have enabled us to identify and track high potential women. Most of our regions have now also adopted the Career Watch programme, which allocates a sponsor with strong organizational authority and influence to high potential women and holds them accountable for their career progression.

At EY, our attitude to learning about and the development and sponsorship of women has paid off. One-third of the nominees to our two-year partner pipeline leadership development programme (Global NextGen) have consistently been women and our percentage of female partners admitted annually has risen steadily from 15% (2010) to 21% (2013).

Julia Jameson, Director, Talent Development, EMEIA Talent Team

The importance of having a sunao mind has been recognized by leadership experts such as Adair (2010), 'managers who don't have a sunao mind are often swayed by their own interests in decision making, inevitably leading to corporate failures'; McGehee (2001), 'a person who does not have a sunao mind is seeing things through filters or a distorting lens … with a sunao mind one can learn from any source, anytime, anyplace'; and Kotter (1997), 'solving different problems requires above all else an open mind and a willingness to learn'.

Kotter attributed much of Panasonic's success, which continued even during global economic depression, to sunao. The founder, Matsushita, 'created visions that were idealistic and compelling which he ensured that all his employees understood' (Kotter, 1997). Through changing his organizational structures he empowered people who rose to the challenges which the founder had given them. By having an open mind to his staff's potential he inspired them to look for superior manufacturing processes and to keep growing themselves. Matsushita also realized at that time the importance of international expansion and started to set ambitious five-year goals.

More recently, the work of Ulrich, Smallwood and Sweetman (2008) noted that being a talent manager was a critical facet of the Leadership Code and that curiosity and open-mindedness were critical to creating a positive work environment for the talented people being managed. They point out that you can put yourself in the path of new ideas and learning opportunities by paying attention to new information 'outside of the usual sources'.

Sunao is important as a leadership quality and hence will translate through to those identified as talent for the following reasons:

- Seeing issues as they really are will mean the management team avoids falling into the trap of making decisions based only on their previous experiences, interests and any biases they may have.
- The view will also allow an appropriate response to changing circumstances such as external market forces or internal restructures.
- Sunao thinking will allow leaders to know when to introduce a new/different approach to a particular issue and when to leave things as they are.

The Conference Board (2013) reinforces this perspective by noting that leaders and managers should have a 'forward looking mind set by translating trends and scenario thinking'. Having an open mind would support any leader in tackling such global challenges as:

- recognizing the cultural challenges of international assignments, e.g. balancing family/work priorities;
- the ability to find solutions to address the differing needs of different demographic groups;
- the difference in culture between those working locally and those in HQ roles.

A sunao mind will help a leader to identify the talent they have in their organization and to develop themselves by having an open mind in their decision making and problem solving.

A sunao mind when making decisions about talent

Having a sunao mindset can add significant value to talent management strategy and implementation. It will help in the process of discovering, developing and retaining talent in selective roles, by ensuring diversity and innovation, and in inclusive roles by an organization-wide transparency that will affect every aspect of the working experience from reward and recognition through to engagement and motivation.

From a talent management perspective there are a number of themes that would apply to the significance of having a sunao mind.

The identification of talented people would be enhanced because sunao would help to prevent, either in recruitment or in selection for promotion, the prejudice of choosing those who fit into a certain, familiar, mould or maybe in a mirror image of the person making the decision. A sunao mind would allow a less-biased view and for a decision to be based on more objective criteria.

The situations in which these dilemmas occur include decisions relating to those new to the business who, as a result, had not yet established a proven track record: to promote or not; to give greater responsibility or not. Having a sunao mind means that a manager can look at each situation and consider the most appropriate timeframe to make a decision rather than applying a single rigid set of criteria based solely on past experience.

Development could be enhanced in two ways. First, a sunao mind would lead to a more considered strategy as to the best type of development taking into account the needs of both the individual and the organization, in addition to the normal standardized, conventional approaches. Second, a sunao mind would facilitate the process by which organizations were more creative in the ways they developed their staff, with potential cost benefits (e.g. using secondments or mentoring).

Finally, a sunao mind would help retention. By approaching the management of selective high-potential employees, for example, with an open mind, new and innovative 'solutions' might be created to help manage expectations. The retention of those in inclusive roles would also benefit from sunao when significant change or uncertainty happened. Most recently, creativity and flexible hours (albeit reduced) working as a response to the recession were seen by many organizations as an alternative to the abruptness of dismissal when the number of orders fell.

Figure 11.1 shows the factors within the sunao mindset and how this could add to the decision making process.

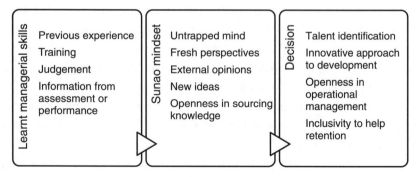

Figure 11.1: A model of decision making with a sunao mind.

Sunao and the learning organization

Successful leaders understand the truth without bias or self-interest 'and are willing to hear different perspectives and have an open mind' (Marquardt, 2011). Such leaders are able to listen and empathize with other people's points of view. One of the popular techniques of developing people is through action-centred learning. And applying a sunao mindset will mean that people will find it easier to accept other interpretations of the challenges they are facing. By having clarity as to the challenge the team can clarify the real issues, thus making it easier to come up with a more effective solution.

An organization which has a culture of learning and development will benefit from promoting a sunao mindset. This may involve having an attitude of learning from everyone, thinking and sharing thoughts, being self-reliant, independent in thought and deed and forgiving of others' mistakes.

In the context of everyone having talent and an inclusive approach to talent management, a leader must demonstrate integrity in their decision making, empowering others and being agile in their behaviour. This is consistent with Goleman's (1996) perspective that 'self-awareness, persistence, motivation, empathy and social deftness are the qualities that mark people who excel, whose relationships flourish and who are stars in the workplace'.

Developing a sunao mindset

Developing a sunao mindset has the advantages of promulgating:

- diversity in skills and experiences to maximize business opportunities;
- creativity and an innovative culture;
- humility instead of hubris;
- the courage to identify people who have the talent to imagine a new direction or enter new markets.

Williams (2013) highlights five main themes that are relevant in the quest for sunao:

- The need to listen more than talk to ensure the contribution of those who need more time and encouragement to speak up to express their views. This is also relevant in multi-lingual environments. From a talent perspective a manager may well recognize 'hidden talents' by listening more to identify their potential.

- To avoid making snap decisions: collecting more information, gathering more facts, finding out what has happened to cause a certain issue will all help in the decision-making process. It might slow things down but the result could well be more favourable. This point is very relevant as there is often a tendency to make snap judgements which could have an adverse impact on motivation. By understanding more, getting the opinion of others and taking time to reflect on the situation a different decision may be reached.

- To thank people for their suggestions: a manager will find that his team are more likely to express their views if they feel their manager has a sunao mind in considering their ideas. Basically, if a manager wants other members of the team to contribute ideas then, when they do, their input needs to be acknowledged and appreciated. As a result a manager may well see their staff in a different light as they become more forthcoming with their inputs, once again seeing their full potential.

- To encourage frankness: in many situations people will tend to accept the view or decision based on the giver's position in the hierarchy or feel uncomfortable to challenge them. A manager with a sunao mind will be more open to the opinions of others and positively encourage his or her team to express their views. Therefore, straight talking can generate different options which can then be considered before a decision is made. In the context of talent management there could be times when perhaps the head of HR needs to challenge a decision of the CEO on the appointment or promotion of a certain individual.

- To hunt for new opportunities: there could well be a new idea or a new approach that could be considered rather than keeping to the same way of doing things. Having a sunao mind would allow a manager to be more creative and innovative in their approach to their responsibilities. From a talent perspective this could result in a particular person being given a different role or challenge which would allow them to demonstrate their potential, which otherwise might have never been fulfilled.

Sunao mind and its impact on cross-cultural relationships

Crossman and Noma (2013) talk about the importance of having a sunao mind in influencing intercultural communication. This is in relation to the point of building and developing trust between Japanese expats and their Australian supervisors. The article reveals that having a sunao mind helped to achieve a trust between people from very different backgrounds to the point that they could both readily accept the organizational culture and become committed to it.

Sunao was related to other concepts of business ethics such as character, empathy and concern for others because it was crucial in the learning and understanding of the perspectives of counterparts so that trust could deepen and flourish.

Living in an age of transparency: Why it is important to have a sunao mind

Ashridge (2006) investigates the merits and demerits of having a culture of transparency in an organization. The merits include a free exchange of information, discussions about career planning, the ability to express views about aspirations freely, a safe background for difficult conversations that in the past have been avoided and it motivates the individuals concerned as they can have clarity as to their possible opportunities and options.

The downsides are that it could be demotivating to those who may not have a clear career path or have not been selected for a particular talent pool and that those selected may have raised expectations which they may struggle to achieve.

One of the most important retention strategies any organization can have is to make their employees feel that they have an important role to play and that their contribution is appreciated. A sunao mind will allow a manager to have the kind of career discussion to take place in a spirit of trust and honesty as they will approach it with no sense of bias or prejudice. This attitude will give all employees the confidence to speak openly without fear of any negative impact.

Chapter 12

Retaining talent

Executive summary

- *Retention is critical to the long-term health and success of the organization.*
- *Retention challenges occur across geographies, business sectors and demographic groups.*
- *Reasons for leaving include failure to recognize and leverage the passions of the employee, failure to challenge them intellectually or to engage their creativity, to develop their skills or to give them a voice. The variability of reasons requires a response that is multifaceted.*
- *Value-adding information and analysis, such as segmentation, are needed to enable the organization to formulate a targeted response for those who would benefit most from such an intervention.*
- *Engaging through meaning is suggested as a powerful retention approach. This includes a transparent communication process, a responsive organization and a philosophy of employees as partners in the venture.*
- *Developing for potential can add some value to the retention process. Providing the opportunity to develop motivates those in leadership roles; in addition there will be organization-wide benefits from a fully trained and engaged workforce.*
- *Rewarding for performance can be used as a retention method. This includes all aspects of work that are both financial and non-financial such as training, learning and development opportunities and the working environment as well as pay and benefits.*
- *The culture of the organization, how it is led and how supportive it is to the developmental aspirations of its workforce will be critical factors in the retention of talent.*

The war for talent will be fought even if you aren't hiring

Making your people before making your products means identi-fying and attracting talent at all levels who are enthusiastic to develop their full potential and can see a convergence of their own work, life and career goals with the business goals of the organiza-tion. Having attracted such people, the organization will want to make sure it keeps them. The retention of talent therefore becomes an important contributor to the overall talent strategy.

Because retention is critical to the long-term health and success of the organization, it is a subject that is attracting increased attention from busi-ness leaders and talent professionals. Retention is a strategic issue as well as an operational one. The departure of talent at any level of the organi-zation can have a significant financial cost and can interrupt productivity, workflow and service, not to mention the loss of expertise.

A renewed focus on retention as the world economy moves out of recession shows that it has the potential to cause problems across geo-graphical boundaries, business sectors and demographic groups.

As the global head of HCL Technologies noted: 'the war for talent will intensify, but will take a different form'. The talent war will go ahead even if you don't want to participate in it.

Retention challenges occur across geographies, business sectors and demographic groups

In the US private sector, retaining top performers and critical skills workers was identified as a significant challenge. Furthermore, a study by Manpower Group (2013b) found that many North American employees planned to pursue new job opportunities in 2014 and concluded that 'engagement, loyalty and job satisfaction should be top concerns for employers who want to keep their best talent'. The willingness to move was probably based on an inherent national optimism on the one hand and greater visibility for new job opportunities on the other. Either way it was a challenge for North American organizations.

Across the globe, a Hays study in China found that there was a significant turnover of staff, in part caused by opportunities created by inward investment from multi-national corporations. Departures had a significant effect on business productivity. The *Shanghai Daily* (26 November, 2013) reported that there had been a 3.5% increase in talent turnover compared with the previous year, as many employees felt confused and uncertain about their futures in a fast-changing environment. Research on multi-national enterprises in China found that there were problems with retention of talent because of intense competition (Hartmann, Feisel and Schober, 2010).

There were similar experiences in Europe but these were more fragmented. When surveyed about their intentions to move job, the majority of workers in Portugal, Denmark, France, Italy and the UK said they were looking to change organizations. There were various reasons for this. Across Europe, the Middle East and Africa less than half of employees felt a sense of 'meaning' in their work, with the UK and Germany reporting the lowest levels and only 39% of employees said they felt valued (behind employees in the Americas, 45%, and Asia Pacific, 51%). Compensation and benefits were not normally the cause of dissatisfaction (Agneus, 2012).

The challenge was not just horizontally across geographies but vertically through business sectors:

- In hospitality, retention was a serious issue, whilst in the accounting and finance sector the lack of career development programmes and the gap between expectations and reality in terms of career management were contributors to employee turnover. Amongst young managers, training, mentoring and coaching were valued but the service received from employers often didn't deliver.
- The challenge of retaining skilled people was identified in the UK engineering sector and it was given such high importance that the Government's Business Secretary looked to develop strategies by which global engineering organizations such as BAE Systems, Rolls-Royce and Nissan could retain their engineering talent. Industry-specific training centres, such as the Siemens facility for the energy sector, and Web-based systems showing national career opportunities were set up. In addition, the UK oil and gas sector felt sufficiently concerned by the loss of experienced people in particular demographic groups to source research into the causes and ways to attract and retain younger workers (which led to a steady rise in people under 30 entering the industry).
- In the US, shortages of skilled talent in software product development, information technology, electronics, software, semiconductors and biotechnology have forced organizations to focus not only on attraction but also on retention through a broad range of reward, engagement and development approaches.

Finally, differences in attitude and behaviour between demographic groups mean that a one-size approach to retention is unlikely to fit all. Amongst the characteristics of difference is that there is less of an inclination to remain at one organization for long periods, particularly, but not exclusively, amongst Generation Y. (Hence the urgency to address the subject and put retention programmes in place including workplace flexibility and mentoring.) Demographic specialists Millennial Branding found that it costs between $15,000 and $25,000 to replace a millennial employee, a particular challenge because 40% of organizations surveyed employed many millennial workers.

Why do people leave organizations in the first place?

Forbes magazine synthesized reasons for leaving as failure to recognize and leverage the passions of the employee; failure to challenge intellect; failure to engage creativity; failure to develop skills and failure to give the employee a voice. The conclusion was that high levels of turnover should be a wake-up call for organizations. The ways to prevent this is by effective employee engagement (Myatt, 2012). Their message to employers was to engage talent through specific interventions. This view is supported by other research which shows that the main indicator of whether millennial workers stay at or leave a company is a lack of career opportunities, line manager relationships, different value sets or a feeling of lack of appreciation or value.

It is clear from the evidence that the variety of reasons for leaving a particular organization requires a response that is multifaceted.

Redesigning the reward package to take account of individual needs would only solve one issue; implementing manager training so that they engage employees better another; and a programme of culture change to free up innovation would by itself do little to improve other circumstances. Any one of these issues would be magnified considerably in a global context. The response to talent retention should be specific to the individual and strategic for the organization.

But before any of these things are put in place, the context of retention needs to be assessed. Hence, a starting point for developing a retention strategy would be to have good information from which decisions could be made.

Turning retention information into insight

It's unlikely that a sustained solution to retention problems would be solved in an organization by implementing change in a single factor (such as pay or communication), nor will it be consistent from geography to geography. The challenge facing global organizations therefore is to understand the reasons why people stay or leave in a way that is evidence based. And then respond in a way that is focused (and cost effective). One way of so doing is the use of segmentation data to build both an accurate position of the here and now and a strategic response for the future.

US organization 3M tackled retention issues by identifying eight segments of employees based on the employees' main motivation for working at 3M. As the Society for Human Resource Management notes, 'all of this is part of a broader HR trend that looks at employee segments in various ways, depending on the problem to solve or the question to answer. Behind segmentation is the explicit or implicit acknowledgment that not all employees fit into the same pigeonhole' (Roberts, 2012). Other types of segmentation include pivotal-role segmentation, high-potential segmentation and succession planning segmentation.

By having more sophisticated information, the organization will be able to formulate a response that is targeted at those individuals or groups of individuals who would benefit most from such an intervention. Instead of a blanket response to retention, using better people metrics enables targeting and positioning. The objectives of focus and fit in talent strategy would then be satisfied.

How do global organizations retain their talented people?

Previously we have seen that retention issues transcend geographic and demographic boundaries. And what's more, there will be additional complexity even within an organization. These factors suggest that a strategic response to retention is needed on the one hand and flexibility or focus in its operation on the other.

The key to effective retention therefore is to regard it not only as a subject within the talent remit but also as a part of a wider employee engagement initiative. There are two reasons behind this twin track:

- The first is based on the assumption that people will leave the organization anyway. Some labour turnover is inevitable and the key is to put forward ideas to prevent key talented people from so doing.
- In the second, engagement of talent should be inherent in the organization's culture, thereby minimizing turnover in the first place (Reitman, 2007).

A holistic view of what factors could influence retention found nine possibilities: process, role challenge, values, work–life balance, information, stake/leverage/reward/recognition, management, work environment and product. The applicability of these as predictors depends on the context within which the organization is operating (Glen, 2006). There's a good argument for linking employee engagement, the psychological contract and talent utilization and retention (Aggarwal, Datta and Bhargava, 2007).

Talented employees are motivated by salary and benefits. And so having competitive rewards in place that are close to those expected in the relevant market or sector is clearly an important step in retention. But, to keep those talented employees motivated in any business means they have to be provided with meaningful, challenging work. However, there is a consensus that the retention of talent needs a multifaceted approach and there is no doubt that a competitive compensation package is important in both the attraction and retention of talent. Monetary rewards cannot, though, substitute for an interesting job, long-term career planning and support from line managers. There are a number of indicators as to the things than can be done to support the retention initiatives.

Recruiting the right people in the first place will help in the engagement process. It's no use taking someone on board based purely on performance. This is important, of course, but there also has to be the right fit of the person's aspirations and ways of working with those of the organization. It is easier to engage someone who is ready to be engaged.

At Japanese company Panasonic, a good deal of importance was attached to employees feeling comfortable with and inspired by the values of the company and its overall mission. The development of a strong management philosophy to this end which was both well understood and implemented was a key reason for its successful retention of key talents. Led by the founder of the company, Konosuke Matsushita, a basic philosophy of contributing to society as a public entity was evolved. This helped to create the important sense of meaning. There were three main themes as to why key talents stayed with the company. These were a clear perspective as to where their career could possibly go, alignment with the company's mission and values and a management team genuinely committed to development.

Designing a strategy for retention that recognizes these factors will be a key part of the 'make your people before you make your products' approach to talent.

A strategy for retention in global organizations

This point shows that retention is about more than money (Cosack, Guthridge and Lawson, 2010). Instead, retaining talent is a holistic process that will span most aspects of people management. From recruitment, as explained above, through the complete employee lifecycle. Figure 12.1 shows four areas to which effort can be given to support the retention process. These are outlined in more detail below.

1. Engage through meaning

Dave and Wendy Ulrich (2010) note that 'those who succeed at creating meaning – either on their own or with the help of their boss – tend to work harder, more creatively, and with more tenacity, giving the companies that employ them a leg up in the marketplace'. But the creation of meaning at work can have additional benefits. It can help to create a sustainable,

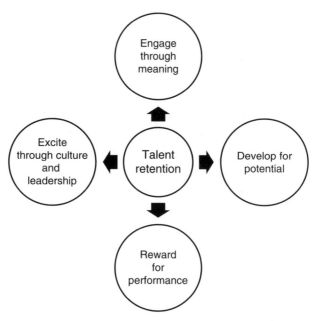

Figure 12.1: Talent retention in global organizations: Four essential approaches.

competitive organization and (of increasing importance) it can help to persuade employees to stay with the organization.

In the first place it's important to understand how employees interpret the concept of 'meaning', because these interpretations will be different. On the one hand meaning could be about role clarity and the direction of the organization; on the other it could be about the organization's greater contribution to corporate social and environmental responsibility. There are some things that can be done at corporate level, such as the creation of a meaningful corporate brand and employee value proposition, but much will emanate from the relationship between employees and their colleagues, employees and their managers and managers and the board.

An innovative approach suggested by the *Wall Street Journal* (2014) was to conduct stay rather than exit interviews. This will enable the organization to understand why employees stay and as importantly what factors provide them with meaning at work.

It goes without saying that all employees should know what is expected of them at work.

Performance management is well established for providing a cascade approach to the achievement of the organization's goals by breaking them down into smaller individual units; but if this process can also include the opportunity to relate what these objectives are to the bigger picture of organizational success then this may add to understanding and meaning on the part of the employee.

If they have meaning and if they can relate this to what is expected of them through their individual business objectives there is a better chance that employees will feel ownership and this will be translated into performance.

A two-way dialogue not only enhances the downward flow of information from the corporate centre to the nodes of the organization; it can also be an upward flow of intelligence about the state of meaning in the organization and what can be done to make more of that. It will be a way of ensuring that employees feel part of the decision making process about where the organization is heading.

Three approaches will help in the process of creating meaning at work (Buahene, 2009):

- **A transparent communication process** where reality rather than an unlikely veneer will help to establish a dialogue of meaning. Whereas once it may have been possible to hold back information about what was happening in the organization it will be less so now. Social media has revolutionized how information is disseminated, who has access to that information and how people communicate about that information (and the speed at which they do so). Engaging with social media is essential for transparency, and clarity of policy about its use is essential.
- **A responsive organization** that not only listens to its employees and their needs but also hears them and does something about it. Social media has largely done for the lack of transparency in organizations and equally so for the time delay in two-way communication. A good deal can be learnt from customer satisfaction systems and processes in this respect. When

the Icelandic ash cloud descended over Europe in 2010 and plane travel was impossible for five days, Dutch Airline KLM's phone lines, email and desks at the airport were jam-packed. It was difficult to give customers answers and deal with their queries in a reasonable time. And so the experiments that had been taking place with social media were brought forward at speed. In 2010, social media customer care was institutionalized within the company. Today responses through Facebook and Twitter are usually within one hour. This isn't to say that an organization's communications with its employees are exclusively through social media platforms. It does mean that once employees recognize that they can get customer care in a short time through social media responses their expectations about their own work life and careers will rise in responses from their own organizations. If organizations don't rise to this challenge they will have problems retaining their employees from other organizations that can rise to the challenge.

- And a philosophy of **employees as partners** in the venture, giving a feeling of ownership and ultimately adding to the meaning of work, or as Dave and Wendy Ulrich put it *The Why of Work* (2010).

If these three things can take place then there is a good chance of an increase in discretionary effort on the part of the employee but also an acceptance of accountability and a connection to the organization.

The International Labour Organization believes in an understanding that 'work is a source of personal dignity'. Its Decent Work project reflects increasing interest in social as well as economic priorities. One of its objectives is to achieve what it refers to as 'fair globalization, reducing poverty and achieving equitable, inclusive, and sustainable development' (International Labour Organization, 2013). Whilst these may be ideals beyond the achievement of any one individual or organization, their sentiment appeals to many. Creating meaning at work will go some way to satisfying that part of the individual which is seeking a contribution to society. Increasingly, global organizations are recognizing this and building it into their own corporate social and environmental responsibility agendas, and individuals into their personal agendas.

2. Develop for potential

The second guideline for retention is about developing for potential.

A focus on career progression has been identified as a powerful intervention in retaining employees at all levels. This can be a structured approach to 'career pathing', that is a way to map a career that is accessible to all or creating the freedom for all employees to take advantage of career and development opportunities wherever they are. In this respect, learning and development that is 'cross-functional and business oriented' (Buahene, 2009) is an approach that is likely to find favour, particularly with millennials.

Providing the opportunity to develop enables employees for leadership roles to test critical thinking skills, change management in a global context and lead cross-cultural teams. In addition, developing global strategy is a core competence for global leaders and those with high potential.

But it is not only at executive level where the opportunity to develop needs to take place if talent is to be retained. Making your people before making your products means developing the potential of all. An excellent example of this was the 'McPassport', which was a McDonald's Europe initiative, providing formal recognition of the training and skills that employees had acquired. This provided access to work and travel in EU countries, Norway and Switzerland. It was a certification of the skills and experiences employees had built up during their time at McDonald's. Their work history was recorded by their restaurant manager in their McPassport and this would be recognized and respected by any participating McDonald's restaurant in the EU, Norway and Switzerland. In short, this meant that an employee could apply for any available vacancy in McDonald's restaurants in 29 countries across Europe, cutting out all the tiresome paperwork usually involved when searching for a new job.

Formal development methods in global organizations include:

- Global leadership programmes. Ericsson, a global technology organization, has a global programme for its aspiring leaders which involves international exposure, job rotation as well as more formal learning modules. The programme is designed to refine important professional skills and to help employees understand Ericsson as a global business. These are complemented by hands-on experience and mentorship.

- International assignments, though even more attention than is usual needs to be given here since the assignment can be a two-edged sword and retention is likely to be achieved through a complex mix of demographics, quality of life and opportunities (De Cieri *et al.*, 2009).
- Support and sponsorship for the talent pool/programme from the very top is a critical success factor to talent development.

Informal ways to develop employees in global organizations include:

- Developing a culture whereby learning at work is considered a part of the success of being an employee.
- Coaching, mentoring and networking above more formal development opportunities.
- Forming Peer Groups CIPD (2011c) research found that 'the power and energy created from the formation of peer groups amongst the highest-performing individuals across the business, as a consequence of talent programmes and pools, provides a significant opportunity for organizations to harness talent'. To make this work 'having a selection process enhances the value the individual perceives from a talent programme and also enhances feelings of self-awareness, confidence and motivation to perform well, for those who are successful applicants'.

Engagement and development are two of the four essentials to retention. The third concerns reward.

3. Reward for performance

Rewarding for performance has long been an approach to retention at several levels, most notably retention bonuses and financial lock-ins for selected staff involved in strategic projects, such as acquisitions. But increasingly, and especially in global organizations, total reward strategy is being used to cover a wider range of employees. Total reward includes all aspects of work that are valued by employees, that are both financial and non-financial and can include training, learning and development opportunities and the working environment as well as pay and benefits.

The challenge is how to implement such an approach around the world. It is likely that reward will be adjusted to suit the local needs of the business unit, albeit in a global framework of reward principles. In one case, Armstrong and Brown (2005) argue that reward management was at the heart of the HR and business agenda in the UK with many organizations there having adopted the US concepts of reward strategy and total rewards. However, in areas of job evaluation, pay structure design and contingent and variable pay, 'a more realistic, tailored, diverse, and long-term approach' was evident. Indeed, it was a melting pot of practices 'with attention to internal equity as well as market rates in pay setting, flexibility, and control in pay structuring and competencies, and results in pay adjustment and individual and collective performance in bonus plans'.

But there are challenges. On the one hand the dimensions of what should be included in the concept of total reward varies from organization to organization (thereby making benchmarking difficult) and this changes over time. On the other hand greater collaboration will be needed in global organizations to ensure that global as well as local goals are achieved. This raises the question of what it takes to motivate local employees to go the extra mile for the sake of the MNC as a whole. The answer to this question will vary from place to place.

Having a strategic approach to reward, for example one that is 'based on the design and implementation of long-term reward policies and practices to closely support and advance business or organisational objectives as well as employee aspirations' (CIPD, 2014) is one way.

Engaging the global workforce with the reward strategy that is being pursued is critical. Research amongst HR professionals in Australia found that there were five reward components: organization reward strategy and philosophy, base pay, base-pay increases, short-term variable pay and benefits. In each of these areas communication about reward was important, 'even to the degree that it affects organizational performance, employee satisfaction with pay, employee retention and employee motivation' (Shields *et al.*, 2009).

But recognizing and rewarding achievement through non-financial means is also a powerful retention strategy since this enhances the individual's reputation and career prospects. Most people feel a greater sense of accomplishment and self-worth when recognized by the organization. It's critical that talented people be recognized regularly and in general provided with real-time feedback on their performance.

4. Excite through culture and leadership

The culture of the organization, how it is led and how supportive it is to the development aspirations of its workforce will be critical factors in the retention of talent. Research in Indian ITES organizations, whilst in diverse organizations in the UK, Thailand and Malaysia, found that line manager engagement in the talent process was also a valuable contribution (Lehmann, 2009). Exciting through culture and leadership therefore has a wide range of perspectives.

Undoubtedly the leader who can create a feeling of excitement in the organization stands a better chance of retaining talented employees than one in which the culture is stilted and unappealing. In addition the quality of the manager–employee relationship can often be the difference between going and staying. Having the relationship of constant feedback, role clarity and fairness are three attributes that lead to a healthy workforce relationship, but in addition the generation of an exciting and progressive culture can add considerable value.

But there are cultural issues. In Accenture, the work–life balance was addressed in retaining talented people. This included such issues as flexitime, job sharing, home working, 'fly backs' for people working away from their home location and other arrangements to help employees achieve a better balance. Accenture significantly reduced the turnover among women through this initiative and increased the number of female partners from less than 6% at the end of the 1990s to more than 10% by 2003.

Chapter 13

Measuring the effectiveness of talent strategy

Executive summary

- An organization-wide understanding of the effectiveness of the investment in people is an essential part of the success of making your people before making your products.
- Metrics of talent effectiveness and value added should include tangible benefits and intangible ones. The latter are critical given that the value of intangibles (corporate reputation, intellectual property, patents) in many organizations far outweighs that of the tangible ones (buildings or fixed assets).
- In providing such metrics those responsible for talent should consider recent developments on the supply side of information – big data and predictive analytics – as well as on the demand side (i.e. moving from data to information to intelligence to insight).
- Data includes: success in filling roles, the supply of sufficient numbers of appropriately skilled employees to meet demand within a given time, turnover rates, employee satisfaction measures, levels of reward-remuneration benchmarked against competitors, total reward package assessed for attractiveness and relevance.
- Information includes: the number of employees required for present operational needs and the number of employees forecast over time in line with the organization's strategic direction as interpreted through the strategic workforce plan.
- Intelligence includes: how gaps between the demand and supply of labour are going to be filled by both internal initiatives and external recruitment campaigns, predictive analysis of optimum talent mix in the workforce, and measures and improvements in corporate reputation.
- Insight includes: how talent has and will contribute to shareholder value, how the competitive position has been improved by talent development and deployment – global, regional or local performance measures such as sales, market share or profitability.
- The role of the talent manager as strategic positioner and capability builder will inevitably lead to the latter as the area of priority.

People management and business performance

An organization-wide understanding of the effectiveness of investment in people is an essential part of the success of making your people before making your products. This goes beyond being an act of faith and will require the smart presentation of business justification on the part of those responsible for its implementation. This will be helped by changes that could revolutionize the way that people initiatives are regarded in terms of their value. The first concerns exciting developments in predictive analytics; the second is in respect of the effect of intangible assets on organizational value, how this can be measured and how it can be incorporated into talent management.

But the process of measurement has been around in global organizations for some years, with mixed results.

The belief that competitive advantage could be secured through the effective deployment of people is one that has inspired researchers to seek evidence of the links between people management and business performance. This is based on the assumption that value can be generated by talent from which employers can derive profit and other forms of benefit.

Amongst the findings are that job satisfaction, organizational commitment and effective HR management practices could account for up to 19%

of the variation in profitability between companies, that effective people management could contribute to enhanced productivity and that 'people factors' have a direct impact on efficiency (Patterson *et al.*, 1997).

Evidence of tangible and intangible value

A body of evidence has been built up over the years to reflect developments in HR metrics and their reporting. The measurement of talent management initiatives has historically focused on the tangible. At an operational level this can be the return on investment from training or development initiatives or costs of attraction and retention. HR and talent metrics measure those factors that contribute to the organization's tangible outputs, such as sales revenue, efficiency measures or ratios and profitability. But the veracity and efficacy of HR metrics continue to be in doubt, resulting in a discipline of HR measurement that has not yet matured sufficiently to be considered a powerful business argument.

The challenge facing those with responsibility for demonstrating the effectiveness of any people investment through the normal method of financial reporting is that the evolution of HR metrics in many ways mirrors that of talent definition (i.e. long and complex arguments with little agreement or consistency of what matters and what should be reported). Indeed, an extensive study of HR management in the USA over a 30-year period concluded 'that strategic human resource management researchers as a group deserve a D to F grade'. Among the problems identified were an overreliance on knowledge areas pertaining to internal dimensions such as organizational behaviour and not enough attention to the external dimension. The author concludes that 'an economics-based framework [could be] a possible way forward' (Kaufman, 2012).

Such a framework will be enhanced considerably by the two particular developments referred to in the introduction to this chapter, namely predictive analytics and the focus on intangible assets. Both developments are critical but the latter point particularly so. This is because the value of a company goes beyond its holdings of tangible assets such as buildings, shops or offices. Up to 80% of the value of some companies can be accounted for by intangible assets.

Stock market flotations reflect the point. The net value of goodwill and other intangible assets on Facebook's balance sheet leapt from $162 million as of the end of December 2011 to $1.4 billion at the end of September 2012. Instagram's value was almost completely made up of intangible assets at its acquisition by Facebook, including 'acquired technology' and 'trade name'. Twitter's flotation value of $30 billion consisted largely of intangible assets, and only 5% of Google's total worth was made up of physical assets.

If the measurement of the effectiveness of making your people before making your products in general, and talent management as part of this process in particular, is to gain credibility then measures of performance will need to include both tangible benefits and those reflected by the value of intangibles on the company's balance sheet.

Tangible benefits: Measurement of talent management effectiveness: Growing sophistication and complexity

There is a quest to provide information systems that educate leaders about the connections between employee engagement, consumer behaviour, unit performance and financial results.

The CIPD (2012) highlighted three types of HR metric that could be adapted to the specific needs of talent and talent management within the 'make your people before you make your products' concept. These are:

- **Measures of talent efficiency:** to what extent is the HR function 'doing things right' and to what extent is talent management operating to achieve its objectives? This relates to two points. In the first place 'efficiency measures are concerned with the extent to which HR processes are undertaken in a way that minimises the use of resources'. In the second place it will be concerned with how talent management is doing on both a comparative and absolute basis. Such aspects as cost of acquisition, retention and deployment and how these compare with competitors or similar-sized organizations. The objective here is to judge operational performance within the talent community and could be referred to as 'reporting data'.

- **Measures of talent effectiveness:** to what extent is the HR function 'doing the right things'? Of critical importance is the metric that assesses effectiveness 'on the extent to which organizational objectives are achieved and specific problems are solved through the contribution that the HR function makes to the organization'. From a talent perspective this means ensuring that the supply of talent is able to match the demand that is identified at corporate, business unit and operational level. Has succession management been effective in identifying and developing people for selective roles? Has the organization secured the services of the best people for new projects or market entry? Is the organization design the right shape for the business (hierarchy, network or matrix, for example)?

- **Measures of HR impact:** to what extent have HR activities met defined priority needs for the organization in its specific and strategic context? The final group of metrics relates to 'the results of bundles of activities on the achievement of strategic priorities through being closely aligned both "vertically" with strategic priorities and "horizontally" with the work of other parts of the organizational system'. This is the least developed area of both HR and talent measurement. It is about identifying links between, say, talent management and shareholder value. By how much has value increased because of effective talent management or the linkage between talent and market growth, financial performance or improved corporate reputation?

These three groups of measures synthesize long-running research and provide an initial framework on which to build. Nonetheless, there is still work to do.

The evolution of HR and talent metrics

Research into the reporting systems and practices for HR management concluded that no single formula could be applied to evaluation. Instead, internal rather than external reporting is preferred with a diversity of human capital evaluation systems across UK organizations.

David Guest's (2011) eloquent historical summary of the evolution of measurement in HR management notes that there had been six phases:

- The first, during the 1980s, attempted to link business strategy or organizational behaviour to human resource management, highlighting the shift from control to commitment.
- The second, during the 1990s, saw the rise of survey-based statistically analysed studies of HR management and performance. Huselid's seminal 1995 work was the most notable feature of this period.
- The third phase, resulting from a backlash about both methodology and concept because of 'the rush to empiricism'. This led to a period of reflection ...
- Resulting in a fourth phase, which can be described as conceptual refinement. Led by Guest, this focused on a better theory about HR practices, about outcomes and about the link between them.
- The fifth phase 'concerns the key role of workers and the importance of workers' perceptions and behaviour in understanding the relationship between HRM and performance'.
- The most recent phase is identified as 'growing sophistication and complexity. This includes increased sophistication in particular with respect to theory and research methods and it provides a stepping-off point for considering future developments'.

What this summary shows is that over a twenty- to thirty-year period the subject of the measurement of the effect of people or HR management practices on performance has either been one of evolution and refinement on the one hand or a lack of understanding about the serious nature of metrics to the future role of people professionals on the other. Today, there is little agreement about how to measure the impact of talent management on business performance, which is an incredible conclusion to reach.

Approaches to tangible outputs of talent management effectiveness

At a strategic level such measures as return on investment in talent or return on human capital employed as outlined in an earlier chapter are the ones on which most focus has been placed.

At an operational level 'Organisations are increasingly using strategy tools such as workforce scorecards to keep track of human resource management related change processes that have been implemented and the effects of these on business unit performance' (Van De Voorde, Paauwe and Van Veldhoven, 2010).

However, the challenge of establishing the links between human resource or talent management practice and business outcomes continues to be fraught with difficulty and a possible lack of belief on the part of business managers. Nevertheless, evidence continues to be revealed about such relationships. One study of 171 branches of a large financial service organization, for example, examined 'to what extent employee surveys can serve as a predictor of better financial performance at the branch level'. The results showed that 'a significant part of branch profits could be predicted using employee surveys' (Van De Voorde, Paauwe and Van Veldhoven, 2010).

It is possible to attribute a range of tangible outcomes to people initiatives in general and talent management initiatives in particular. The more straightforward ones are typically performance related (sales training, customer service training and so on). In these cases it is possible to see a direct link between the training or development and the improvement in outcome.

The less straightforward ones come from those people initiatives that are more tangentially related to performance such as team building or leadership development. Whilst tangible outcomes have been shown for these, there is less of an acceptance of a causal relationship between the two.

The following section investigates some of the tangible outcomes of people initiatives.

Examples of tangible outcomes of talent management initiatives

- Increased sales, market share or profitability through sales or marketing training; the development of a product management function (by recruiting expertise or developing it internally).
- Improvements in customer satisfaction not only by specific customer-relations training but also by improvements in culture, engagement and communication.
- Improvements in number of products or services that the customer buys by investment in marketing expertise (again by recruitment or training).
- Enhanced revenue opportunities identified by the development of a culture of innovation or specific initiatives such as quality initiatives
- Improved cost structure by initiatives in reward management or organizational design.
- Better-managed projects that deliver on time and on budget because of the selection and training of talented people to undertake them.
- Reduced turnover therefore reducing costs of recruitment or productivity owing to bedding in and climbing the learning curve.
- More new products or services by the encouragement and development of a culture of innovation.

Such findings confirm the beliefs of the believers. The challenge is to convince those in non-HR or talent positions that these results have credibility and can be included in business strategy settings and decision making.

The effect on organizational value through increases in the value of intangible assets

It is the potential contribution of people to the value of the organization through its intangible assets that offers new potential for the advancement of the case for making your people before making your products.

An organization's intangible assets (up to 80% of its value in many cases) include such things as goodwill, patents and licences, trademarks, trade names, intellectual capital and corporate reputation.

The value of these assets can be influenced by things beyond the control of the organization, such as time: patents often have a time limitation. But of powerful significance is the fact that so many intangible assets and therefore the value of the company are directly influenced by people.

It is easy to see why this should be the case with intellectual capital and patents since these are both inside the heads of the people who work within the organization. The case for making your people before making your products can be proven and financially justified. This is why companies are acquired even before they have made a profit – teams of scientific researchers and investment bankers are recruited wholesale. Value can accrue almost immediately on the part of the latter and over the medium to long term on the part of the former.

An area of intangible asset that is less obvious but has equal potential is that of corporate reputation. There is a view that the elements that make up corporate reputation and its management are core competences: 'a set of differentiated skills, complementary assets and routines that provide the basis for a firm's competitive capabilities and sustainable advantage in a particular business and … encompass the cognitive processes by which the stock is understood and translated into action' (Brown and Turner, 2011). Furthermore 'those companies with a reputation for a high quality of management are likely to recognize the importance of the reputation for people management and develop culture, systems and processes to enhance the actuality and hence the reputation. Indeed, where companies focused on improving the performance of their managers in "bridging the gap" between the best and worst performers, profitability improved' (Brown and Turner, 2011).

There is a strong case for building metrics on the effect of talent management on the value of the company through its intangible assets.

From data to information to intelligence to insight: The DI³ approach

The convergence of the concepts of evidence-based and insight-driven HR with the exciting developments in predictive analytics and big data gives a new opportunity to make a step function from the reporting of HR data to the provision of insights that will deliver competitive advantage through people.

This approach is consistent with that of strategic workforce planning and contains the elements of data, information, intelligence and insight, referred to as 'DI³' and shown in Figure 13.1 It is based on the assumption that organizations need more than data. They need insight about their people to be competitive in world markets. This is because people are often the only source of competitive advantage.

HR professionals provide insight through being strategic positioners, capability builders, change champions, innovators and integrators and an evidence-based approach to people management. From a talent perspective this means a radical rethink about performance. It means going beyond the preparation of what could be called 'reporting data', such as numbers and status of successors to selective posts, numbers of people on development programmes, training days per employee and so on, to

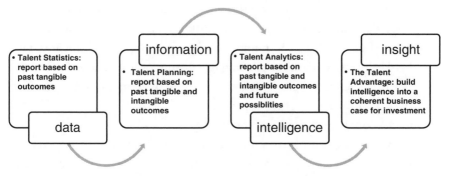

Figure 13.1: The DI³ approach to talent measurement (Turner, 2013).

insights using predictive analytics: what is the optimum mix of knowledge, skills, attitudes and behavioural attributes to achieve competitive advantage? How will investment in the workforce improve customer satisfaction or shareholder value and at what rate? What organizational design and constitution will allow us to achieve the competitive edge?

Not all organizations will be in a position to move straight to providing insights into the outcomes from people activities. In a global context this is particularly challenging because the maturity of data collection may vary from region to region and collating this into a global whole may be difficult, and extrapolating the outcomes of an initiative that is global to measurable benefits in each region can be open to interpretation.

Nevertheless, as workforce information systems and practices continue to evolve, these challenges should diminish. What remains will be an exercise in demonstrating, through intelligence and insight, that real shareholder value can be delivered. The adoption and success of making your people before making your products will depend on persuading business leaders that this is the case.

The component parts of the four sections of 'data to insight' could be summarized as:

- Data-talent statistics, including:
  - attraction: success in filling roles, the supply of sufficient numbers of appropriately-skilled employees to meet demand within a given time
  - retention: turnover rates; employee satisfaction measures
  - levels of reward–remuneration benchmarked against competitors; total reward package assessed for attractiveness and relevance
  - amount of development: number of days per employee compared with market average; investment in training per employee as a financial measure
  - performance management data: target achievement (sales, productivity); numbers meeting objectives.
- Information: talent planning, including:
  - the number of employees required for present operational needs
  - the number of employees forecast over time in line with the organization's strategic direction as interpreted through the strategic workforce plan

- the state of the internal labour market: turnover; numbers available and trained for new roles
- the identification of any gaps between the demand for labour and its supply
- employee satisfaction using EAS or employee surveys and how these vary from one period to the next (together with external benchmarking for organizations of similar size or business).

■ Intelligence: talent analytics, including:
  - how gaps between the demand and supply of labour are going to be filled by both internal initiatives and external recruitment campaigns
  - predictive analysis of optimum talent mix in the workforce
  - measures and improvements in corporate reputation.

■ Insight: creating the talent advantage, including:
  - how talent has and will contribute to shareholder value
  - how the competitive position has been improved by talent development and deployment: global, regional or local performance measures such as sales, market share or profitability.

The measurement of talent initiatives is a developing science. Advances in technology, application and analytical techniques will bring a spotlight onto this area which, to date, has been neglected. The case for making your people before making your products can be enhanced by the judicious use of insight. Such insight will be evidence based.

The talent-balanced scorecard: Developing credibility with the board

The creation of HR metrics will not per se give the credibility to the case. It will, however, generate a dialogue with the organization's executives on the value of doing so. A methodology of reporting the outcomes of the analysis is the balanced scorecard approach. Kaplan and Norton's (1996) work on balanced scorecards in a wider business context provided a foundation on which organizations could review their performance in the round since several measures of effectiveness were included. This approach can be adapted to the measurement and reporting of people issues and talent in particular.

From a business perspective the balanced scorecard 'defines what management means by "performance" and measures whether management is achieving desired results. The Balanced Scorecard translates Mission and Vision Statements into a comprehensive set of objectives and performance measures that can be quantified and appraised' (Bain & Company, 2013). These measures typically include:

- financial performance, such as revenues and cash
- customer performance, such as market share or customer satisfaction
- quality and productivity rates
- innovation performance, such as revenue from new products
- employee performance, such as morale (EAS) or turnover.

Translating this concept into a talent-balanced scorecard would take account of both tangible and intangible measures, as shown in Figure 13.2.

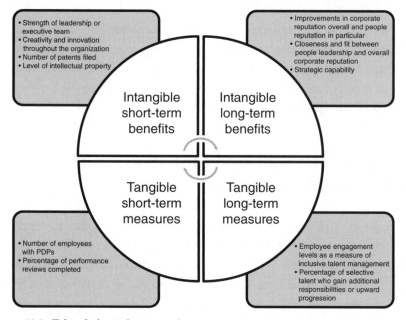

Figure 13.2: Talent balanced scorecard.

In this model, both tangible and intangible outcomes would be reported and used as the platform for board or executive team level dialogue. The information used in the balanced scorecard would include comparisons with prior periods to show progress in each of the areas. But most importantly it, together with other measures discussed above, would be used to generate insight on the part of the people professionals about the wisdom of investment. Justifying investment in people moves on from being an act of faith to an act of competitive positioning.

Insights for making your people before making your products

The CIPD argues that a shift of mindset and focus is required by HR professionals which complements their 'getting things done' service and process orientation with one of being 'able to challenge and influence business because of their penetrating vision, and who create highly individualised solutions rather than relying on tried-and-tested HR levers' (CIPD, 2011d).

To do so will require insights at three levels:

- Having **business** understanding of what makes a business successful. HR acts as an applied business discipline.
- Understanding the **context** of the business, including not only market forces but also demographic and macroeconomic trends.
- Having knowledge of the dynamics of the **organization**, of people, culture, global and local dynamics.

HR has a vantage point at the intersection of these three areas and this is where 'powerful and game-changing perspectives can be developed' (CIPD, 2011d).

Measuring the effectiveness of making your people before making your products and the resulting talent strategy will require those responsible to provide insight above and beyond the reporting of historical data, though the latter is important as a measure of progress.

At the business level making your people before making your products will have to demonstrate that it has contributed materially to the success of the organization by enhancing those things that are core to competitive advantage. In a selective sense this means showing that the interventions that were made to identify, attract, retain and develop those in the executive cadre were value adding and successful across the world. In an inclusive sense there is the onus to show how providing a culture of opportunity led to innovation in design, manufacture and delivery which in turn led to revenue and profit. Both selective and inclusive approaches will have to have contributed to the increase in the value of the organization through its intangible assets: corporate reputation, IP, know-how and patents.

The insights provided at the contextual level will include:

- The application of knowledge and understanding of demographic change to the advantage of the organization through providing an effective workforce mix, a culture that supports such a mix, and leaders who are comfortable in this environment.
- Recognizing that the world is an open market for talented people and building such understanding into people strategy and the measures that show its efficacy: labour turnover, retention, attraction success rates and so on.
- Using knowledge of the context within which the business is operating to ensure that an agile and fluid organizational structure is put in place that moves with the prevailing economic climate without losing competitive advantage. The measures by which this can be demonstrated will be the employee response to organizational change, whether projects are delivered on time and within budget and once again the overall reputation of the organization and the effect this has on intangible assets and ultimately value.

Insight into the third area, that of organization, will include predictive analysis of the outcomes of the type of organization, its workforce mix and its culture. What kind of skills are needed in what type of organization structure? How can cultural differences around the globe be used for advantage rather than be seen as a disadvantage and how can the interventions in this type of organizational dynamic be measured and the cost justified? Insights here will result from the analysis of big data as well as the sharp intuition of the skilled people professionals. Making your people before making your products will be enhanced if people professionals can use their insights into both external and internal forces as they relate to labour markets and organizational dynamics. This will require the development of measureable outcomes as well as the commitment that people will deliver competitive advantage. A combination of both attributes is necessary.

Chapter 14

Joining up the 'ownership' of talent management

Executive summary

- *Successful talent management will occur when there is a convergence of talent knowledge, HR or people business partner insight and specialist HR expertise in the achievement of business objectives.*
- *Those with responsibility for talent management will know about the importance of having an inclusive and selective approach.*
- *HR business partners will have insights into what will work and what won't in their own geographic or functional areas, whilst HR specialists will have expertise on the effects of a specialist activity such as reward on the overall approach to people management.*
- *Where talent management is selective there will be specific additional activities such as assessment and development programmes, executive or performance coaching, secondments or project-based assignments. To make this approach work it will be necessary for an agreed modus operandi between those with specific talent responsibilities.*
- *For an inclusive approach the objective is to provide an environment for all talent to flourish and people policies that facilitate this. Since this is organization wide, it will require coherence, cooperation and coordination on the part of those responsible for talent, HR generalists and business managers.*
- *Global talent managers will act as strategic positioners. This means understanding the context of talent in the overall business environment.*
- *Capability alignment will be a key part of responding to organizational need. Creating a strong organization requires an understanding of the organizational capabilities needed to achieve its goals. These capabilities exist at all levels, and making your people before making your products is about making sure that they are recognized, developed and applied in practice.*
- *A shift in organizational attitudes to ones which encourage and foster the 'make your people before you make your products' philosophy will be significant. As change champions, HR professionals will need to understand exactly how they can effect this new approach.*

The difference between talent management and people or HR management

Regardless of how an organization defines talent, or the strategy it deploys to ensure the effective contribution of talented people, it's important that there is role clarity in the areas of people and talent management responsible for delivery of the strategy. This is necessary to avoid duplication, mixed messages or conflicts of interest. However, there is an ongoing debate amongst both academics and practitioners about the differences between talent management and people management. The two often seem to overlap.

The difference between people and talent management will vary from organization to organization. But in all, talent management facilitates the contribution made over and above that which would normally be expected within performance management goals and objectives. Many organizations have spent years of effort in finessing talent management processes, but it remains one of the single most challenging of all people management activities.

A review of the literature of talent management and HR management concluded that there were three possible scenarios:

- Talent management is not essentially different from HR management.
- Talent management is integrated HR management with a selective focus.

- Talent management is organizationally-focused competence development through managing flows of talent through the organization (Iles *et al.*, 2010).

In an international context Tarique and Schuler's (2010) study found that there were also identifiable differences:

- In the first place they argue that international human resource management (IHRM) includes more stakeholders and 'the field of IHRM is broad in its inclusion for the concerns of a wide variety of stakeholders' including customers, investors, suppliers, employees, society and the organization itself; whilst 'the most immediate and significant impact of GTM (Global Talent Management) is on the employees and the organization itself'.
- Second, they conclude that because of the greater number of stakeholders IHRM has a broader sphere of concern than attracting, developing and retaining employees and included such issues as morale and engagement, productivity and innovation.
- Third, IHRM covers the whole regime of HR policies and practices such as planning, 'staffing, compensating, training and developing, appraising, labor relations and safety and health'.

In addition to these three major differences, talent management is a more focused topic or issue, similar to diversity management or knowledge management. They conclude that talent management 'can be examined *in the context of IHRM'*, building on work already undertaken in IHRM and applying those theories and models to talent management.

The challenges within the people management function can be exacerbated by those facing line managers. These may be barriers to 'corporate advancement' of talented people in subsidiary companies or divisions possibly because of 'self-serving mechanisms displayed by subsidiary managers that might hinder effective talent management systems' throughout the organization. Furthermore, limited information systems that are used to make decisions about talent by top management teams could result in talented people being overlooked at subsidiary level (Mellahi and Collings, 2010).

Hence, the risk associated with a lack of clarity over 'ownership' of talent management in national or regional organizations is multiplied when looking at organizations in a global context. The challenge facing those responsible for talent management include not only doing the right things (through strategy) but also doing things right (through implementation).

In a global organization, with operations in several countries, it is likely that the people management part of the business will have evolved either in a different way or at a different pace. The challenge for those whose objective is to move to a 'make your people before you make your products' approach is to move to a new platform for people management whilst respecting the history and evolution of that which exists at the moment.

Doing the right things, doing things right

It's important that there is clarity and agreement about roles and responsibilities within the people management function, and that this clarity is then transmitted to executives and managers so that they are engaged in the overall objectives of the 'make your people before making your products' idea. Indeed, Cheese (2008, 2010) suggests that amongst the key processes to enhance the talent approach is an understanding of how to encourage and reward line managers for nurturing talent. To do so would require a modern outlook to identify, develop and deploy talent to the best effect.

Successful talent management will occur when there is a convergence of talent management knowledge, HR or people business partner insight, specialist HR expertise and business objectives, as shown in Figure 14.1.

In this convergence, the overall objective is to make sure that talent management contributes to the delivery of the business's objectives, and, as we saw in an earlier chapter, this could even generate new revenue streams through the freeing-up of innovation and creativity.

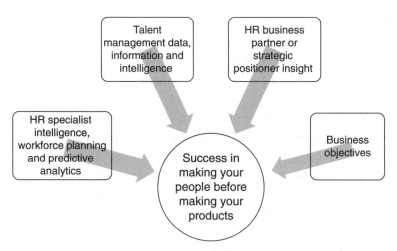

Figure 14.1: Make your people before you make your products: A convergence of interests.

Those with responsibility for talent management will know about the importance of having an inclusive and selective approach, the ways in which such strategies can be developed and the kind of tools and techniques needed for its delivery. HR business partners will have insights into what will work and what won't in their own geographic or functional areas, whilst HR specialists will have expert knowledge of the effects of a specialist activity, such as reward, on the overall approach to people management.

Any one of these areas going it alone won't succeed at a strategic level, although they will be able to deliver short-term benefits in a single area. A combination of effort has the possibility to deliver competitive advantage for the whole organization as opposed to tactical advantage for one part of it. Figure 14.2 suggests responsibilities to ensure this combination of effort.

Figure 14.1 may provide a framework for the various responsibilities for talent management allocated to individual stakeholders, bearing in mind that there will still be areas of ambiguity, particularly in a global context.

Figure 14.2: Global talent responsibility framework.

Organizational stakeholder	Area of responsibility	Deliverables
Global CEO, president or managing director	• Strategy, stewardship and policy for talent across the organization • Ownership of global talent strategy • Delivering successors and executives in business critical positions across the world • Creating a culture of inclusivity so that the potential of all can be maximized • Ensuring buy-in from regional or local organizations to the core principles of 'make your people' • Providing resources for the delivery of talent strategy worldwide • Communicating and engaging the global workforce in the principles of talent management	• Increasing the value of the company by 'making your people before making your products' • Gaining board agreement to a global talent strategy that is both inclusive and selective • With sufficient resource allocated to deliver both parts of the 'make your people' equation • A global culture of potential fulfilment • An organization that has diversity at its heart by ensuring that all employees have the chance to develop and progress
Regional or local CEO, president or managing director	• Regional stewardship of talent • Ensuring that the talent strategy is implemented effectively at regional or local level • Regional or local 'selective talent' identification and management	• Increase in the business performance through the effective implementation of a 'make your people before you make your products' approach • A workforce that is engaged and motivated and fulfils its potential

(continued)

Figure 14.2: (*continued*)

Organizational stakeholder	Area of responsibility	Deliverables
	• Creating a culture of opportunity for all employees in regional or local businesses • Allocating resources for the delivery of the 'make your people' approach	• Employees who are advocates of the organization because of its approach to 'make your people'
Regional or local managers	• Delivering a culture of opportunity, progress and development for all employees in their own business units • Ensuring talented people at all levels have the chance to develop and progress • Sharing information on high-performing people with managers in other business units	• The achievement of business results through maximization of the skills and potential of the workforce • An engaged and motivated workforce
Global people executive	• Ensuring that the talent strategy is integrated and aligned with other people management strategies and practices across the world	• A global people strategy that includes the principles of make your people before you make your products in every aspect, including reward, engagement, training and development
Regional or local people executive	• Ensuring that the regional or local talent strategy is integrated with other people management practices in the region or business unit	• Insights into the benefits of applying the talent strategy in the region • The adaptation and delivery of the strategy in a regional context

Role	Responsibilities
Global people management specialists	• Ensuring that strategies for reward, employee relations, performance management or organizational design are consistent with and supportive of the global talent strategy • A set of joined-up policies and practices that span all people management specialisms
Regional or local people management partners	• Ensuring the effective implementation of the talent strategy in the region in a way that is consistent with other people strategies and policies • The implementation of the strategy in their own business units • Monitoring and measuring the effectiveness of the strategy
Global talent executive	• The preparation of a global talent strategy • Including a succession plan for selective roles and development policy for all employees • And a talent pool for selective positions • A global process for identifying and developing those in selective positions • A global policy for the development and inclusion of the whole workforce • The succession plan for global roles • The succession process for regional or local roles
Regional or local talent executive	• Delivery of the talent strategy • Tracking information and progress • Regional or local insights into both strategy and implementation • Providing measures of success

269

Talent management and HR responsibilities for selective roles

Whilst all employees, from the CEO onwards, are covered by the organization's people or HR policies and procedures including pay and reward, employee engagement, diversity and inclusion, and training and development, some employees will be regarded as having potential to achieve more 'senior' positions than others. Traditionally this latter group will have specific additional activities covered by the concept of talent management. These will include assessment and development programmes, executive or performance coaching, secondments and project-based assignments.

To make this approach work and ensure that there is no duplication or conflict of interest it will be necessary for an agreed modus operandi between those with specific talent responsibilities, HR or people management generalists, and functional specialists (such as reward). The following are some approaches that would support clarity.

- Agreement about how to converge the objectives of the talent strategy and the overall people strategy. If this decision rests within the aegis of an overall people or HR director then a dialogue can be set up between the various policy owners and those with responsibility for talent. This should be done at the pre-strategy setting phase since 'doing the right things' won't happen by presenting a fait accompli from any of the specialist areas.
- At this stage it is useful to test the ideas with the various global, regional or local stakeholders identifying blockages or potential hot spots. For example, the concept that those in selective roles (e.g. on the succession plan) are in fact 'group' employees and not 'regional' ones may cause problems if the person identified has a particularly critical role in the region for a fixed period of time (during an acquisition, new product launch or restructuring). Understanding these positions, identifying scenarios for their resolution and gaining agreement across the group

will facilitate the acceptance and implementation of the strategy once agreed. The people responsible for this dialogue will mirror the overall structure of the people management function.

- In addition the implications of the inclusive approach will need to be tested. Questions about relevance and applicability and how it may be adapted in different regions will be the precursors for how it is implemented. There is also the question of the allocation of sufficient resource to make the concept work.

- Once strategies have been agreed, clarification with the CEO and executive teams will also be necessary since ultimately they will be the ones responsible for implementation. A cascade approach is possible here starting with the global board or executive committee and engaging regional or local executives.

- The responsibility for the delivery of the 'make your people before you make your products' approach does not sit within the remit of any one single people management professional. The chances of success will increase significantly if there is consensus between talent, people generalist and functional specialists.

These considerations will be complemented by the need to ensure that talent management is closely followed by business strategy.

Talent management and HR responsibilities for inclusive roles

Where the assumption is that everyone has talent, which after all is the basic objective of the 'make your people before you make your products' concept, the objective is to provide an environment for talent to flourish and people policies that facilitate this. To achieve this will require cooperation on the part of those responsible for talent and HR generalists if the two roles are separate. If they are one and the same it means making sure that there is coherence about talent policies with others relating to people management.

Since a key part of talent management is creating the context as well as providing the process within which this takes place, attention will also need to be given to the recipient of this beneficial approach (i.e. those members of the workforce who are enthused about the opportunities on offer).

The likely hot spots here are concerned with the roles and responsibilities of people generalists and where these come up against the specialist knowledge of those responsible for talent management. Typically, this will be around boundaries of responsibility (who is responsible for inclusive talent management in a country or a region), regional or local knowledge (understanding what will work in a specific region or country) and power.

If these constraints don't exist then so much the better. If they do then it's possible to deal with these challenges as follows:

- Two sets of insights can influence the strategy. The first is the overall direction of people management through a wide range of activities from performance management through to organization design; the second is the unique knowledge of those who are responsible for talent management and in this case the inclusive part of the strategy. Combining both sets of insights will enhance the chances of a successful outcome to the setting of strategy and business performance. A dialogue between the various parties involved, agreement about roles and responsibilities and a resourcing plan to make sure that whatever is agreed can be delivered are three important areas. At a global level this dialogue will take place with the global people executive and the global talent executive (or equivalent). The output will be a direction for inclusivity and some overall group-wide objectives and measures.

- A rough guideline is that those with talent management responsibility develop strategy and policy, whereas HR generalists will advise on variations or adaptations to ensure it resonates in the region and then be responsible for actually making it work. And they will make sure that the talent initiatives are consistent with other people policies, and vice versa.

- So it's important to ensure that there is a dialogue at the pre-strategy-setting stage. People managers at regional level, such as business partners, will have a unique understanding of business strategy to which the 'talent' manager may not be party, how the function works in their own business units and the possible cultural implications of the 'make your people before you make your products' principle. They will want to have an input as to what it means in their areas and will want this input before decisions are made. Talent managers will understand the criticality of accepting the concept and will have ideas as to how this can be applied. Where the two meet is the point of success.

Once there is a fit between the talent approach and what the organization needs to deliver success, the implementation of a 'make your people before you make your products' strategy can begin, though in reality this will be an ongoing crafted approach rather than a one-off project with a beginning and an end. At a global level, implementation will be complex and will almost certainly require adaptation as the concept hits reality in the regions or business units.

Where flexibility is logical and reasonable and doesn't derail the overall approach, the learning from such adaptations can be shared across all organizations. However, where the required adaptation is too far away from the original concept and has the potential to create fragmentation and disharmony elsewhere, there needs to be a forum where discussion can take place. Ultimately, the CEO will have the casting vote for exceptions, but this should be seen as a last resort.

Whatever situations arise will require focus on the part of all people professionals involved and excellence in project management and implementation skills, a set of competences that don't always feature in HR competency lists and yet can be the difference between success and failure.

The professional attributes of a world-class talent leader

The role of HR professionals in the process of talent management has developed. Ulrich *et al.* (2012) define six HR competency domains – strategic positioner, capability builder, change champion, human resource innovator and integrator, credible activist and technology proponent – that can be translated from the general to the specific in the role of talent managers and emphasize the importance of taking a strategic approach to talent and talent management. Whilst all six domains are important for talent management, it is worth considering the first three in more detail:

- In the first, the role of strategic positioner means understanding the context of talent in the overall business environment, external factors such as the state of labour markets and dynamics and internal factors such as business objectives and customer requirements. In future, HR professionals as strategic positioners will think from the outside in and 'co-create their organization's strategic responses to business conditions and customer expectations by helping frame and make strategic and organization choices'.

- Second, as capability builders, HR professionals will have a critical part to play in ensuring that their organizations have enough people to ensure business success. Capability alignment will be a key part of responding to organizational need. In addition and following the 'make your people' philosophy, the HR professional will have a wider remit to ensure an organizational culture (and structure) that facilitates the development and encouragement of creativity outside of an established business strategy. Creating a strong organization requires an understanding of the organizational capabilities needed to achieve its goals. These capabilities exist at all levels, and making your people before making your products is about making sure that they are recognized, developed and applied in practice.

- A shift in organizational attitudes to ones which encourage and foster the making of people before products will be significant. As change champions – the third of the Ulrich domains – HR professionals will need to understand exactly how they can effect this new approach.

The personal attributes of the world-class talent leader

Given the scope of the role of the talent leader in global organizations in both an inclusive and a selective domain, it is assumed that the level of professionalism has to be extremely high. Dealing with the global board requires one set of skills; having a dialogue with a country manager or regional HR executive another set. There are also personal attributes that would seem to fit the role.

- **Cultural sensitivity, cultural awareness, cultural capability:** There are two definitions of culture that apply in this attribute. The first is the awareness of organizational cultures and the differences between what could be called 'head office' and that of working in a region or business unit. Recognizing the nuances of politics and power plays through the organization (although we all probably regard these as undesirable) and being able to manage through them successfully may be the difference between success and failure. Second, the ability to live, work and be comfortable with different geographic cultures is also important to success in the role. This isn't about understanding Hofstede's power distance ratio country by country but about a personal inclination to thrive in different cultures.
- **A willingness to learn and adapt, having a sunao mind:** The role of the global talent professional owes a lot to understanding and being comfortable with business issues. This means developing into someone who 'knows and loves business, understands the strategy, products and services, is fiscally savvy' (Effron and Shanley, 2011). So as well as the constant updating of talent management skills, cultural developments (inside and outside of the organization), the global talent manager will also require an updating of business knowledge. This will require someone with the attribute of a willingness to learn and as a result possibly adapt his or her behaviour.
- **Being someone with authority:** Being a global talent manager is not a role for a shrinking violet. The challenges of developing a strategy

that has worldwide resonance and gaining acceptance of this throughout each of the organization's business units will require someone who not only understands the backgrounds, strengths, weaknesses, and development needs of the top talent, has met them personally and can respond to CEO requests quickly, but also is robust, able to back up argument with evidence and knows when to hold ground and when to concede it. This is tough enough in a national context, but in a global one it requires authority.

A combination of outstanding professional skills with a set of personal attributes or characteristics that will allow the global talent manager to thrive wherever they are in the world will form the foundation on which the process can flourish.

However, they will not be enough to carry the 'make your people before you make your products' concept if they are delivered in a vacuum. Hence, close cooperation and integration with other HR or people processes will be required together with a close alignment to the needs and objectives of the business.

CONCLUSION

A historic shift in the business landscape

The tectonic plates of economic, technological and demographic change are realigning into a new global business landscape which is having a dramatic effect on the supply of and demand for talent. This shift is creating significant challenges for global organizations in the way they manage their workforces. These include how to become a learning organization, how to manage the work–life balance, change and cultural transformation (Boston Consulting Group, 2013). But uppermost is the management of talent. The reward for getting it right, however, is the chance to create and sustain a competitive advantage that can't be copied: the competitive advantage of a skilled, engaged and motivated workforce.

Finding the right people with the right skills to work in companies around the world continues to test business executives. To support their efforts, HR professionals are rethinking their 'techniques for managing talent [to] ensure they are aligned with the new strategic objectives of their organization. Increasingly they will need to develop more evidence-based approaches to manage global talent – drawing on improved analytics to identify talent segments and gaps, optimize resource allocation, integrate workforce plans and manage unavoidable risk' (Oxford Economics, 2012). This move will be a step function in the role of HR.

Hence, the study of talent management in a global context is one that is growing in importance. The search is for an 'integrative conceptual framework' for global talent management that involves a cross-cultural perspective as well as proposals for effective implementation (Sehoon and McLean, 2012).

There is evidence of how to do so. Research has shown that the success of talent strategy relies on both a focus (a clear strategy and how this will contribute to the achievement of the organization's objectives) and fit (how well it sits within other HR processes). But questions still remain about who falls within the remit of 'talent', about the nature of talent strategy, about who is responsible for its delivery and, most importantly, about how it can be made to work in a global as opposed to a national context.

The assumption of this book is that if you make your people before you make your products then energy, engagement and innovation will follow; the workforce will be aligned to the goals of the organization whilst at the same time having meaning in their roles in the organization. Ultimately, people will become a competitive differentiator.

In this concept, 'talent' is an inclusive term. Everyone in the organization has talent, and a strategy that looks to invest in them, engage them in development and treat them as a community will create an environment of innovation. All of this has to be done whilst making sure that selective roles are filled in line with succession plans or the need to head up strategic projects or business units around the world.

Such a process is complex. Not only does it require expert skills on the part of people professionals in general and talent managers in particular; it requires the demonstration of insight and the ability to execute the strategy with utmost professionalism. Such things can't be oversimplified. But they do lend themselves to a few critical steps, and these are outlined below.

8 important steps in making your people before making your products

1. Provide insight into the value of people to organizational success

The ongoing debates about the contribution of people management to organizational success and the best ways in which talent management can be delivered sometimes conspire to deter progress. And the debate about what constitutes talent is the most fundamental blocker of all.

On the one hand talent can mean those chosen few who have delivered outstanding performance and have shown high potential and have survived the ordeal of the corporate assessment centre. On the other hand talent can mean everyone who works for the organization. Definitions sit at exact opposite poles.

And so the first step is using outside-in thinking in the preparation of the case for making your people before making your products. This means having insights drawn from labour market data and relating these to the business context. It means engaging in the process of business strategy setting and making sure that the 'make your people' objective becomes ingrained in the dialogue of strategy setting as well as its outcomes. It means having acceptance at board and executive level that the concept is legitimate and value adding. And more than this it means ensuring that the people agenda becomes an integral part of the business agenda. To help in this process new techniques such as predictive analytics and new measures of performance such as the increase in the value of intangibles can provide insightful information.

2. Make the business case for making your people before making your products

Providing insight is one part of the story. Converting insight into a business case is another, and this constitutes the second step. Relying on adages such as 'people are our greatest asset' to persuade executives to support the concept of making your people before making your products is no longer enough. There are strategic reasons for doing so but these need to be backed up by a business case if they are to secure a level of resource that may put people in competition with other strategic projects such as product management or technology investment. On the assumption that an organization's resource is finite, the strategy process will be about resource allocation. Securing a level of resource that will allow the delivery of make your people before you make your products is the objective. A business case is the solution.

The case needs to be accepted and actively managed by the organization. In this respect there is a paradox in the search for a talent strategy that will deliver a winning competitive position in intensely competitive global markets. On the one hand there was a strong correlation between financial performance as measured by profit per employee and companies that achieved the best scores for their talent management abilities and yet on the other a lack of consistency about global HR processes (Guthridge and Komm, 2008). It is surprising that process issues have prevented the maximization of benefits. How to deal with this paradox is at the heart of global talent management.

3. Ensure an organization-wide understanding and buy in to the talent definition

Having made the case and secured resources, stakeholders will have to be engaged with and buy into what the concept means to them and to the whole organization. The idea that everyone has talent will be recognized and understood; the idea that the organization will invest in talent before or at the level of previously dominant alternatives may be new. If the execution of the concept is to be as successful as its articulation at board level then a broad range of stakeholders will have to give their support – from the executives themselves who have to turn the concept into practice in their business units around the world, to line managers who are going to have to be prepared for their most talented people moving to new roles outside of their areas, and shareholders who will see more focus on people and may want to understand why this is going beyond the chosen few of the succession plan.

Equally, the employees in a dispersed workforce will need to recognize that opportunities exist but aren't automatically awarded. Making your people before making your products is an earned concept. Willingness to learn, willingness to take ownership and responsibility for their own careers and willingness to acquire new skills in a rapidly changing landscape are part of the culture change. This isn't a top-down initiative but a 360-degree one.

4. Have an inclusive/selective talent strategy with equal emphasis on each area

This approach will require the development of a strategy that balances the need to fill key positions (succession planning, selective roles and people development) with the need to develop the potential of the whole of the workforce in an inclusive way. Once again, this won't happen unless resource is allocated to do so. In addition to the tangibility of training and development budgets there will be the need to allocate executive and management time to making sure that the concept is delivered effectively.

Gaining acceptance and promulgating belief will ultimately come about when there are visible signs of the strategy in action, transparency in the process, perhaps surprise or unexpected appointments, workforce mobility, a performance management process that is embraced rather than rejected as a chore and a willingness to work in cross-functional or cross-business-unit teams to create innovative products, services or processes. These are possible outputs of the concept.

5. Make the CEO the talent champion

Critical to the success of this will be the role of the CEO as talent champion. For most CEOs this will merely be putting a name to what they do anyway. But it is worth ensuring that this is sustained by engaging the CEO in all of the talent processes, by clarifying what is expected through his or her leadership in terms of a culture of inclusivity and potential and, having done so, making sure that these attitudes and behaviours are emulated by executives and managers throughout the organization.

The CEO as a talent champion will reinforce the concept of making your people before making your products, and the elevation of the topic to an executive committee agenda item will cement the understanding.

6. Join up talent management activity with business activity and other people-management strategies

Of prime importance will be to ensure that talent management is not a stand-alone activity. On the one hand it is a critical part of business management; on the other it needs to be joined up with other parts of HR throughout the world. Since for most organizations there are likely to be many variants on the way that talent is defined and talent management administered, this objective will be a challenging one and will require a sustained unrelenting commitment throughout all of those within the people-management function, be they talent specialists, people specialists or business partners.

There are some critical decisions to be made here. Can a business unit in one part of the world opt out of the process claiming other priorities or can the concept as agreed centrally be diluted or implemented selectively? The answer to these questions lies in the context of the organization, its history and the stage of its people development. We have seen examples of an unflinching commitment to the implementation of consistent talent management processes worldwide; we have also seen a tolerant attitude which favours other business priorities (such as the trade-off between standardization and innovation.) There are advantages to global consistency, including cost and equality. The disadvantages will be where such an approach gets in the way of the unique competitive position of the business unit.

7. Deliver talent management brilliantly throughout the world and have excellence in implementation

The agreement of a strategy for making your people before making your products, the allocation of resource and the support of the CEO and executive team will count for nothing unless the strategy is expertly implemented. It will be necessary therefore to spend as much time on implementation as on strategy setting. The creation of a coherent project plan for the delivery of the strategy necessitates the creation of goals and targets, the allocation of responsibilities and actions, risk management and thinking through and anticipating implementation issues as they will occur throughout the world. A cross-functional, multi-discipline project team will be the vehicle by which these measures are dealt with.

It will also be important to have as much clarity as possible about what is expected of all stakeholders.

8. Make sure there is involvement from all of the organization's stakeholders

The finding of talent management in the German and Irish subsidiaries of a US multi-national suggested that the success of talent management practices is a function of effective stakeholder involvement, senior level support and relevant information. Those responsible for delivering the concept of 'making your people' (i.e. talent managers or people professionals) are likely to have more influence than power. And so their success will depend on a broad range of stakeholders who will need to be engaged in both the setting and the delivery of the strategy.

These stakeholders will include:

- Board members who will discuss the strategic impact of the idea on shareholders and customers alike.
- The executive team, some of whom will have vested interests in securing enough resource for their unit or functional area and will have to agree to trade-offs.

- Managers throughout the world who will be responsible for making it happen and may have to give up some of their precious high-performing or high-potential people.
- Employees who will need to understand that the 'make your people before you make your products' idea is not an automatic right to extra investment or a higher reward package but something that has to be actively sought, managed and earned.

Account will need to be taken of the needs and perceptions of each of these groups and an engagement plan put in place that incorporates and deals with their interpretation, understanding, doubts and concerns.

Finally: The question of resource

Inevitably, the subject of making your people before making your product will come back to the question of resource. There are several ways to overcome some of the challenges that may be encountered. These include devoting more senior management time to the subject, liberating talent trapped in national silos and overcoming barriers to international mobility. It shouldn't be ignored that such solutions have a cost attached to them. And as we have stated previously, the investment is likely to come at the expense of other projects. So, at some point, those responsible for persuading the organization to make its people before making its products will have to answer the question, 'Why should I invest in this project instead of buying a new technology system/creating a corporate treasury or building a new production line?'

How to get to grips with such an important subject is one that continues to focus the minds of global managers. If this can be mastered, the rewards are enormous. The organization will have a unique competitive advantage: the talent advantage.

REFERENCES

Adair, J. (2010) *Effective Strategic Leadership*. Macmillan Publishing, London.

Aggarwal, U., Datta, S., Bhargava, S. (2007) The relationship between human resource practices, psychological contract and employee engagement: Implications for managing talent. *IIMB Management Review*, 19(3).

Agneus, L. (2012) 8 signs talent retention strategies are faltering. *Kelly Global Workforce Index*, http://www.kellyocg.com/Knowledge/Ebooks/8_Signs_Talent_Retention_Strategies_are_Faltering_-_EMEA/, accessed 24 May 2014.

Aguinis, H. and Kraiger, K. (2009) Benefits of training and development for individuals and teams, organizations, and society. *Annual Review of Psychology*, 60.

Amagoh, F. (2009) Leadership development and leadership effectiveness. *Management Decision*, 47(6).

Armstrong, M. and Brown, D. (2005) Reward strategies and trends in the United Kingdom: The land of diverse and pragmatic dreams. *Benefits Review*, 37(4).

Ashridge (2006) *Developing Future Leaders: The contribution of talent management*, http://www.ashridge.org.uk/Website/IC.nsf/wFARATT/Developing+Future+Leaders:+The+contribution+of+Talent+Management/$File/DevelopingFutureLeaders-TheContributionOfTalentManagement.pdf, accessed 24 May 2014.

Bain & Company (2013) *Balanced Scorecard*, http://www.bain.com/publications/articles/management-tools-balanced-scorecard.aspx, accessed 24 May 2013.

Barrow, S. and Mosley, R. (2005) *The Employer Brand: Bringing the best of brand management to people at work*. John Wiley & Sons, Ltd, Chichester.

Benett, A. (2013) *The Talent Mandate: Why smart companies put people first*. Palgrave Macmillan, New York.

Benko, C. and Weisberg, A. (2007) *Mass Career Customization: Aligning the workplace with today's non-traditional workforce*. Harvard Business School Publishing, Boston.

Berkshire Hathaway (2012) Inclusive letter to shareholders, http://everythingwarren-buffett.blogspot.co.uk/2013/03/warren-buffetts-2012-letter-feb-28.html, accessed 24 May 2014.

Berlin, I. (1953) *The Hedgehog and the Fox*. Weidenfeld & Nicolson, London.

Biro, M.M. (2013) Big Data Is A Big Deal. *Forbes*, www.forbes.com/sites/meghanbiro/2013/06/23/big-data-is-a-big-deal, accessed 24 May 2014.

Bjorkman, I., Ehrnrooth, M., Smale, A. and John, S. (2011) The determinants of line management internalisation of HRM practices in MNC subsidiaries. *International Journal of Human Resources Management*, 22(8).

Boston Consulting Group (2012) Creating People Advantage: Mastering HR challenges in a two-speed world. BCG, WFPMA and the EAPM, https://www.bcgperspectives.com/content/articles/people_management_human_resources_leadership_creating_people_advantage_2012/ accessed 24 May 2014.

Boston Consulting Group (2013) The future of HR in Europe key challenges through 2015, https://www.bcg.com/documents/file15033.pdf, accessed 24 May 2014.

Boudreau, J.W. (2012) Will predictive analytics impact the future of talent management? *Talent Management*, http://talentmgt.com/articles/view/will-predictive-analytics-impact-the-future-of-talent-management/print:1, accessed 24 May 2014.

Boudreau, J.W. and Ramstad, P.M. (2005) Talentship, talent segmentation and sustainability: A new HR decision science paradigm for a new strategy definition. *Human Resource Management*, 44(2).

Boussebaa, M. and Morgan, G. (2008) Managing talent across national borders: The challenges faced by an international retail group. *Critical Perspectives on International Business*, 4(1).

Brown, M. and Turner, P. (2008) *The Admirable Company*. Profile Books, London.

Brown, M. and Turner, P. (2011) People Management, Business Performance and Corporate Reputation-research findings from the Britain's Most Admired Company surveys 1990–2010. British Academy of Management Conference, Aston University, Birmingham.

Buahene, A.K. (2009) Engaging a multigenerational workforce: The why and the how. Society of Human Resource Management Conference, New Orleans, 28 June to 1 July 2009.

Burke, E. (November 2013) Where's the value in talent analytics? *Talent Management Magazine*, http://talentmgt.com/articles/view/where-s-the-value-in-talent-analytics/1, accessed 24 May 2014.

Cabrera, E. (2009) Protean organisations: Reshaping work and careers to retain female talent. *Career Development International* 14(2).

Caplan, J. (2011) *The Value of Talent*. Kogan Page, London.

Cappelli, P. (2008) Talent management for the twenty-first century. *Harvard Business Review* 86(March).

Cappelli, P. (2011) *Talent Partnerships Throughout and Beyond the Organisation*. Chartered Institute of Personnel and Development, London, http://www.cipd.co.uk/NR/rdonlyres/0CE8F45C-3F85-49E9-95DD-3631FC7D8C07/0/Talent5.pdf, accessed 24 May 2014.

Cheese, P. (2008) Driving high performance in the talent powered organisation. *Strategic HR Review*, 7(4).

Cheese, P. (2010) Talent management for a new era: what we have learned from the recession and what we need to focus on next. *Human Resource International Digest*, 18(3).

Chia, R. (2003) From knowledge-creation to the perfecting of action: Tao, Basho and pure experience as the ultimate ground of knowing. *Human Relations*, 56(8).

ChiefExecutive.net (2013) *Four Steps to Better Talent Management*. Chief Executive Group, Greenwich, CT, http://chiefexecutive.net/four-steps-to-better-talent-management-2, accessed 24 May 2014.

Churchard, C. (2013) There are no great workplaces. *People Management*, November.

CIPD (2008) Employer branding: A no-nonsense approach, http://www.cipd.co.uk/nr/rdonlyres/d0ac3cb0-bc5f-44f5-886d-4c00276f2208/0/empbrandguid.pdf, accessed 24 May 2014.

CIPD (2011a) *Is There a Bigger and Better Sustainable Future for Talent Management?* Talent Forward Series, Part 6. Chartered Institute of Personnel and Development, London.

CIPD (2011b) *Tackling the New Global Talent Realities*, Talent Forward Series, Part 1. Chartered Institute of Personnel and Development, London.

CIPD (2011c) *Talent Clusters*, Talent Forward, Part 3. Chartered Institute of Personnel and Development, London.

CIPD (2011d) *Next Generation HR: Insight driven*. Chartered Institute of Personnel and Development, London.

CIPD (2012) Using HR metrics for maximum impact, http://www.cipd.co.uk/hr-resources/practical-tools/using-hr-metrics-for-maximum-impact.aspx, accessed 24 May 2012.

CIPD/Cornerstone(2013a) Annual Survey Report: Learning and Talent Development, https://www.cipd.co.uk/hr-resources/survey-reports/learning-talent-development-2013.aspx, accessed 24 May 2014.

CIPD/Hays (2013b) Resourcing and Talent Planning Survey, http://www.hays.co.uk/cipd/, accessed 24 May 2014.

CIPD (2014) Strategic reward and total reward, CIPD fact sheet, http://www.cipd.co.uk/hr-resources/factsheets/strategic-reward-total-reward.aspx, accessed 24 May 2014.

Citi (2013) *Hot Spots 2025: Benchmarking the future competitiveness of cities*. The Economist Intelligence Unit, London, http://www.citigroup.com/citi/citiforcities/pdfs/hotspots2025.pdf, accessed 24 May 2014.

Clutterbuck, D. (2012) *The Talent Wave: Why succession planning fails and what to do about it*. Kogan Page, London.

Collings, D.G. and Mellahi, K. (2009) Strategic talent management: A review and research agenda. *Human Resource Management Review*, 19(4).

Conference Board (2013) *Strategic Talent Management*. The Conference Board Inc., New York.

Corporate Leadership Council (2002) *The Compelling Offer Revisited*. Corporate Executive Board, Washington.

Cosack, S., Guthridge, M. and Lawson, E. (2010) Retaining key employees in times of change. *McKinsey Quarterly*, August, http://www.mckinsey.com/insights/ organization/retaining_key_employees_in_times_of_change, accessed 24 May 2014.

Crossman, J. and Noma, H. (2013) Sunao as characteristics: Its implications within subsidiaries of Japanese Multinationals in Australia. *Journal of Business Ethics*, 113(3).

De Cieri, H., Sheehan, C., Costa, C., Fenwick, M. and Copper, B.K. (2009) International talent flow and intention to repatriate: An identity explanation. *Human Resource Development International*, 12(3).

De Voorde, V., Paauwe, J. and Veldhoven, M.V. (January 2010) Predicting business unit performance using employee surveys: Monitoring HRM related changes. *Human Resource Management Journal*, 20(1).

Dejoux, C. and Thevenet, M. (2012) The shift in talent management for French MNC's in Asia. *Revue de gestion des resources humaines*.

Deloitte (2010) Talent Edge 2020: Blueprints for the new normal, http://www.deloitte. com/assets/dcom-unitedstates/local%20assets/documents/imos/talent/ us_talentedge2020_121710.pdf, accessed 24 May 2014.

Deloitte (2011) The global talent challenge-getting new people in new jobs in new places.

Deloitte (2013) Human Capital Trends Report: Leading indicators, http://www. deloitte.com/view/en_US/us/Services/consulting/human-capital/human-capital-trends/index.htm, accessed 24 May 2014.

Dewhirst, M., Pettigrew, M. and Srinivasan, R. (2012) How multinationals can attract talent they need. *McKinsey Quarterly* 3(8).

Dewhurst, M., Harris, J. and Heywood, S. (2012) The global company's challenge. *McKinsey Quarterly*, http://www.mckinsey.com/insights/organization/the_global_ companys_challenge, accessed 24 May 2014.

Dobbs, R., Remes, J., Manyika, J., Roxburgh, C., Smit, S. and Schaer, F. (2012) Report, McKinsey Global Institute, http://www.mckinsey.com/insights/urbanization/ urban_world_cities_and_the_rise_of_the_consuming_class, accessed 24 May 2014.

Donlon, J.P. (2012) 40 Best Companies for Leaders 2012: How top companies excel. *Chief Executive.net*, http://chiefexecutive.net/40-best-companies-for-leaders-list, accessed 23 May 2014.

Economist, The (2012) The world's most valuable resource is talent: No country grows enough of it, 13 October.

Edger, C. (2012) *Effective Multi-Unit Leadership*. Gower Publishing, Aldershot.

Effron, M. and Shanley, J. (2011) What qualities make a world class talent management leader? In: *The Talent Management Handbook*, L. Berger and D. Berger (eds). McGraw-Hill, New York.

Erickson, R., Schwartz, J. and Ensell, J. (2014) The Talent Paradox: Critical skills, recession and the illusion of plenitude. *Deloitte Review*, http://www.deloitte. com/view/en_US/us/Insights/Browse-by-Content-Type/deloitte-review/ eadd148c49305310VgnVCM1000001a56f00aRCRD.htm, accessed 24 May 2014.

REFERENCES

Ernst & Young (2012) Growing Beyond, http://www.ey.com/GL/en/Issues/Driving-growth/Growing-Beyond/Growing-Beyond, accessed 24 May 2014.

Fast Company (2013) Most daring CEOs, http://www.fastcompany.com/3019228/the-most-daring-ceos, accessed 24 May 2014.

Fast Company (2000) War for talent: Seven ways to win, http://www.fastcompany.com/42093/war-talent-ii-seven-ways-win, accessed 24 May 2014.

Florida, R. (2005) *The Flight of the Creative Class: The new global competition for talent*. HarperCollins, New York.

Fuller, A. and Unwin, L. (2004) *Expansive Learning Environments: Workplace learning in context*. Routledge, London.

Garavan, T.N., Carbery, R. and Rock, A. (2012) Mapping talent development: Definition, scope and architecture. *European Journal of Training and Development*, 36(1).

Glen, C. (2006) Key skills retention and motivation: The war for talent still rages and retention is the high ground. *Industrial and Commercial Training*, 38(1).

Glover, G. (2012) From traditional HR to building a healthy organisation. Stamford Global Nordic-Baltic Human Asset, 26–27 April 2012, Helsinki.

Goffee, R. and Jones, G. (2006) *Why Should Anyone Be Led by You? What it takes to be an authentic leader*. Harvard Business School Publishing, Boston.

Goldsmith, M. and Carter, L. (2010) *Best Practices in Talent Management*. John Wiley & Sons, Ltd, San Francisco.

Goleman, D. (1996) *Emotional Intelligence*. Bloomsbury Publishing, London.

Groves, K.S. (2007) Integrating leadership development and succession planning best practices. *Journal of Management Development*, 26(3).

Guest, D. (2011) Human resource management and performance: Still searching for some answers. *Human Resource Management Journal*, 21(1).

Guthridge, M. and Komm, A.B. (2008) Why multinationals struggle to manage talent. *McKinsey Quarterly*, May.

Han, Y. and Zhang, Z. (2011) Enhancing managerial mindfulness: A way for middle managers to handle the uncertain situations, IACM 24th Annual Conference Paper, 24 June 2011.

Hanson, E. (2011) Talent reviews and high potential identification. *DDI*, http://www.ddiworld.com/DDIWorld/media/white-papers/talentreviewsandhighpotential-identification_wp_ddi.pdf?ext=.pdf, accessed 24 May 2014.

Harris, J.G., Craig, E. and Light, D.A. (2011) Talent and analytics: New approaches, higher ROI. *Journal of Business Strategy*, 2(6).

Hartmann, E., Feisel, E. and Schober, H. (2010) Talent management of western MNCs in China: Balancing global integration and local responsiveness. *Journal of World Business*, 45(2).

Hatum, A. (2010) *Next Generation Talent Management*. Palgrave Macmillan, Basingstoke.

He, L. (2013) Google's secrets of innovation: Empowering its employees. *Forbes*, March, http://www.forbes.com/sites/laurahe/2013/03/29/googles-secrets-of-innovation-empowering-its-employees/, accessed 24 May 2014.

Horwitz, F.M., Teng, C., Ahmed, H. and Quazi, A. (2003) Attracting, motivating and retaining knowledge workers. *Human Resource Management Journal*, 13(4).

Hoyte, M. and Newman, P. (2008) *Simply a Great Manager: The 15 fundamentals of being a successful manager*. Marshall Cavendish, London.

Huselid, M. (1995) The impact of human resource management practices on turnover, productivity and corporate financial performance. *Academy of Management Journal*, 38(3).

Huselid, M.A. and Becker, B.E. (2011) Bridging micro and macro domains: Workforce differentiation and strategic human resource management. *Journal of Management*, 37(2).

Huselid, M.A., Jackson, S.E. and Schuler, R.S. (1997) Technical and strategic human resources management effectiveness as determinants of firm performance. *Academy of Management Journal*, 40(1).

Huy, Q. and Shipilov, A. (2012) The key to social media success within organizations. *MIT Sloan Management Review*, 54(1).

Iles, P., Chuai, X. and Preece, D. (2010) Talent management and HRM in multinational companies in Beijing: Definitions, differences and drivers. *Journal of World Business*, 45(2).

International Labour Organization (2013) Decent Work Agenda, http://www.ilo.org/global/about-the-ilo/decent-work-agenda/lang--en/index.htm, accessed 24 May 2014.

Jesuthasan, R. (2013) Transforming talent management through segmentation. *HR Executive Online*, http://www.hreonline.com/HRE/view/story.jhtml?id=534355414, accessed 24 May 2014.

Jiang, T. and Iles, P. (2011) Employer brand equity, organizational attractiveness and talent management in the Zhejiang private sector. *Journal of Technology Management in China*, 6(1).

Johnson, G., Scholes, F. and Whittington, R. (2007) *Exploring Corporate Strategy*, 8th edn. FT Prentice Hall, Harlow.

Kaplan, R.S. and Norton, D. (1996) *The Balanced Scorecard: Translating strategy into action*. Harvard Business Press Books, Boston.

Kapoor, V. (2010) Employer branding: A study of its relevance in India. *The IUP Journal of Brand Management*, 7(1–2).

Kaufman, B.E. (2012) Strategic human resource management research in the United States: A failing grade after 30 years? *Academy of Management Executive*, 26(2).

Kempster, K. and Iszatt-White, M. (2013) Towards co-constructed coaching: Exploring the integration of coaching and co-constructed autoethnography in leadership development. *Management Learning*, 44(4).

Kimpakorn, N. and Tocquer, G. (2009) Employees' commitment to brands in the service sector: Luxury hotel chains in Thailand. *Journal of Brand Management*, 16.

Kotter, J.P. (1997) *Matsushita Leadership*. Simon & Schuster, New York.

Kucherov, D. and Zavyalova, E. (2012) HRD practices and talent management in the Companies with the Employer brand. *Emerald*, 36.

Kunerth, B. and Mosley, R. (2011) Applying employer brand management to employee engagement. *Strategic HR Review*, 10(3).

Lawler, E.E. (2008) *Talent: Making people your competitive advantage.* Jossey-Bass, San Francisco.

Lehmann, S. (2009) Motivating talents in Thai and Malaysian service firms. *Human Resource Development International*, 12(2).

Leverone, K. (2013) Six ways to develop home-grown talent and boost engagement, http://workplaceinsights.lhh.com/2013/09/12/six-ways-to-develop-home-grown-talent-and-boost-engagement/, accessed 24 May 2014.

Lewin, A.Y., Massini, S. and Peeters, C. (2009) Why are companies offshoring innovation? *Journal of International Business Studies*, 40.

Lombardo, M.M. and Eichinger, R.W. (1996) *The Career Architect Development Planner.* Lominger, Minneapolis.

Mackey, J. and Sisoda, R. (2013) *Conscious Capitalism: Liberating the heroic spirit of business.* Harvard Business Review Press, Boston.

Makela, K., Bjorkman, I. and Ehrnrooth, M. (2010) How do MNC's establish their talent pools? Influences on individual's likelihood of being labelled as talent. *Journal of World Business*, 45(2).

Mancesti, M. (2012) Retaining talent: Are we missing the real battle? *IMD*, http://www.imd.org/research/challenges/retaining-talent-marco-mancesti.cfm, accessed 24 May 2014.

ManpowerGroup Press Release (2013) ManpowerGroup Advises CEOs to Access, Mobilize and Optimize Talent to Remain Competitive in Economic Uncertainty, 8 November.

ManpowerGroup (2013a) *Talent Shortage Survey: Research results.* ManpowerGroup, Milwaukee, WI.

ManpowerGroup (2013b) Employers Advised to Connect Engagement to Performance to Retain Top Talent in the New Year. Media Centre, November, http://www.manpowergroup.com/wps/wcm/connect/manpowergroup-en/home/newsroom/news-releases/most+employees+plan+to+pursue+new+job+opportunities+in+2014+reveals+right+management+poll#.U43ika1OWzk, accessed 24 May 2014.

Mansharamani, V. (2012) All hail the generalist. HBR Blog Network, *Harvard Business Review*, http://blogs.hbr.org/2012/06/all-hail-the-generalist/, accessed 24 May 2014.

Manyika, J., Chui, M., Brown, B., Bughin, J. *et al.* (2011) Big data: The next frontier for innovation, competition, and productivity. Report, McKinsey Global Institute, http://www.mckinsey.com/insights/business_technology/big_data_the_next_frontier_for_innovation, accessed 24 May 2014.

Marquardt, M.J. (2011) *Building the Learning Organisation: Achieving strategic advantage through a commitment to Learning.* Nicholas Brealey Publishing, Boston.

Martin, G., Gollan, P.J. and Grigg, K. (2011) Is there a bigger and better future for employer branding? Facing up to innovation, corporate reputations and wicked problems in SHRM. *International Journal of Human Resource Management*, 22(17).

Mascarenhas, B. (2009) The emerging CEO agenda in multinational companies. *Journal of International Management*, 15(3).

Matsushita, K. (1978) *Practical Management Philosophy*. PHP Institute, New York.

Matsushita, K. (1988) *My way of life and thinking*. PHP Institute, New York.

McCartney, C. (2010) *The Talent Perspective: What does it feel like to be talent-managed?* Chartered Institute of Personnel and Development, London.

McDonnell, A., Lamarre, R., Gunnigle, P. and Lavelle, J. (2010) Developing tomorrow's leaders. *Journal of World Business*, 45(2).

McDonnell, A. and Hickey, C. (2011) Global talent management: Exploring talent identification in the multinational enterprise. *European Journal of International Management*, 5(2).

McGehee, T. (2001) *Whoosh: Business in the fast lane*. Perseus Publishing, Cambridge, MA.

McKinsey and Company (2008) *Strategic Talent Management*. CIPD Conference, Harrogate, September.

Mellahi, K. and Collings, D.G. (2010) The barriers to effective global talent management: The example of corporate elites in MNE's. *Journal of World Business*, 45(2).

Mendenhall, M.E., Osland, J.S., Bird, A., Odour, G.R. and Maznevski, M.L. (2008) *Global Leadership*. Routledge, Abingdon.

Michaels, E., Handfield-Jones, H. and Axelrod, B. (2001) *The War for Talent*. Harvard Business Press, Boston.

Mintzberg, H. (2011) *Managing*. Pearson, London.

Mitchell, S. (July 2013) The people challenges of going global. *Europe and Middle East Business Review Europe*, www.businessrevieweurope.eu/feature.html, accessed 24 May 2014.

Moroko, L. and Uncles, M.D. (2008) Characteristics of successful employer brands. *Journal of Brand Management*, 16(3).

Mosley, R.W. (2007) Customer experience, organisational culture and the employer brand. *Journal of Brand Management*, 15(2).

Myatt, M. (2012) 10 reasons why your top talent will leave you. *Forbes* magazine, http://www.forbes.com/sites/mikemyatt/2012/12/13/10-reasons-your-top-talent-will-leave-you/, accessed 24 May 2014.

Neal, A. (2013) *Brave New World: Recruiting talent in the digital age*. Research Report R-1534-13-RR. Conference Board.

Nikravan, L. (2012) The CEO's role in talent. *Talent Management*, http://talentmgt.com/articles/view/the-ceo-s-role-in-talent/print:1, accessed 24 May 2014.

Nooyi, I. (2012) Letter from CEO, http://www.pepsico.com/Purpose/Performance-with-Purpose/Letter-from-the-CEO, accessed 24 May 2014.

Oxford Economics (2012) Global Talent 2021: How the new geography of talent will transform human resource strategies, http://www.oxfordeconomics.com/Media/Default/Thought%20Leadership/global-talent-2021.pdf, accessed 24 May 2014.

Patterson, M.G., West, M.A., Lawthorn, R. and Nickell, S. (1997) *Impact of People Management Practices on Business Performance*. Chartered Institute of Personnel and Development, London.

Peck, D. (2013) They're watching you at work. *The Atlantic*, December, http://www.theatlantic.com/magazine/archive/2013/12/theyre-watching-you-at-work/354681/, accessed 24 May 2014.

People Management (2013) *Don't Lick the Burger*. Chartered Institute of Personnel and Development, London.

Peters, T. (2013) *Re-Imagine EXCELLENCE!* HR Summit and Expo 2013. Dubai International Convention and Exhibition Center, 7 October 2013.

Pless, N., Maak, T. and Stahl, G.S. (2013) Developing responsible global leaders through international service-learning programmes: The Ulysses experience. *Academy of Management Learning*, 10(2).

PwC (2011) 14th Annual CEO Survey, downloadable from http://www.pwc.tw/en/publications/events-and-trends/e244.jhtml, accessed 24 May 2014.

PwC (2012) 15th Annual Global CEO Survey, http://www.pwc.com/gx/en/ceo-survey/2012/index.jhtml, accessed 24 May 2014.

PwC Saratoga (2012) A Question of Talent: India Human Capital Effectiveness Survey, July, http://www.pwc.in/en_IN/in/assets/pdfs/Home/saratoga.pdf, accessed 24 May 2014.

Ready, D.A. and Conger, J.A. (2007) Make your company a talent factory. *Harvard Business Review*, 85(6).

Reitman, A. (2007) *Talent Retention*. ASTD Press, Alexandria, VA.

Right Management (2005) *Wachovia Case Study: Using an employee value proposition*. Right Management, London.

Rice, C., Marlow, F. and Masarech, M. (2012) *The Engagement Equation*. John Wiley & Sons, Ltd, New Jersey.

Right Management (2012) The struggle over talent management strategy: A North American Progress Report. *Manpower Group*.

Roberts, B. (2012) Celebrate differences: Meet diverse needs through employee segmentation. *HR Magazine*, 57 (12), www.shrm.org/publications/hrmagazine/editorialcontent/2012/1212/pages/1212-employee-segmentation.aspx#sthash.PKSnjebv.dpuf, accessed 24 May 2014.

Roberts, D. (2008) Building brand loyalty, creating brand equity-brand loyalty and the long good-bye CIPD.

Ross, S. (2013) How definitions of talent suppress talent management. *Industrial and Commercial Training*, 45(3).

Rumelt, R. (2011) *Good Strategy, Bad Strategy: The difference and why it matters*. Profile Books, London.

Savitz, A. (2013) *Talent, Transformation and the Triple Bottom Line*. John Wiley & Sons, Ltd, San Francisco.

Scott-Ladd, B., Travaglione, A., Perryer, C. and Pick, D. (2010) Attracting and retaining talent: Social organisational support as an emergent concept. *Research and Practice in Human Resource Management*, 18(2).

Scullion, H. and Collings, D.C. (eds) (2011) *Global Talent Management*. Routledge, New York.

Sehoon, K. and McLean, G.N. (2012) Global talent management: Necessity, challenges and the roles of HRD. *Advances in Developing Human Resources*, 14(4).

Selvaretnam, S.V. (2013) Talent boomerang. *HRM Asia*, http://www.hrmasia.com/case-studies/talent-boomerang/180023/, accessed 24 May 2014.

Sengupta, D. and Mukherjee, W. (2011) Talent management tops company CEO's task list. *The Economic Times*, 28 June.

Shields, J. (2009) Managing employee performance and reward: Concepts, practices, strategies. *Industrial Relations Journal*, 40(2): 173–175.

Sohota, H. (2013) *Supra Modernity: Complexity and the new now*. Purple Beach Conference, London.

Sonnenberg, M. (2010) Talent key ingredients. *Accenture Report*, http://www.accenture.com/SiteCollectionDocuments/Local_Netherlands/Accenture_Talent_Key_Ingredients_Brochure_2011.pdf, accessed 24 May 2014.

Stahl, G.K., Bjorkman, I., Farndale, E., Morris, S.S. *et al.* (2012) Six principles of effective global talent management. *MIT Sloan Management Review*, Winter.

Tansley, C., Turner, P.A., Foster, C., Harris, L. *et al.* (2007) *Talent: Strategy, management and measurement*. Chartered Institute of Personnel and Development, London.

Tarique, I. and Schuler, R.S. (2010) Global talent management: Literature review, integrative framework, and suggestions for further research. *Journal of World Business*, 45(2).

Tobin, R. (2013) The six traps of global organisation development and how to avoid them. Keio University (Japan), www.tobinkeio.com/pdf/six-traps.pdf, accessed 24 May 2014.

Toegel, G. and Barsoux, J.L. (2013) Cut out to lead? How personality plays a role in effective leadership. IMD Business School, http://www.imd.org/research/challenges/personality-effective-leadership-ginka-toegel-jean-louis-barsoux.cfm, accessed 24 May 2014.

Tomer, J.F. (2006) *Organisational Capital and Personal Capital Handbook of Contemporary Behavioural Economics: Foundations and developments*. ME Sharpe Inc, New York.

Towers Watson (2012) Employee value proposition: Key to getting and keeping the best, www.towerswatson.com/en-GB/Insights/IC-Types/Ad-hoc-Point-of-View/Perspectives/2012/Employee-Value-Proposition-Key-to-Getting-and-Keeping-the-Best, accessed 24 May 2014.

Tubbs, S. and Schultz, E. (2006) Exploring a taxonomy of global leadership competencies and meta competencies. *Journal of Academy of Business*, 8(2).

Turner, P. (2012) *Talent Management in Europe*. Stamford Global Talent for Tomorrow Summit, 23–25 April 2012, Vienna.

Turner, P. (2013) *Strategic Workforce Planning: A core process of human resource management*. IIR Middle East HR Summit and Expo, Dubai, 6–10 October 2013.

Uhl-Bien, M. (2003) Relationship development as a key ingredient for leadership development. In: *The Future of Leadership Development*, S.E.Murphy and R.E. Riggio (eds). Psychology Press, Hove.

Ulrich, D. (1996) *Human Resource Champions*. Harvard Business School Press, Boston.

Ulrich, D. (2011) *Talent: A formula for success*. Human Asset Summit. Budapest, 25–26 October 2011.

Ulrich, D. and Ulrich, W. (2010) *The Why of Work*. McGraw-Hill, New York.

Ulrich, D., Brockbank, W. and The RBL Group. (2012) 2012 Human Resource Competency Study, http://rbl.net/index.php/news/detail/the-rbl-group-announces-the-results-of-the-2012-hr-competency-study, accessed 24 May 2014.

Ulrich, D., Smallwood, N. and Sweetman, K. (2008) *The Leadership Code*. Harvard University Press, Boston.

Ulrich, D., Younger, W., Brockbank, W. and Ulrich, M. (2013) The state of the HR profession. *Human Resource Management*, 52(3).

Universum (2013) The world's most attractive employer's, http://universumglobal. com/ideal-employer-rankings/global-results/, accessed 24 May 2014.

Unoki, K. (2013) *Mergers, Acquisitions and Mergers*. Routledge, London.

Uren, L. (2011) What talent wants: The journey to talent segmentation. *Strategic HR Review*, 10(6).

Vaiman, V. and Vance, C. (2008) *Smart Talent Management: Building knowledge assets for competitive advantage*. Edward Elgar Publishing Ltd, Cheltenham.

Vaiman, V., Scullion, H. and Collings, D. (2012) Talent management decision making. *Management Decision*, 50(5).

Van De Voorde, K., Paauwe, J. and Van Veldhoven, M. (2010) Predicting business unit performance using employee surveys: Monitoring HRM-related changes. *Human Resource Management Journal*, 20(1).

Van Dijk, H.G. (2008) The talent management approach to human resource management: Attracting and retaining the right people. South African Association of Public Administration and Management, 9th Annual Conference, University of the Free State, Bloemfontein.

Vance, A. (2012) Steve Ballmer Reboots, http://www.businessweek.com/magazine/steve-ballmer-reboots-01122012.html, accessed 24 May 2014.

Vorhauser-Smith, S. (2012) China's talent equation still doesn't add up. *Forbes*, 4 April 2012, http://www.forbes.com/sites/sylviavorhausersmith/2012/04/18/chinas-talent-equation-still-doesnt-add-up/, accessed 24 May 2014.

Waddock, S. and Lozano, J.M. (2013) Developing more holistic management education: Lessons learned from two programs. *Academy of Management Learning* 12(2).

Walgreen's (2012) Walgreen's Annual Report 2012, http://files.shareholder.com/downloads/WAG/3213181221x0x608988/5A4CA423-70A4-46A7-876E-0EA1FBD-F14AA/WAG_2012_AR_lo.pdf, accessed 24 May 2014.

Wall Street Journal (2014) Employee Retention: How to retain employees, http://guides.wsj.com/small-business/hiring-and-managing-employees/how-to-retain-employees/, accessed 24 May 2014.

Wallace, M., Lings, I. and Cameron, R. (2012) Industry branding: Attracting talent to weaker profile industries. *Asia Pacific Journal of Human Resources Special Issue: Talent management in Asia Pacific*, 50(4).

Waller, D. (2013) Pipeline is no longer a tap for talent. *The Times*, 14 October 2013.

Walumbwa, F., Avolio, B., Gardner, W. Wernsing, T. and Peterson, S. (2008) Authentic leadership: Development and validation of a theory based measure. *Journal of Management*, 34(1).

Wakeman, C.Y. (2013) How to evaluate the ROI of an employee, http://www.forbes.com/sites/danschawbel/2013/05/28/cy-wakeman-how-to-evaluate-the-roi-of-an-employee/, accessed 24 May 2014.

Warner, M. (2009) Making sense of HRM in China: Setting the scene. *International Journal of Human Resource Management*, 20(11).

Weyland, A. (2011) Engagement and talent management of Gen Y. *Industrial and Commercial Training*, 43(7).

Williams, D. (2013) The 5 secret strategies of great people: How to become open-minded. *Forbes*, http://www.forbes.com/sites/davidkwilliams/2013/01/07/the-5-secret-tricks-of-great-people-how-to-become-open-minded-in-2013/, accessed 24 May 2014.

Wilson, A., Lenssen, G. and Hind, P. (2006) *Leadership Qualities and Management Competencies for Corporate Responsibility*. Ashridge Business School, Berkhamsted.

Yarnall, J. (2011) Maximising the effectiveness of talent pools: A review of case study literature. *Leadership & Organization Development Journal*, 32(5).

Young, J. and Chapman, E. (2010) Generic competency frameworks: A brief historical overview. *Education Research and Perspectives*, 37(1).

Zhang, S. and Bright, D. (2012) Talent definition and talent management recognition in Chinese private-owned enterprises. *Journal of Chinese Entrepreneurship*, 4(2).

INDEX

Accenture 242
action learning 113, 201, 206, 215–16, 223
Adair, J. 219
Admiral Group 3
agile thinking 2, 113
Alcatel 187
Alfa SAB de CV 41
Alstom 174
American Express 114
analytics 114, 124, 135–7, 277–8
    see also predictive analytics
Anshan Iron and Steel Group Corporation 78
AOL 67
Apple 13, 20, 112, 163
ArcelorMittal 152
Armstrong, M. 241
Ashridge 225
assessment centres 69, 143
attitudes 93, 120, 262, 274
attraction 1, 12, 14, 145, 161–83
    digital narrative through social media
        176–8
    employee value proposition 173–6, 182–3
    employer brand 164–73, 183
    global roles 179
    high potentials 180–1
    metrics 246, 254, 258
    multi-cultural environments 181–2
    networked organizations 45–6
    regional or local roles 180
    social organization and support 178
    specialists 181
    talent strategy 88, 93, 99
    see also recruitment

attractiveness 171
Australia 29, 241
authority 275–6
Avon 13
awareness 171–2

Baby Boomers 40, 41
BAE Systems 231
Bain 164
balanced scorecard 255–7
Balfour Beatty 112
Ballmer, Steve 19
Barrow, S. 165
Barsoux, Jean-Louis 109–10
BASF 13, 112
Becker, B.E. 101
benchmarking 14, 16, 82, 92
benefits, organizational 165, 173, 178, 181, 234
Benett, Andrew 31
Benko, C. 203
Berkshire Hathaway 112, 114
Berlin, Isaiah 192
Bersin model 195–6
Bertelsmann 198
Best Practice Institute 13
big data 114, 135–6, 139, 259
Bjorkman, I. 126, 158
BMW 164
board commitment 95–6
bonuses 69, 241
Boston Consulting Group (BCG) 3, 39–40,
    164, 179
Bottger, Preston C. 109–10
bottom line 114

Boudreau, J.W. 88, 137
Brazil 36
Bright, D. 57, 154
Brown, D. 241
Brown, M. 252
BSkyB 112
Buffett, Warren 114
Burke, E. 137
business case 22–4, 279–80
business strategy 84, 86–7, 90, 94, 96, 99–101, 103, 208, 279
business unit strategy 89, 96–7

Cabrera, E. 182
Canada 29
Canon 164
capability alignment 262, 274
Caplan, J. 25
Cappelli, Peter 32, 59, 143
Carbery, R. 191
career development 196, 199, 231, 239–40
    employee value proposition 173, 175
    Generation Y 41
    Jerónimo Martins 17–18
    lattice structure 202–3
    Thomson Reuters 33–4
    see also development
Carlson Rezidor 77
CEOs see chief executive officers
change champions 274
Chartered Institute of Personnel and Development (CIPD) 24, 26, 37, 52, 55, 134, 214
    global consistency/local relevance 151
    labour migration 36
    metrics 247–8
    peer groups 240
    rewards 241
    shift of mindset 257
    talent strategy 87, 196
Cheese, P. 265
CHG Healthcare 3
chief executive officers (CEOs) 8, 15, 19, 66, 73, 105–21, 273
    board commitment 96
    bottom line 114
    buy-in from 62
    characteristics and qualities 108–11
    employer branding 118–19
    hierarchical organizations 43–4
    internal and external recruitment 117–18
    'leadership code' 119–20
    networked organizations 46
    predictive analytics 139
    resource allocation 133

responsibilities 267
    skills shortages 39
    straight talking to 224
    succession planning 153
    surveys 29
    talent as strategic priority 112–13
    as talent champions 281–2
    talent retention 116–17
    talent strategy 7, 98, 103
    transition to inclusive approach 82
    Unilever 148–9
China 29, 30, 36, 154, 164–5, 230
China Vanke 3
Chuai, X. 58
CIPD see Chartered Institute of Personnel and Development
Clutterbuck, David 143
coaching 24, 69, 113, 197, 240, 270
    accounting and finance sectors 231
    CEO role 116
    co-constructed 201
    Panasonic 128
    Rio Tinto 148
    workforce development 202
Coca-Cola 112, 114
coherence 103, 124, 129–34
Collings, D.G. 53, 86
commitment 56, 176, 245–6, 282
communication
    cross-cultural relationships 225
    employer brand 166
    leadership meta-competences 193, 194
    skills 2
    social media 177
    sunao 217
    transparent 228, 237
communities of talent 6
compensation 166, 234
    see also rewards
competences 56, 85–6, 101, 252
    generic or technical 190–1, 192, 194, 195
    global workforce 195–6
    leadership meta-competences 186, 193–5
    world-class talent leaders 273–4
competency profiles 146, 154–5
competitive advantage 1, 14, 20, 21, 51–2, 266, 277, 284
    demographic edge 30
    global organizations 188
    insight 253, 258, 259
    people management 245
    potential talent 50
    talent strategy 84, 87, 90, 102–3
    workforce development 186, 209

Conference Board 178, 207, 220–1
Conger, J.A. 22, 35
consistency 85, 133, 151, 174, 282
contribution 56
cooperation, culture of 19
coordination of actions and policies 131–3
corporate brand 167–8
Corporate Leadership Council 176
corporate social responsibility 173, 175, 178, 179, 236, 238
corporate strategy 88–9, 96
Craig, E. 138
creativity 6, 22, 23, 256, 265, 274
    generic competences 190, 191
    leadership meta-competences 193
    sunao 223, 225
cross-functional teams 131, 186, 189, 191, 281, 283
Crossman, J. 225
cultural issues 21, 86, 196, 212
    competency profiles 154–5
    cultural awareness 37, 199, 206, 275
    generic competences 191
    international assignments 221
    management style 213
    sunao influence 225
    workforce development 189, 190, 206
    world-class talent leaders 275
customer satisfaction 237–8, 251
customization 182, 203

Danone 174
data 62–3, 134–9, 244, 248, 253–4, 266
    big data 114, 135–6, 139, 259
    Hitachi 170
    labour market 81–2
    performance review 159
    retention 232–3
    social networking sites 172–3
    see also information
Dejoux, C. 174
Deloitte 35, 41, 164
demand 2, 31, 35–6, 37, 38, 248
    gap analysis 98
    identification of talent 145, 146, 152
    intelligence 244, 255
    talent strategy 84, 94
demographic changes 28, 30, 36, 39–42, 258
Denmark 230
development 1, 12, 13, 19, 23–5, 52
    culture of 114
    employee value proposition 175
    global roles 179
    high potential talent reviews 151

Jerónimo Martins 17–18
Merlin Entertainments 203–4
metrics 246, 254
networked organizations 46
NHS 79–80
nine-box model 157
opportunities for 130
Panasonic 127–8, 217
personal 175, 199
retention 228
selective roles 200–2
sunao 222
talent pools 158
talent strategy 88, 93, 99
Thomson Reuters 33–4
total reward 241
    see also career development; training; workforce development
Dewhirst, M. 37
Dewhurst, M. 166
DI3 approach 253–5
Diageo 3, 112
differentiation 172, 175
disabled people 92
Disney 112
diversity 23, 26, 37, 84, 100, 110, 168, 186, 267
    employee value proposition 173
    global development strategy 197
    global roles 179
    identification of talent 142
    leadership 152
    London Olympics 91–3
    management style 213
    Rio Tinto 148
    sunao 221, 223
    Thomson Reuters 33
    workforce development 206, 209
Dobbs 30
Donlon, J.P. 14

e-learning 205–6
Edger, Chris 118, 155
Effron, M. 275
Ehrnrooth, M. 158
elitism 73
employee satisfaction 255
employee value 134
employee value proposition (EVP) 119, 162, 166, 173–6, 179, 182–3
employer brand 86, 90, 118–19, 162, 164–73, 179, 181, 182, 183
engagement 5, 12, 23, 28, 47, 61, 72, 90
    balanced scorecard 256
    Employee Engagement Index 176

engagement *(continued)*
  employer brand 167
  'engagement vigilance' 117
  IHRM 264
  nine-box model 157
  retention 230, 232, 234, 235–8
engineering sector 29, 165, 231
Ensell, J. 35
Erickson, R. 35
Ericsson 239–40
Ernst & Young 163, 164, 218–19
ethics 173, 225
ethnicity 142, 158, 168
Europe 55–6, 60–1, 86, 176–7, 230, 239
European Commission 201
EVP *see* employee value proposition
exclusive approach 4–5, 12, 17, 19, 21, 72–3
  balanced approach 60, 61–2
  geography/scope matrix 68–72
  McKinsey research 55
  multi-national enterprises 58
  resource allocation 133
  see also selectivity
executive search 146
experiential learning 200, 201, 202

Facebook 13, 177, 247
fairness 23, 80, 183, 242
feedback 242
Finland 3
'fit' 110, 153, 168, 234
Florida, R. 37
Forbes 3, 136, 232
France 230

gap analysis 25, 95, 97–8
Garavan, T.N. 191
gender 142, 158, 218–19
  see also women
General Electric 17
General Motors 137
generalists 192, 270, 271, 272
Generation X 40, 41
Generation Y 40, 41, 175, 231
generational differences 25, 26, 28, 39, 40–1,
  42, 231
generic competences 190–1, 192, 194, 195
geography/scope matrix 68–72
Germany 3, 40, 230
GlaxoSmithKline 112
global organizations 20–1, 31, 132–3, 187, 254
  attraction 179
  employee value proposition 174
  generic competences 191

global consistency/local relevance 151
  leadership meta-competences 193–5
  ownership of talent management 265
  retention 233–42
  skills shortages 39
  workforce development 186, 188–90, 196–7,
    200–2
  see also multi-national enterprises
global talent management 57–8, 62, 69–70, 71, 72
  inclusive approach 74, 76–7
  inclusive/selective approach 78
  responsibilities 267–9, 272
  selective approach 74, 75
  strategy 85–6
globalization 25, 36–9, 60, 150, 238
Goffee, R. 194
Goldman Sachs 196
Goleman, D. 223
Gollan, P.J. 164
Google 3, 13, 20, 100, 112, 136–7, 149, 163, 164,
  177, 214, 247
graduates 180
Greene King 118
Grigg, K. 164
group interviews 92
Groves, K.S. 194, 195
guanxi 154
Guest, David 249

Han, Y. 215
Harris, J. 166
Harris, J.G. 138
HCL Technologies 13, 19, 229
Hewlett-Packard (HP) 137, 206
Heywood, S. 166
hierarchies 43–4
high potentials 50, 55, 198, 200, 203–4, 222
  attraction of 180–1
  geography/scope matrix 69, 70–1
  leadership development 194
  multi-national enterprises 57–8
  talent reviews 151
Hilti 3
Hitachi 168–70
hospitality 56, 231
HR *see* human resources
human capital 58–9, 106, 120, 138
  return on 132, 135, 250
  talent strategy 196
human resources (HR) 8–9, 15, 66, 115, 257,
  266, 277–8
  big data 136
  global talent management 58
  metrics 134–5, 138, 139, 246, 247–50

performance 125, 144, 245–6
responsibilities 270–3
succession planning 154
talent management compared with 263–4
talent specialists 102
talent strategy 84, 87, 90
world-class talent leaders 273–6
Huselid, M.A. 101, 144, 249
Huy, Q. 177

IBM 112, 114, 135
identification of talent 57–8, 141–59, 163
behaviours 144
competency profiles 154–5
culture of innovation 145–7
high potential talent reviews 151
internal and external 148–9
leadership assessment 151–2
nine-box model 155–7
performance review data 159
segmentation 150
strategic workforce plan 149–50
succession process 152–4
talent pools 157–8
IHRM *see* international human resource
    management
IKEA 164
Iles, P. 58, 164–5
IMD 109–10, 116
inclusive approach 5, 6, 12, 16, 19, 21, 262
balanced approach 60, 61–2
CEO role 111
demonstrating effectiveness 258
geography/scope matrix 68–72
global organizations 74, 76–7, 189, 197
identification of talent 146
learning interventions 206
London Olympics 91–3
McKinsey research 55
multi-national enterprises 58
regional or local approach 74, 77
resource allocation 133
Rio Tinto 148
sunao mindset 223
talent management and HR responsibilities
    271–3
talent strategy 93–4
tourism sector 56
transition to 81–2
workforce development 202–5, 208, 209
inclusive/selective approach 66, 72–3, 74,
    78–81, 82, 94, 103, 281
CEO role 108
coherence 130

global strategy 196–7
identification of talent 146, 159
succession process 152
India 29, 36, 166, 242
information 62, 97–9, 149, 232–3, 244, 253,
    254–5, 266
see also data
innovation 22, 23, 84, 164, 258, 265
balanced scorecard 256
culture of 80, 142, 145–7, 232, 251
Google 149
IHRM 264
leadership meta-competences 193
sunao 221, 223, 225
workforce development 209
insight 98–9, 232–3, 244, 253–4, 255, 257–9,
    266, 278
Instagram 247
intangible assets 244, 245, 246–7, 252–3, 258,
    279
Intel 137
intellectual capital 252, 256
intelligence 244, 253, 255, 266
Internal Revenue Service 13
international assignments 221, 240
international human resource management
    (IHRM) 58, 87, 264
International Labour Organization 238
interpersonal skills 2, 55
Ireland 29
Italy 230

Jackson, S.E. 144
Japan 29, 40
Jerónimo Martins 17–18
Jesuthasan, R. 150
Jiang, T. 164–5
job satisfaction 1, 230, 245–6
joined-up approach 94, 126, 282
Jones, G. 194

Kaplan, R.S. 255–6
Kapoor, V. 166
Kaufman, B.E. 246
'key roles' 73, 78, 80, 93, 113, 153
Kimpakorn, N. 168
Kingfisher 112
KLM 238
Kotter, J.P. 220
Kucherov, D. 165
Kunerth, B. 166

labour markets 8, 38, 47, 66, 81–2, 90, 96, 166
Lawler, E.E. 90

leadership 4, 28, 46–7, 55–6, 70
   assessment 146, 151–2
   balanced scorecard 256
   classic talent management 14–15
   competency profiles 154–5
   Generation X 41
   global organizations 75, 187, 239–40
   inclusive/selective approach 73
   'leadership code' 119–20, 220
   leading through experience 200
   meta-competences 186, 193–5
   retention 228, 239, 242
   sunao 217–21
   world-class talent leaders 273–6
   see also chief executive officers
leadership development 90, 158, 194, 199, 202
   global development strategy 197
   leading through experience 200
   meta-competences 193
   nine-box model 157
   Panasonic 127–8
   talent strategy 93
   tangible outcomes 250–1
   see also development
learning 128, 195, 240, 241
   action learning 113, 201, 206, 215–16, 223
   by doing 215
   e-learning 205–6
   experiential 200, 201, 202
   informal 202, 206
   sunao 223
   workforce development 200, 204–5
learning needs analysis 146
Lenovo 13, 115
Light, D.A. 138
LinkedIn 177
listening 224
local approach 69, 70, 74, 76, 77, 85, 267–9
London 2012 Olympic and Paralympic Games
   91–3
L'Oréal 172, 174
loyalty 230
Lozano, J.M. 201

Maak, T. 201
Makela, K. 158
management development 57, 93, 94, 99, 158,
   199, 201
   see also leadership development
management tools 7, 8
Mancesti, M. 116
ManpowerGroup 29, 107, 179, 230
Mansharamani, Vikram 191–2
Marquardt, M.J. 215–16, 223

Martin, G. 164
Matsushita, Konosuke 1, 215, 216, 220, 235
McCartney, C. 24
McDonald's 72, 174, 239
McDonnell, A. 57–8
McGehee, T. 219–20
McKee Foods 137
McKinsey 32, 55, 136, 155
meaning at work 40, 41–2, 230, 235–8
meetings 120
Mellahi, K. 53
Mendenhall, M.E. 187
mentoring 24, 77, 200, 231
   CEO role 116
   global organizations 240
   Panasonic 128
   workforce development 206
mergers and acquisitions (M&A) 100–1, 146,
   198, 217
meritocracy 74
Merlin Entertainments 203–4
metrics 132, 134–9, 207, 244, 246–51, 253–5, 258
Microsoft 19, 164
migration 36–8
Millennial Branding 231
mindset 12, 21, 209, 223–5, 257
   see also sunao
Mintzberg, Henry 108
MNEs see multi-national enterprises
mobility 86, 113, 131, 201, 281
Mosley, R. 165, 166, 167
Most Admired Companies 112
motivation 51, 143, 234, 240, 242
Mukherjee, W. 115
multi-cultural environments 37, 181–2
multi-generational workforce 40–1, 42, 202
multi-national enterprises (MNEs) 57–8,
   131, 158
   see also global organizations

National Health Service (NHS) 78–80
Nayar, Vineet 19
Nestlé 164
networked organizations 44–6, 70–1, 188
networking events 179
new products or services 100, 146, 148, 198, 251
NHS see National Health Service
Nikravan, L. 115
nine-box models 25, 75, 133, 146, 155–7, 159
Nissan 231
Noma, H. 225
Nooyi, I. 115
Norton, D. 255–6
Novartis 16

objectives 12, 120, 183, 265–6
  performance management 237
  succession planning 153
  talent strategy 84, 89, 93, 95, 96–7, 99, 103
  workforce development 197, 198–9
Offer-Fit Index 176
oil and gas sector 29, 231
Old Navy 42
Olympic and Paralympic Games (London 2012) 91–3
on-the-job training 195, 206
open-mindedness 190, 212, 213–14, 217, 220, 221, 223
  see also sunao
operational strategy 89, 97, 98
opportunity 51, 66, 72, 75
  culture of 31, 84, 90, 93–4, 108–11, 130, 149, 153, 183, 258, 268
  inclusive/selective approach 80, 81, 82
organizational culture 12, 20, 25, 31, 102, 186
  capability alignment 274
  CEO role 106, 108, 115, 118, 119
  consultative 159
  cross-cultural relationships 225
  cultural awareness 275
  employer brand 166, 172
  inclusive/selective approach 130
  resource allocation 133
  retention 228, 232, 234, 242
  sunao mindset 223
  supportive 194
organizational paradox 3–4
organizational structure 28, 36, 42–6, 60, 133, 258
outside-in thinking 26, 62, 113, 130, 279
Oxford Economics 277–8

Paauwe, J. 250
Panasonic 1, 127–8, 196, 199, 215–17, 220, 235
partners, employees as 238
patents 252, 256, 258
Peck, D. 136–7
peer groups 240
people management 3, 5, 15, 52
  employer brand 168
  performance and 245–6
  succession planning 154
  talent management compared with 263–4
  see also human resources
PepsiCo 115
performance 23, 114, 125–6, 144, 253, 280
  balanced scorecard 255–7
  generic or technical competences 191

global organizations 186, 189
  metrics 134–5, 247, 249–51
  nine-box model 155–7
  people management and 245–6
  performance review data 159
  rewards 228, 240–2
performance management 3, 16, 146, 156, 254, 281
  global organizations 21
  Hitachi 170
  retention 237
  talent linked to 214
  workforce development 202
Pettigrew, M. 37
Philippines 29
Pless, N. 201
Portugal 29, 230
potential 21–2, 50, 51–2, 69, 71
  development for 239–40
  global organizations 186, 189
  identification of talent 70, 143
  inclusive/selective approach 78, 82
  nine-box model 155–7, 159
  talent strategy 94, 97
  see also high potentials
predictive analytics 82, 90, 96, 103, 137–9, 150, 163, 176, 244, 245, 253–4, 279
Preece, D. 58
PriceWaterhouseCoopers (PWC) 29, 59, 117, 164
Procter & Gamble 14, 22, 137
project management 20, 273
'Project Ulysses' 201
promotion 41, 82, 152, 218

Ramstad, P.M. 88
Ready, D.A. 22, 35
recession 4, 31, 35
recognition 242
recruitment 37, 93, 152, 234
  employer brand 86, 165, 173
  internal and external 117–18, 244
  London Olympics 91–2
  networked organizations 46
  selective local approach 76
  transparency 82
  see also attraction
regiocentrism 85
regional approach 69–70, 71, 74, 76, 77, 267–9
reputation 23, 86, 112, 116, 145
  employee value proposition 175, 183
  employer brand 118–19, 167–8
  as intangible asset 252, 258
  measures of 244, 255, 256

resource allocation 132, 133–4, 138, 267, 268, 271, 280, 281, 284
responsibilities 266–73, 283
retention 1, 12, 14, 42, 77, 145, 227–42
  bonuses 69
  business sectors 231
  CEO role 116–17
  culture and leadership 242
  demographic differences 231
  development for potential 239–40
  Employee Retention Index 176
  employer brand 86, 167, 173
  engagement through meaning 235–8
  geographical comparisons 230
  information and insight 232–3
  metrics 246, 254, 258
  networked organizations 45–6
  reasons for leaving 228, 232
  reward for performance 240–2
  selective local approach 76
  sunao 222, 226
  talent strategy 88, 93, 99
  war for talent 229
return on investment 25, 26, 68, 94, 103, 132
  benchmarking 92
  exclusive approach to talent 73
  metrics 135, 246, 250
  predictive analytics 90
rewards 69, 88, 90, 132–3, 179
  data 244, 254
  employee value proposition 173, 175
  graduate recruitment 180
  retention 228, 232, 234, 240–2
  standardized packages 3
  team-based 71
Rio Tinto 147–8
Roberts, B. 233
Roberts, D. 167
role clarity 236, 242, 265
Rolls-Royce 112, 231
Ross, S. 60
Rumelt, R. 97, 126, 129, 134
Russia 29, 36, 165

Sainsbury's 118
SAS 3
Savitz, A. 40
Schuler, R.S. 35, 57, 58, 144, 264
Schultz, E. 193
Schwab, Klaus 2–3
Schwartz, J. 35
Scullion 86
segmentation 145, 150, 158, 182, 228, 233
selectivity 73, 74–6, 81, 130, 262

CEO role 106
demonstrating effectiveness 258
identification of talent 146
talent management and HR responsibilities 270–1
see also exclusive approach; inclusive/ selective approach
self-development 82, 134, 201
Sengupta, D. 115
Shanley, J. 275
shareholder value 12, 16, 244, 248, 255
Shell 112
Shields, - 241–2
Shipilov, A. 177
Siemens 206, 231
Singapore 3
Singapore Airlines 13
skills 2, 30, 35, 71, 144
  big data 136
  generic competences 191
  leadership 70
  project management and implementation 273
  selectivity 73
  shortages 38–9
  specialists with global 181
  talent strategy 86, 87, 89–90, 93, 97
  workforce development 188, 189–90, 195, 209
  world-class talent leaders 275–6
Smallwood, N. 195, 220
social capital 58, 177, 208
social media 26, 99, 121, 146, 237–8
  attraction of talent 162, 163, 176–8, 180, 181, 182
  employer brand 171, 172–3
social networking events 179
social organization and support 178
Sodexo 53–4
Southwest Airlines 112
Spain 29
specialists 55, 69, 70, 149, 192
  attraction of 181
  HR 262, 266
  networked organizations 45, 46
  nine-box model 156
  responsibilities 269, 270, 271, 272
  talent 102–3
Srinivasan, R. 37
Stahl, G.K. 21
Stahl, G.S. 201
stakeholder involvement 283–4
Standard Chartered Bank 214
Starbucks 112
strategic positioners 274

strategy 23, 25, 26, 43, 83–103, 126, 278
  alignment of business to people 100–1
  alignment of people to business 90–4
  assessment of talent supply 97
  board commitment 95–6
  business objectives 96–7, 99, 103
  case for talent 86–7
  CEO role 107, 109–10, 112–13, 115
  characteristics of 87–8
  coherence 103
  data-gathering 63
  definition of 88
  global influences on 85–6
  identification of talent 145
  implementation 124, 126–7, 129, 132–3, 269,
    271, 273, 283
  insights from talent analysis 98–9
  measuring the effectiveness of 243–59
  multiple levels 88–90
  outside-in thinking 279
  preparation of 99
  responsibilities 267, 268, 269, 270, 271,
    272–3
  retention 229
  talent specialists 102–3
  workforce development 196–7, 200,
    207–9
subsidiaries 264–5
succession management 69, 73, 75, 90,
  152–4
succession planning 19, 52, 74, 113, 130,
  152–4, 194
  high potential talent reviews 151
  identification of talent 145–6
  MNEs 57
  nine-box model 157
  responsibilities 269
  workforce development 198, 200
sunao 212–26, 275
  as critical leadership skill 217–21
  cross-cultural relationships 225
  decisions about talent 221–2
  developing a sunao mindset 223–5
  learning organization 223
  Panasonic 215–17
supply 2, 35–6, 37, 248
  gap analysis 98
  identification of talent 145, 146, 152
  intelligence 244, 255
  talent strategy 84, 94, 97
surveys 112, 164, 170, 172, 179, 250, 255
sustainability 88
Sweetman, K. 220
Switzerland 3

talent 5–6, 8, 278
  CEO role 109–10
  definitions of 15–16, 17, 50, 59–61, 109, 279,
    280
  flows 36–8
  geography/scope matrix 68–72
  global strategy for 83–103
  identification of 57–8, 141–59, 163
  potential 21–2
  shortages 2, 15, 28, 29–30, 35, 38–9, 82
  talent formula 56–7
Talent 4.0 19–20
talent factories 22, 34–5
talent management 4, 6–7, 8, 12, 277–8
  big data 136
  business case for 22–4, 279–80
  CEO role 107–8, 109–10, 115–16
  classic approach to 14–15, 43–4
  comparison with HR management 263–4
  complex history of 32
  critical success factors 25–6, 129
  definitions of 52–3
  8 steps 279–84
  identification of talent 143, 146, 149
  implementation 123–40, 283
  metrics 137–9, 247–8, 250–1, 253
  Novartis 16
  organizational structure 42–6
  ownership of 261–76
  'people case' for 22, 24–5
  potential 21–2
  sunao 211–26
  time spent on 13–14
  see also exclusive approach; global talent
    management; inclusive approach;
    inclusive/selective approach
talent pools 60, 75, 77, 84, 111
  identification of talent 142, 145–7, 157–8
  London Olympics 91
  responsibilities 269
  segmentation 150
  top management support for 240
talent reviews 146, 151
Tarique, I. 35, 57, 58, 264
Tata 3, 164
technical competences 190–1, 192, 194, 195
technology 2, 205–6
technology industries 231
Tesco 13, 112
Thevenet, M. 174
Thomson Reuters 32–4
3M 233
Tobin, R. 188–9
Tocquer, G. 168

Tomer, J.F. 125
top management team (TMT) 53, 264–5
'top talent' 4, 15, 112, 156
    see also high potentials
total reward 240–1, 244
Towers Watson 173
Toyota 206
training 3, 113, 206, 231, 232, 246
    impact on performance 250, 251
    Jerónimo Martins 17–18
    on-the-job 195, 206
    technical competences 191
    total reward 241
    workforce development 199, 200, 206, 207
    see also development
transparency 75, 82, 196, 213, 217, 221, 225–6,
    228, 237, 281
trust 154, 217, 225, 226
Tubbs, S. 193
Tumblr 13, 177
Turner, D. 252
Turner, P. 56, 60
turnover 230, 234, 242, 251
    balanced scorecard 256
    metrics 135, 137, 244, 255, 258
    reasons for leaving 232
    see also retention
Twitter 177, 247

Ulrich, Dave 23, 42, 51, 56, 102, 119, 195, 220,
    235, 238, 273–4
Ulrich, Wendy 42, 235, 238
uncertainty 4, 31, 191, 194
Unilever 81, 148–9, 205
United Kingdom 29, 112, 230, 231, 241
United States 29–30, 32, 40, 112, 230, 231, 246
Universum 164
Uren, L. 24

values 165, 168, 171, 172, 175, 193, 234, 235
Van de Voorde, K. 250
Van Veldhoven, M. 250
Volvo 19–20
Vorhauser-Smith, S. 30

Waddock, S. 201
Walgreens 144
Wall Street Journal 236
Waller, D. 100
'war for talent' 2, 4, 5, 55, 76, 110, 229
Weisberg, A. 203
Wells Fargo 114
Weyland, A. 40
Wharf Holdings 3
Williams, D. 224
women 53–4, 168, 182, 218–19, 242
work-life balance 33, 175, 178, 181, 234,
    242, 277
workforce development 185–209
    creating a strategy 196–7
    e-learning 205–6
    generic or technical competences 190–1,
        192, 195
    global workforce competences
        195–6
    inclusive roles 202–5
    leadership meta-competences 193–5
    objectives 198–9
    selective roles 200–2
    specialists and generalists 191–2
    strategic orientation 207–9
    three dimensions 189–90
workforce planning 52, 82, 87
    NHS 79, 80
    strategic workforce plan 62, 142, 145, 146,
        149–50, 254
working environment 166, 175, 234, 241
World Economic Forum (WEF) 2, 38
World Federation of People Management
    Associations 22

Yahoo 13
Yarnall, J. 158
YouTube 177–8

Zappos 42
Zavyalova, E. 165
Zhang, S. 57, 154
Zhang, Z. 215

Berkeley College